120 CONTENT STRATEGIES FOR ENGLISH LANGUAGE LEARNERS

TEACHING FOR ACADEMIC SUCCESS IN SECONDARY SCHOOL

SECOND EDITION

Jodi Reiss

Florida International University, Emerita

Boston   Columbus   Indianapolis   New York   San Francisco   Upper Saddle River
Amsterdam   Cape Town   Dubai   London   Madrid   Milan   Munich   Paris   Montreal   Toronto
Delhi   Mexico City   Sao Paulo   Sydney   Hong Kong   Seoul   Singapore   Taipei   Tokyo

Vice President, Editor in Chief: Aurora Martínez Ramos
Editor: Erin K.L. Grelak
Editorial Assistant: Meagan French
Marketing Manager: Danae April
Production Editor: Karen Mason
Project Manager: Susan Hannahs
Cover Designer: Karen Salzbach
Cover Art: Somos Images/Alamy RF
Photo Researcher: Annie Pickert
Full-Service Project Management: Sudip Sinha/Aptara®, Inc.
Composition: Aptara®, Inc.
Text Printer/Bindery: LSC Communications
Cover Printer: LSC Communications
Text Font: Garamond

Credits and acknowledgments borrowed from other sources and reproduced, with permission, in this textbook appear on appropriate page within the text.

Library of Congress Cataloging-in-Publication Data
Reiss, Jodi.
    120 content strategies for English language learners: teaching for academic success in secondary
school / Jodi Reiss.—2nd ed.
        p. cm.
    Includes bibliographical references and index.
    ISBN-13: 978-0-13-247975-2
    ISBN-10: 0-13-247975-3
    1. English language—Study and teaching (Secondary)—Foreign speakers. 2. Content area reading.
3. Education, Bilingual. I. Title. II. Title: One hundred twenty content strategies for English language
learners. III. Title: One hundred and twenty content strategies for English language learners.
    PE1128.A2R4547 2012
    428.0071'2—dc22

                                                                    2010033834

17 2021

www.pearsonhighered.com

ISBN-10:   0-13-247975-3
ISBN-13: 978-0-13-247975-2

DEDICATION

This book, *120 Content Strategies for English Language Learners: Teaching for Academic Success in Secondary School,* Second Edition is dedicated to those who teach content to English language learners. It is written in the belief that mainstream teachers, as much as English language development teachers, have much to contribute to the academic success of these students.

QUICK REFERENCE STRATEGIES

**CHAPTER 7   DID THEY GET WHAT I TAUGHT?
CHECKING COMPREHENSION 87**

**CHAPTER 8   EXTENDING COMPREHENSION:
TEXTBOOK VOCABULARY STRATEGIES 101**

BRIEF CONTENTS

CONTENTS

FOREWORD: TEN QUESTIONS

I. Is this book primarily for teachers of English language learners?

No, it is for all teachers with English language learners in their classes. It is for middle and high school teachers of math, science, social studies, and language arts who want to find ways to teach their content to students who are in the process of learning English. And it is for English language development (ELD) teachers who need to teach their students the language skills they need for academic success. In actuality, both groups teach language and content: Content teachers use language to teach content, and ELD teachers use content to teach language.

2. Is this book primarily for middle and high school teachers?

Yes, although many of the strategies presented here can be used by elementary school teachers of fourth grade or higher.

English language learners in the primary grades have the advantage of learning to read and write English at the same time as their native English-speaking peers. By third or fourth grade, however, a shift occurs—from learning to read to reading to learn.

For those who teach upper elementary school grades, I believe you will find a number of strategies in this book that are appropriate for your students and your content. As content complexity increases with each successive grade, more strategies can be successfully incorporated into classroom instruction.

3. Is this book for practicing teachers?

Yes, it is for practicing teachers, *and* for preservice teachers.

For the preservice teacher, I hope this book will inspire you with new and exciting ideas. From your first day in the classroom, you will have a wide range of creative strategies to meet your students' needs.

For the practicing teacher, I hope this book will offer innovative approaches to the content you teach. You may find in it some strategies that you use regularly and some that you recall knowing once but have long ago forgotten. Mostly, I hope you discover inspiring new strategies that give you many "Aha!" moments.

4. Do I have to be in a teacher training program to benefit from this book?

No, not at all. Although this book is written primarily as a text for teacher training courses, it is equally appropriate for group study in a book club setting and for individual teachers who seek ideas for working with the English language learners in their classrooms. The strategies are formatted in a manner that facilitates comprehension for all readers.

5. Will reading this book give me new ideas about ways to teach content to my English language learners?

Yes, and I'd be very disappointed if it did not! My goal is to share with you a multitude of solutions that will work with your English language learners and your content. You should find strategies in this text that expand your repertoire of approaches to instruction and assessment, as well as strategies that enrich your daily activities of teaching in ways that will be more effective for your language-learning students.

6. Do I have to change the way I teach to incorporate the strategies in this book?

No. I know that today's teachers already face enough challenges to their time and resources. The purpose of this book is to provide you with practical, easy-to-incorporate ideas that fit right in with the techniques and activities you currently use in your classroom. You do not have to change the way you teach at all; the strategies are designed to offer you versatile options. Choose the ones that fit your content, your teaching style, and your students.

7. Will reading this book give me new ideas about ways to assess what my English language learners really know about the content I teach?

Again, yes, I certainly hope so! I believe that teachers use traditional forms of classroom assessment simply because that's what they've always used. The strategies for classroom assessment in this book offer interesting alternatives to multiple-choice and essay tests. I hope they inspire you to try new approaches to assessing the achievement of your English language learners.

8. Do I need to know a lot of specialized jargon to understand this book?

No. By design, this book is reader-friendly. The writing is light on jargon and technical terminology.

9. Do I need to know a lot about second-language acquisition theory to read this book?

No. The more you know, of course, the better your knowledge base will be. However, out of the vast body of research and theory that constitutes the field of second-language acquisition, I have selected and included here the theories that most strongly inform these strategies. Chapter 1 explains first the need for some basic theoretical background and then the pertinent theories and principles. The final pages of that chapter put everything together into a cohesive whole that forms the foundation upon which all the strategies are based. Understanding the theoretical foundation is essential to making informed choices of strategies that will work best for you, your students, and the content you teach.

10. Will reading this book make me a better teacher?

Reading it will not make you a better teacher; using the strategies in the book will.

Let me start by saying that I believe that those who choose teaching as a profession do so because they enjoy it. (We know they don't do it for financial reward!) They strive to be the very best they can be. They love finding solutions to issues they face in the classroom.

The strategies in this book offer you many creative solutions. Using them will help you to become a more accomplished professional. And successful teachers are happy teachers. It is my hope that these strategies will add to your pleasure in teaching. I wish you great success!

PREFACE

Purpose of This Book

Teaching content to students who are in the process of learning English is a challenge, both for teachers whose expertise lies in subjects such as math, science, and social studies and for those who teach English either as a new language or as language arts and literature. I have written this book for all of them.

This is a reader-friendly resource book that presents content teaching strategies built on a foundation of second-language acquisition theory. I had two goals in writing this book. The first was to balance theory and application—to provide readers with a wealth of practical instructional and assessment strategies for teaching content to English language learners, along with the theoretical understanding to make informed pedagogical decisions about when, how, why, and with whom to use which strategies. For this reason, the strategies are presented in a two-part format. The concept underlying each strategy is discussed first, followed by the practical application section.

The second goal involved the adage "Nothing succeeds like success." Teachers care about their students' success. I wanted to write a book that offered teachers practical, adaptable strategies to help English language learners experience academic success in content classrooms. For these students and their teachers, even the beginnings of success can be their own reward.

New to This Edition

Through my continued interactions with the teachers participating in my workshops, I became aware of a need to enhance certain sections of my original book. Their questions and comments about issues with the English language learners in their classes challenged me to create new strategies and techniques, which I share with you in this second edition.

In this new edition you will find the following:

- 18 new strategies
- 15 new practical application techniques
- Substantial additions in the areas of reading a textbook, review techniques and products, and questioning techniques for increased participation
- Expanded and updated TechConnection websites
- Book Club section with questions for self-directed discussion
- Chart of select strategies cross-referenced with core content areas in addition to previously included chart of strategies that support the four language skills

Organization

This book is divided into three parts. Part I presents the foundations that inform the strategies.

- Chapter 1 provides an overview of select theories and principles of second-language acquisition that form the theoretical basis for the strategies. The end of the chapter unifies the separate theories into an application called *12 Guidelines for Practice*.
- Chapter 2 aims to develop teacher awareness of the deep roots of culture that may lead to cross-cultural misunderstandings. The chapter examines culture as a potential determinant of English language learners' classroom behavior patterns and presents details of specific cultural considerations for teaching math, science, social studies, and language arts.

Part II takes readers through sets of strategies that follow the developmental steps in the instructional process.

- Chapter 3 looks at state standards in relation to English language learners and offers strategies for making sound curricular choices.
- Chapter 4 presents first an overview of learning strategies in general, followed by learning strategies for English language learners. It looks at the need to incorporate learning strategies into daily instruction and provides strategies to explicitly teach them to students.
- Chapter 5 deals with the relationship between background knowledge and learning and then presents strategies to build and activate background knowledge for English language learners.
- Chapter 6 analyzes teacher talk and offers strategies to facilitate comprehension for English language learners during periods of oral instruction. It then focuses on the importance of and strategies for classroom routine and review.
- Chapter 7 examines question-and-answer patterns in the classroom and presents strategies to increase the quality and quantity of participation for all students.
- Chapters 8 and 9 focus on facilitating English language learners' comprehension of the textbook. Chapter 8 details vocabulary strategies, and Chapter 9 describes reading strategies.
- Chapter 10 presents strategies for in-class and at-home activities and assignments to reinforce conceptual learning for students at varying stages of English language development. These strategies maintain the cognitive challenge of activities and assignments while reducing the linguistic complexity.

Part III covers assessment practices as they relate to English language learners.

- Chapter 11 examines the difficulties of traditional essay and multiple-choice tests for English language learners and presents strategies for modifying classroom tests and creating alternative testing formats. The chapter ends with a section on grading, advocating the need and offering the strategies to evaluate English language learners in ways that promote academic success.
- Chapter 12 focuses on the topic of accountability and high-stakes tests. The chapter offers strategies to prepare English language learners for high-stakes tests and then examines test accommodation strategies to maximize students' performance potential at every level of English language development.

Features

The theories that inform the strategies are kept in continual focus throughout the strategy chapters in Parts II and III. In the *Questions for Discussion* section ending each chapter, the first question asks students to review the *12 Guidelines for Practice* appearing at the end of Chapter 1 in order to select those that are foundational to the set of strategies that were the focus of that chapter.

The strategy chapters (Chapters 3–12) follow an organized and practical format. Each chapter contains these sections:

- An introductory examination of the needs and difficulties that English language learners may encounter with the lesson segment under consideration.
- *The Objective* succinctly states the goal toward which teachers must strive in leading English language learners toward academic success.
- *The Rationale* explains the reasoning underlying each objective.
- Each *Strategy* presents practical and widely adaptable techniques that teachers can use to help English language learners experience success within the objective. (All strategies are listed on pp. iii–viii.) Each strategy is presented in two sections, which are described next.
- The *In Concept* section introduces the strategy and explains why the strategy will be advantageous to English language learners.
- The *In Practice* section details how to use the strategy, showing through graphic illustration and clear explanation, often with examples, specific techniques for classroom application.
- The *In Summary* segment ends each chapter with concluding thoughts, pointers, and suggestions.

Postreading questions and a resource section end each chapter. The *Questions for Discussion* section includes reflective, research, and observational activities to extend and apply the reader's conceptual understanding of the strategies and the theories that inform them. The listings in *References and Resources* include reference citations as well as informative articles and books on the various topics, and *The TechConnection* offers helpful websites.

End matter includes a *Glossary* listing acronyms relating to all aspects of English language development, including, but not limited to, those used in this book. A *Book Club* section follows with questions for self-directed group discussion. *Appendix I* contains additional teacher resources—books and websites that are excellent sources of valuable information for teaching content to English language learners. Their scope is simply too broad to have been included in the reference section of any single chapter. Finally, on the inside back cover is a chart of select strategies that support the four language skills: reading, writing, speaking, and listening.

ACKNOWLEDGMENTS

I owe much to the prospective and practicing teachers who have filled my university classes and my workshops. Many of the strategies in this book were developed in a spirit of mutual cooperation and collaboration to meet specific challenges they faced. I must also thank them for the many times they asked, "When are you going to write a book?"

I thank Meagan French for her patience in answering my many emailed questions and Mary Benis for her clear thinking and careful editing. I am also most appreciative of the reviewers of the first edition for their incredibly thorough critiques and detailed suggestions: John McAndrew, Kutztown University of Pennsylvania; Imelda Basurto, California State University, Fresno; Juanita N. Benioni, Utah Valley State College; George C. Bunch, University of California, Santa Cruz; Sandy Cmajdalka, University of Houston–Downtown; Dana L. Grisham, San Diego State University; Linda Holley Mohr, Texas A&M University; Oneyda M. Paneque, Barry University; and W. Robert Walker, Northern Arizona University, Yuma. In addition, I thank the reviewers whose suggestions contributed to the second edition: Mary Carol Combs, University of Arizona; Timothy A. Rodriguez, Ohio State University; Dr. Laura A. Staal, University of North Carolina at Pembroke; and Jennifer Stengel-Mohr, Queens College, CUNY. The efforts of these dedicated educators made this a much better book.

ABOUT THE AUTHOR

Photograph by Ron Elkind

JODI REISS   Before retiring from Florida International University in Miami, Jodi Reiss served as the director of the TESOL master's program. In her nine years there, she adapted, developed, and taught a variety of graduate and undergraduate TESOL courses. She particularly enjoyed teaching Methods of TESOL, Assessment for English Language Learners, and the final seminar in the master's program, in which her teachers directed their full attention toward analyzing their own teaching behaviors. These courses in how to teach, how to evaluate, and how to become a reflective practitioner served as a rich source of material for her books.

Since her retirement, Ms. Reiss has written four books for secondary school teachers on strategies for teaching content to English language learners. In conjunction with these books, she conducts teacher workshops and presentations for school districts throughout the United States. Although no longer in the classroom, her clearly written books and popular workshops have allowed her to continue to provide information and inspiration to teachers of English language learners.

PART

I

PERSPECTIVES FOR CLASSROOM PRACTICE: THEORY AND CULTURE

CHAPTER 1

THEORETICAL CONSIDERATIONS

The director of the United States Census Bureau, Robert Groves, was asked, "What do you think will be the most surprising information the [2010] Census will reveal?" This was his reply:

> What's going to . . . surprise us all is the dispersion of new ethnic groups all over the country. Immigration doesn't just come to the East Coast or to the West Coast the way it did in earlier generations. It's everywhere now." ("10 Questions," 2010)

Teachers will undoubtedly not find this quite so surprising. A year earlier, the *New York Times* wrote:

> Students learning English, labeled as English Language Learners by education officials, are among the nation's fastest-growing group of students. In recent years these students have flooded small towns and suburban school districts in states like Arkansas, Georgia and North Carolina, which have little experience with immigrants. ("New to English," 2009)

Indeed, school districts in every state in the nation face the challenge of developing programs and services to help these students learn English, as well as math, science, social studies, and language arts. Schools and teachers are held accountable to demonstrate yearly progress for all students, including the English language learners (ELLs). The challenge affects teachers of every grade level and subject area. The challenge is hard, and stakes are high—each year they seem to get harder and higher.

WHY CONTENT TEACHERS CAN HELP

Learning content is difficult for ELLs for reasons discussed later in this chapter and in Chapter 2. Teachers who are aware of these challenges and use techniques to make their content material more learnable can make a real difference in the academic lives of the ELLs in their classrooms by helping them begin to experience success as learners. Content teachers can help ELLs develop an I-can-do-it attitude toward learning that promotes their self-confidence and increases their motivation to learn. Thinking you can do it goes a long way toward academic success, and success breeds more success.

HOW CONTENT TEACHERS CAN HELP

Content teachers can help by using instructional strategies that increase the comprehensibility of the content they teach and by choosing assignment and assessment strategies that separate content knowledge from English language knowledge. These are the strategies presented in this text. However, to choose and use the strategies that work best for you, your content, and your students, you will first need a set of basic theoretical understandings.

THEORETICAL FOUNDATIONS

Good teachers make good choices, and good choices are grounded in theory. The theories, hypotheses, and principles of these six theorists inform the strategies presented in this text:

- Cummins's differentiation between social and academic language
- Krashen's separate concepts of the affective filter and comprehensible input
- Vygotsky's zone of proximal development
- Swain's ideas about meaningful interaction
- Brown's principles of language teaching and language learning
- Bloom's taxonomy classifying levels of cognitive challenge

The sections that follow examine each of these important contributions. A final section shows how together they form a cohesive support system for teaching content to ELLs.

Cummins: Differentiation of Social and Academic Language

Jim Cummins (1984) contributed the concept that *academic language,* the language of the classroom, requires more cognitively demanding language skills than *social language,* the language of the outside world. This differentiation forms a foundation for understanding why the process and product of content instruction are challenging for ELLs. The concept of academic language underlies virtually every strategy in this text and deserves to be examined in detail.

Understanding Social Language

Language is a social construct: The purpose of language is communication. In a process closely resembling first-language acquisition, children learning English as a second language communicate to make friends with other children and to participate in the youth culture of sports, music, movies, TV, video games, Internet, fads, and fashion. They develop the social language skills of everyday activities through a process of natural acquisition by becoming immersed in the English-language-rich environments surrounding these activities. They learn to retell events, describe activities, express personal opinions, and maintain conversation. Children learning English develop these social language skills with an apparent ease that often awes adult learners. Because these children are so immersed in an English-speaking environment, it takes only six months to two years for them to develop this type of language competence (Cummins, 1981).

Understanding Academic Language

Schools have traditionally judged the proficiency level of ELLs by assessing their oral language communication skills, an often highly misleading indicator. Students can function at high levels in face-to-face social interaction and yet lack critical language skills for learning academic content.

Unlike social language, the language of the classroom requires students to use language that is conceptually demanding and cognitively complex. Academic assignments require students to use different forms of language to do the following:

define	describe	explain
list	order	classify
discuss	compare	contrast
analyze	explain	infer
integrate	predict	deduce
evaluate	justify	defend

The challenge inherent in these uses of academic language for ELLs is increased by the need to apply them in all modalities of communication: speaking, listening, reading,

Social Language	Academic Language
Tell me about the girls in your gymnastics class.	Compare and contrast the main characters in the book.
Why do you want to do that?	Explain what you believe to be the most effective choice.
Is there an easier way to do this?	Can you propose and support an alternative technique to facilitate this procedure?
What do you think is going to happen? Why?	Formulate a hypothesis that predicts the most probable outcome. Explain your reasoning.
Who's your favorite teacher? Why?	Which of the characters do you find the most interesting? Justify and explain you choice.

Figure 1.1   Comparing Social and Academic Language

and writing. The examples in Figure 1.1, which contrast social and academic language usage, illustrate the distinct differences in the choice of words, the way the words are used, and the type of thought processing the two types of usage require.

The complex skills associated with academic language are situation specific, cognitively challenging, and context reduced. Academic language is *situation specific* because it is used exclusively in a classroom environment and must be learned. Students cannot acquire it naturally through immersion in activities of everyday life. With such limited exposure, it takes from five to seven years to reach full development (Cummins, 1981). More recent research has shown that this type of language competence can take up to 10 years to develop in language learners, depending on the amount of formal schooling students have received in their first language (Thomas & Collier, 1995).

Academic language is *cognitively challenging* because it deals largely with abstract concepts. It is beyond the realm of the here-and-now—those concrete personal experiences and activities that make social language easier to understand.

And finally, it is *context reduced* because oral and written academic tasks frequently lack the environmental clues to meaning that facilitate comprehension of social language.

Making Academic Language More Comprehensible

Cummins next addressed the issue of how to make the cognitive challenge of classroom oral and written academic language more comprehensible for ELLs. Embedding academic language in context, he found, provides the support of environmental clues to make cognitively demanding content easier for ELLs to understand. This concept is reminiscent of the adage "A picture is worth a thousand words."

Figure 1.2 shows the graphic framework Cummins created to show what makes language easier or more difficult for these students. Difficulty is based on the relationship between two factors: the degree of *cognitive demand* and the amount of available *contextual support.*

The cognitive challenge of oral or written tasks is represented in the framework as undemanding (easy) in the two quadrants across the top of Cummins's chart or demanding (difficult) in the two lower quadrants. *Cognitively undemanding* tasks are either largely social or simply academically easy; *cognitively demanding* tasks are academically difficult, requiring higher levels of thought processing and language skills.

Contextual support, the second factor in Cummins's framework, assists comprehension by providing clues to the meanings of words. The more that spoken and written words are supported, or embedded, in context, the easier they are to understand. Contextual support for oral tasks comes from supplementing spoken language with facial expressions, gestures, body language, demonstration, and graphic and visual representation. Contextual support for written tasks comes from supplementing text with pictures,

I Cognitively Undemanding + Context Embedded	II Cognitively Undemanding + Context Reduced
III Cognitively Demanding + Context Embedded	IV Cognitively Demanding + Context Reduced

Figure 1.2 Cummins' Framework for Evaluating Language Demand in Content Activities (Modified Format)

Cummins, J. (1984). *Bilingualism and Special Education: Issues in Assessment and Pedogogy.* San Francisco, CA: College-Hill Press. Used with permission.

graphs, charts, tables, and other textbook aids. Tasks—both oral and written—with a high level of contextual support are *context embedded*. Tasks in which students must derive meaning solely from the spoken or written words themselves are *context reduced*.

The two quadrants on the left side of Cummins's chart represent tasks that are highly embedded and contextually supported. Tasks in the two quadrants on the right side are those that are context reduced. Combining the two elements of cognitive challenge and contextual support, the quadrants move in difficulty from I to IV. ELLs will generally find Quadrant I tasks easy because they are low in cognitive demand and high in contextual support. Quadrant IV tasks, at the other end of the spectrum, will be difficult for ELLs because they are academically demanding and lack contextual support.

Examples of tasks in each of the four quadrants, as shown in Figure 1.3, help to clarify Cummins's chart. Face-to-face conversation is classified as a Quadrant I task because the

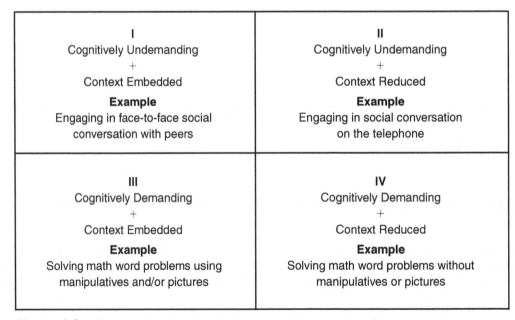

I Cognitively Undemanding + Context Embedded **Example** Engaging in face-to-face social conversation with peers	II Cognitively Undemanding + Context Reduced **Example** Engaging in social conversation on the telephone
III Cognitively Demanding + Context Embedded **Example** Solving math word problems using manipulatives and/or pictures	IV Cognitively Demanding + Context Reduced **Example** Solving math word problems without manipulatives or pictures

Figure 1.3 Cummins' Framework with Examples of Tasks for Each Quadrant

Cummins, J. (1984). *Bilingualism and Special Education: Issues in Assessment and Pedagogy.* San Francisco, CA: College-Hill Press. Used with permission.

cognitive demand is low (most conversation is purely social) and the contextual support is high (observing the speaker's lips, facial expressions, and body language). The task moves to Quadrant II when the same conversation takes place over the telephone. The task is still social and, thus, cognitively undemanding, but here the listener loses the speaker's contextual support and must rely completely on auditory input for comprehension.

The tasks illustrating Quadrants III and IV are similar. On the lower half of the chart, the tasks are cognitively challenging. ELLs (and other students) will find mathematical word problems that offer the contextual support of manipulatives, graphics, and/or pictures easier to solve than problems without these environmental clues. Again, the level of difficulty changes in accordance with the degree to which words are embedded in context.

Not every task can be neatly placed in a quadrant. Variables within a task or within a student's prior knowledge or experience can affect its placement on the chart. Solving simple computational problems in math, for example, would normally be considered a Quadrant III task. However, it would move to Quadrant IV if a student's native language used a different system of notation for writing numerals.

An even more complex example involves students' participation in physical education classes. Demonstrating how to play a sports game is clearly a Quadrant I task. However, it would fall into Quadrant II if the rules of play were explained orally with no accompanying demonstration. Reading and discussing complex rules and regulations of play or the history of a sport would move these tasks into the cognitively demanding quadrants. And whether they fell in Quadrant III or Quadrant IV would depend upon the amount of available contextual support.

Using Cummins' Principles

Strategies to embed academic tasks in context—to move them from Quadrant IV to Quadrant III—are commonly called *scaffolded instruction,* or simply *scaffolding.* The term derives from the construction trades, in which temporary external structures, *scaffolds,* provide support for workers as they construct a building. These scaffolds allow access to parts of the construction that would otherwise be impossible to reach. So, too, it is with scaffolded instruction. In academics, scaffolds provide ELLs with the support they need to learn content while they are developing their English language skills. In ways figuratively similar to those of construction, these scaffolding strategies allow language learners better access to content material and are then progressively dismantled and discarded as they are no longer needed for support.

Scaffolding strategies facilitate comprehension for ELLs by moving academic tasks from Cummins's Quadrant IV to Quadrant III. For example, consider the Quadrant IV task of reading about materials that conduct electricity. Science teachers can shift this to Quadrant III by using the direct inquiry process. In class, students test materials such as plastics, woods, metals, and glass in a closed-circuit battery experiment to discover which materials are good conductors of electricity and which are not. Manipulating real-life objects turns abstract concepts into concrete academic tasks. It is a scaffolding strategy that allows students to formulate their own conclusions; real learning is taking place, independent of English language knowledge.

This example also illustrates the goal of maintaining a high level of cognitive challenge for ELLs. Direct inquiry learning of this type does not water down the curriculum. Embedding content in context maintains high levels of cognitive demand at the same time that it facilitates comprehension of important academic concepts.

Learning tasks in content classrooms frequently fall into Quadrant IV because they are cognitively demanding and context reduced. ELLs (and struggling readers, as well) typically find these tasks overwhelming and frustrating. Teachers can use the dual perspectives of cognitive challenge and contextual support to evaluate the difficulty of class instruction, activities, assignments, and assessments for their ELLs. This approach offers teachers a valuable tool to assist in selecting, planning, and using appropriate strategies to scaffold content learning, moving it from Quadrant IV to Quadrant III.

Krashen: The Affective Filter

As part of his five-hypothesis monitor model of second language acquisition, Stephen Krashen (1982) proposed the existence of an emotional filter that influences how much actual learning takes place in relation to input. The strength of the filter itself is determined by affective factors of learner anxiety, self-confidence, and motivation.

The affective filter may be conceived of as an emotional wall that blocks input from reaching the brain. Students who experience high learner anxiety, low self-confidence, and low motivation are said to have high affective filters that prevent them from successfully processing input. At the other extreme are learners with low affective filters who, with little anxiety, good self-confidence, and high motivation, will learn much more from the same amount of input.

Using the Affective Filter Concept

Content teachers who use the strategies in this text give their ELLs the opportunity to experience academic success. With every small success comes an increase in a student's self-confidence. The greater the gain in self-confidence, the more motivated the student becomes to continue learning. Increased self-confidence and motivation lower the affective filter and allow more academic input to be processed. The rewards of being a good learner are self-perpetuating.

Krashen: The Comprehensible Input Hypothesis

Krashen's second hypothesis that impacts content teaching deals with the concept of comprehensible input. He represented his idea in the formula $i + 1$, in which i is input—meaningful input based on real communication that is immediately comprehensible to the language learner—and $+ 1$ is the next level at which language is advanced just enough so that the learner is challenged by it but is able to learn it. This is the teachable/learnable area—the area between a student's actual and potential language development.

Extending the formula by logical implication, it is apparent that $i + 2$ would present too much challenge to be learnable and $i + 0$ would present no challenge toward more advanced levels of language development at all. To successfully advance language learning, then, comprehensible language input ideally should be $i + 1$.

Krashen's concept of language development can be compared to the experience of tennis players who, wanting to improve their skills, arrange games with players whose skill level is slightly more advanced than their own. The challenge motivates the less skilled players, and the effort is rewarding. Playing only with those whose skills are equal offers little input that might lead to improvement; playing with those whose skills are substantially higher leads to feelings of frustration and defeat. As with language learning, tennis skills develop best in an environment of $i + 1$.

Using i + 1

Teachers can facilitate comprehension for ELLs by incorporating strategies that expand the area between students' actual and potential levels of language ability. Scaffolding strategies that embed language in context use the $i + 1$ concept to allow students to advance to the next level of achievement.

Vygotsky: Zone of Proximal Development

Lev Vygotsky (1978) contributed the concept of the zone of proximal development (ZPD), which he defines as "the distance between [a student's] actual developmental level as determined by independent problem solving, and the level of potential development as determined through problem solving under adult guidance or in collaboration with

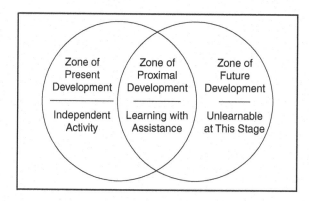

Figure 1.4 Understanding Vygotsky's Zone of Proximal Development

more capable peers" (p. 87). Figure 1.4 shows the three zones of possible development: the first, in which a learner can solve problems independently; the middle, in which the learner can solve them with assistance; and the third, in which the learner is unable to solve them at all because they are too advanced. Within the middle zone, according to Vygotsky, learning occurs only when teachers offer opportunities for students to actively interact with their academic environment.

Although Vygotsky's ZPD and Krashen's *i + 1* appear similar in content, the two differ in focus. Krashen applied his ideas narrowly to second-language skill development and focused on the need to make language input comprehensible. Vygotsky applied his ideas more broadly to learning in general and focused on the importance of meaningful interaction with others who are more advanced. Both concepts are useful for content teachers with ELLs in their classrooms.

Using the Zone of Proximal Development

Applying the ZPD to the content classroom addresses process issues rather than product issues. Students learn most effectively by becoming active participants in their own learning through interaction in the classroom. Students will progress to their fullest potential when teachers scaffold instruction with activity and assignment strategies that encourage working with teachers and peers, individually and in groups, in an atmosphere of guidance and collaboration.

Swain: Meaningful Output

Merrill Swain's 1985 concept of meaningful output supports Vygotsky's ZPD and enriches Krashen's comprehensible input. Swain views meaningful output as central to the process of language acquisition because it provides learners with opportunities to work with developing language in contextualized, meaningful situations. Swain believes that "it is not input per se that is important to second language acquisition but input that occurs in interaction where meaning is negotiated" (1985, p. 246).

The concept of *negotiated meaning* comes from the way people communicate with each other. To clarify meaning in conversation, native speakers often participate in a series of back-and-forth exchanges that lead to more complete understanding. However, when native and *nonnative* speakers converse, they engage in a series of trial-and-error exchanges in which language becomes successively modified until both parties understand the communication. Nonnative speakers receive input from their conversational partners. If words are not understood, language learners request more comprehensible input by asking for repetition or clarification, causing the native speaker to paraphrase or offer environmental clues—for example, gestures, facial expressions, drawings—to make meaning clearer. This is how meaning is negotiated through interaction.

Using Meaningful Output

Swain's concept of meaningful output has direct bearing on learning in content classrooms. The concept highlights the importance of small group interaction in long-term retention of both language and conceptual knowledge. Content teachers can choose strategies that encourage students to negotiate meaning through paired or small group discussion. ELLs, in meaningful academic conversation with their peers, receive input and feedback that allow them to compare their language use (vocabulary, pronunciation, structures) and their conceptual understandings with those of their native-speaking peers. Manipulating language in meaningful classroom interaction clarifies input and makes it more comprehensible for ELLs.

Brown: Principles of Language Teaching and Learning

Of the 12 language teaching and learning principles upon which H. Douglas Brown (2007) based his entire methodology, five have direct bearing on teaching content to ELLs. In some you will recognize the tribute he pays to the theorists discussed in the preceding sections.

Principle 2, *meaningful learning*, is the conceptual opposite of rote learning. Unlike the isolated, memorized facts of rote learning, meaningful learning promotes long-term retention of knowledge. Brown says that learning can be made meaningful for ELLs by appealing to their interests, by associating new topics and concepts with their existing knowledge and experience, by making abstract learning more concrete, and by choosing activities and assignments that go beyond drill and memorization (Brown, 2007, p. 66).

Principle 4, the *intrinsic motivation principle*, says that all human beings work, act, or behave in anticipation of a reward, but "the most powerful rewards are those that are intrinsically motivated within the learner" (Brown, 2007, p. 68). When one's own needs, wants, and/or desires are the source of behavior, the behavior itself becomes self-rewarding. Tangible rewards of praise and grades motivate students, but more long-term learning takes place when students are motivated to learn because they perceive classroom activities and assignments to be "fun, interesting, useful, or challenging" (Brown, 2007, p. 68).

Principle 5, *strategic investment*, says that successful learning largely depends on the learner developing a set of strategies for understanding and producing the language involved in content learning. The greater the variety of strategies a learner can develop for processing information, the greater the possibility of academic success. Because students vary in their abilities to use individual strategies, teachers need to create opportunities to unlock the "secrets" of learning as a means of promoting academic success among students.

Principle 8, *willingness to communicate,* combines the closely related concepts of self-confidence and risk-taking. When language learners develop an I-can-do-it attitude, they will be more willing to risk using language "for meaningful purposes, to ask questions, and to assert themselves" (Brown, 2007, p. 73). Most educational research has shown that willingness to communicate leads to increased long-term retention and intrinsic motivation. This concept is particularly interesting in light of certain academic cultures that instead encourage correctness and discourage even educated guesses.

Teachers can build student confidence and encourage risk-taking behavior by using verbal and nonverbal approval and encouragement and by assigning tasks in sequence from easier to more difficult. Early successes motivate students to deal with successively more challenging tasks. In addition, students will be more willing to take language risks when the classroom atmosphere "encourages students to try out language [and] to venture a response" (Brown, 2007, p. 74). Teachers need to reward students' attempts with a response that encourages future attempts. ELLs who feel assured that language errors are a normal part of language learning will ultimately be more successful learners.

Principle 9, the *language–culture connection*, presents the concept that learning a new language involves learning a new culture: all the customs, beliefs, and values that deal with ways of thinking, feeling, and acting. Content teachers who are aware that culture determines expectations of "proper" classroom behavior will avoid misinterpretation by recognizing that the way ELLs act in class may be rooted in strong cultural components.

Meaningful Learning	Make learning meaningful and interesting to promote long-term retention of knowledge
Intrinsic Motivation	Motivate student learning by making it interesting, useful, challenging, and fun
Strategic Investment	Teach learners *how* to learn by actively teaching a variety of learning strategies
Willingness to Communicate	Encourage communication by building student self-confidence, by supporting students' efforts to use language in meaningful ways, and by fostering students' understanding that errors are a normal part of the learning process
Language–Culture Connection	Recognize that learning a new language involves learning a new culture and new ways of thinking, feeling, and acting

Figure 1.5 Brown's Principles at a Glance

Indeed, culture can even lead ELLs to confusion about particular concepts or topics. Brown suggests that teachers "discuss cross-cultural differences with [their] students . . . [and] make explicit to [the] students what [the teachers] may take for granted in [their] own culture" (Brown, 2007, p. 75).

Using Brown's Principles

Brown's principles, shown in summary form in Figure 1.5, form a humanistic foundation for teaching language and, by extension, for teaching content. They serve as a guide to understanding, evaluating, and selecting sets of strategies to make the content you teach more accessible and enjoyable for the ELLs in your classroom.

Bloom: Taxonomy

Benjamin Bloom (Bloom & Krathwohl, 1977) examined teacher question patterns and devised a system to categorize them according to the degree of cognitive challenge they posed. He identified six levels of question types in his taxonomy and termed them *knowledge, comprehension, application, analysis, synthesis,* and *evaluation.* Questions at the knowledge and comprehension levels are simple and concrete, requiring only rote learning. Increasing in cognitive challenge, questions designated as application, analysis, synthesis, and evaluation are more abstract and increasingly complex. These are the questions that encourage critical thinking.

At the lower levels of cognitive challenge, *knowledge questions* demand only isolated, memorized facts as answers, testing recall and recognition of information. Questions of this type often start with *who, what, when,* and *where,* as in "Who wrote the Declaration of Independence?" *Comprehension questions* ask for short explanations or definitions of basic meaning in the students' own words, as in "What does each part of the Declaration of Independence say?" *Application questions* require students to apply known information to new situations, using rules and principles to produce a result, as in the question "How is the Constitution used today?"

Moving up the ladder of cognitive challenge, *analysis questions* focus on individual elements. They ask students to consider the relationship of the separate parts to each other and to the whole, as in "What qualities did the heroes of the War of Independence have in common? How were they different?" *Synthesis questions* require putting elements together in a novel way, as in "How might life have been different for the colonists if they had lost the War of Independence?" *Evaluation questions,* the most cognitively challenging level, ask students to make, justify, and defend judgments based on the information under consideration. In this category are questions such as this: "Benjamin Franklin was one of the most important people in early American history, but he went to school for only two years. How can you explain this? Could this happen today? Why or why not?" Figure 1.6 summarizes types of thought processing, associated verbs, and additional questions for each of the six levels of cognitive demand.

Level	What Students Are Asked to Do	Useful Verbs	Sample Questions
Knowledge	• memorize • recognize • recall • remember • identify	tell state locate relate list find name choose define label select match	Who, what, when where, how? What happened after _____? How many _____? Which is true or false? Which one shows _____?
Comprehension	• interpret • paraphrase • organize facts • classify • condense • compare • contrast • summarize	explain restate outline compare describe distinguish convert estimate rewrite arrange	What was the main idea? Can you state this in your own words? What do you think is meant by _____ ? Does X mean the same as Y? What are the differences between _____? Which statements support _____? What information does the graph (table) give?
Application	• solve problems • use information to produce a result • extend what is learned to an unknown • make predictions • apply facts, rules, principles	apply interpret solve use demonstrate dramatize change compute calculate construct modify predict	How is X an example of _____ ? Why is _____ significant? How is X related to _____ ? How might you group these _____ ? What factors would change if _____ ? What would happen if _____ ?
Analysis	• identify component parts of a whole • examine relationship of parts to whole • understand underlying structures • find patterns • draw conclusions	analyze separate probe categorize connect arrange	What are the elements of _____? How would you classify _____ according to _____? How does _____ affect the whole? What are some different ways to categorize _____?

Figure 1.6 Bloom's Toxonomy (*continued*)

Level	What Students Are Asked to Do	Useful Verbs	Sample Questions
	• distinguish between fact and inference • recognize hidden meaning	divide dissect deconstruct group compare infer	Why did _____ changes occur? What were the motives behind _____? What assumptions are part of _____? What is the implication of _____?
Synthesis	• combine ideas or elements to form a new whole • generalize from given facts • relate knowledge from separate areas • predict, draw conclusions	combine integrate create design devise invent develop compose modify rearrange reorganize generate propose formulate hypothesize	What if _____? What would you predict from _____? How would you design a _____ to _____? What might happen if you combined _____? What solutions might you offer for _____? What are some unusual ways to use _____? What are some alternative ways to _____?
Evaluation	• make value decisions about issues and ideas • compare and discriminate information • verify value of evidence • recognize subjectivity • develop opinions, judgments, and decisions • make and justify choices	assess appraise evaluate decide rank rate recommend support defend convince judge discriminate prioritize deduce conclude criticize critique	What is your position on _____? Why? Is there a better solution for _____? How would you have handled _____? What evidence supports your position on _____? Do you believe _____ was a positive or negative influence? Why? What criteria are you using to evaluate _____?

Figure 1.6 Bloom's Toxonomy

Using Bloom's Taxonomy

It is discouraging to note that the great majority of teachers' oral and written questions fall into the two lowest levels of Bloom's taxonomy. Developing an awareness of question types focuses teacher attention on the levels of cognitive demand in teacher-directed discussions, classroom activities and assignments, and teacher-made quizzes and tests. An important objective of the strategies in this text is to maintain a high level of critical thinking for ELLs (actually, for all students) while simultaneously facilitating their comprehension.

APPLYING THE THEORIES AND PRINCIPLES

The theories and principles presented in this chapter individually contribute to the understanding of teaching content to ELLs. However, to be of real value, they must be combined in a way that addresses this central question:

> How can content teachers use these theories and principles to promote more effective learning for the ELLs in their classrooms?

The answer lies in distilling the essential elements of these separate theories and principles into a practical application that can guide all aspects of instruction and assessment of ELLs in content classrooms. The *12 Guidelines for Practice* are the outcome of this process.

THEORY TO APPLICATION: 12 GUIDELINES FOR PRACTICE

1. Use scaffolding strategies with ELLs to facilitate comprehension of the specialized academic language of content classrooms.
2. Use scaffolding strategies to challenge ELLs to advance beyond their present state of independent activity, into the areas of potential learning in which content is learnable with the assistance of teachers and peers.
3. Use scaffolding strategies that embed the oral and written language of content material in a context-rich environment to facilitate learning for ELLs.
4. Use scaffolding strategies that maintain a high level of cognitive challenge, but lower the language demand by embedding it in context.
5. Maintain a high level of cognitive challenge for ELLS by selecting content material that is meaningful, interesting, and relevant.
6. Actively teach learning strategies to give students a "menu" of ways to process and learn new information.
7. Be aware that cultural differences may affect ELLs' models of classroom behavior and interpretation of specific content material.
8. Activate and develop background knowledge to make new content meaningful and to form a foundation upon which new learning can be built.
9. Provide opportunities for ELLs to negotiate conceptual understandings and to explore language usage through classroom interaction.
10. Lower learner anxiety in the classroom to create students who are more willing to participate in class, to become risk takers in the learning process, and ultimately to become more successful learners.
11. Use scaffolding strategies to assess content knowledge separately from English language knowledge so students can show what they know.
12. Provide opportunities for students to experience success in the classroom: Success in learning promotes more success by increasing learner motivation, interest, and self-confidence.

Together, these theory-based guidelines form the cornerstone of effective instruction and assessment of ELLs in content classrooms. They also serve as a solid foundation upon which the strategies in each chapter of this text are based. Let these guidelines inform your choices of strategies to maximize your ELLs' academic achievements.

Scaffolding strategies offer rewards to students that go beyond just learning the content being taught. These strategies offer students the beginnings of academic success, bringing with it renewed interest and motivation to learn. Students' feelings of self-confidence as learners will grow, and they will begin to view school as a place of positive rewards.

Scaffolding strategies give you, the content teacher, a range and variety of options to help you make better instructional decisions. You will see that using these techniques, ideas, and activities in your classroom makes a real difference in the academic lives of your ELLs. And like your students, you will derive greater satisfaction from your teaching. You will enjoy the renewed confidence that comes with being an even more accomplished professional.

QUESTIONS FOR DISCUSSION

1. Locate statistics in your state and/or district for the number of ELLs enrolled in K–12 schools over the last five years. Compare that to the total enrollment in the same time period. What are the enrollment projections for the next five years?

2. Using Cummins' quadrants, how would you classify each of the following tasks? The final three tasks can be placed in more than one quadrant; for those, justify and explain your placement.

   a. Listening to a tape-recorded presentation about caring for pets
   b. Listening to a presentation about pet animals that includes pictures and video
   c. Listening to a lecture on an unfamiliar topic
   d. Participating in a conversation with friends about politics or economics
   e. Understanding written text through pictures and graphics
   f. Understanding written text through small group discussion
   g. Reading Shakespeare's *Romeo and Juliet* in its original format
   h. Reading the illustrated (comic book) version of Shakespeare's *Romeo and Juliet*
   i. Writing research reports on assigned topics in social studies
   j. Reading a list of required school supplies
   k. Solving math problems
   l. Doing a science experiment

3. Observe a content class and keep a written log of the questions the teacher asks. Classify them according to Bloom's taxonomy. What percentage of the total is made up of questions classified as knowledge and comprehension? Make up some additional higher level questions that the teacher could have used in this lesson.

4. If you have ever studied a foreign language, how successful were you in learning it? Can you explain your success or lack of it based on these theories, principles, and guidelines?

REFERENCES AND RESOURCES

Bloom, B. (Ed.). (1956). *Taxonomy of educational objectives: Handbook I—Cognitive domain.* White Plains, NY: Addison Wesley.

Bloom, B., & Krathwohl, D. (1977). *Taxonomy of educational objectives: Handbook 1—Cognitive domain.* San Diego, CA: College-Hill Press.

Brown, H. D. (2007). *Teaching by principles: An interactive approach to language pedagogy* (3rd ed.). White Plains, NY: Pearson Education.

Cummins, J. (1981). The role of primary language development in promoting educational success for language minority students. In California Department of Education (Ed.), *Schooling and language minority students: A theoretical framework* (pp. 3–49). Los Angeles: Evaluation, Dissemination and Assessment Center, California State University.

Cummins, J. (1984). *Bilingualism and special education: Issues in assessment pedagogy.* San Francisco: College-Hill Press.

Krashen, S. (1982). *Principles and practice in second language acquisition.* Oxford, England: Pergamon Press.

Krashen, S. (1985). *The input hypothesis: Issues and implications.* London: Longman.

New to English. (2009, March 13). *New York Times.* Retrieved May 6, 2010, from http://www.nytimes.com/interactive/2009/03/13/us/ELL-students.html

Richard-Amato, P. A., & Snow, M. A. (Eds.). (2005). *Academic success for English language learners: Strategies for K–12 mainstream teachers.* White Plains, NY: Pearson Education.

Swain, M. (1985). Communicative competence: Some roles of comprehensible input and comprehensible output in its development. In S. Gass & C. Madden (Eds.), *Input in second language acquisition* (pp. 235–253). Rowley, MA: Newbury House.

10 Questions. (2010, April 5). *Time, 175*(13), 2.

Thomas, W. P., & Collier, V. P. (1995). Language minority student achievement and program effectiveness. *California Association for Bilingual Education Newletter, 17*(5), 19, 24.

Vygotsky, L. (1978). *Mind in society: Development of higher psychological processes.* Cambridge, MA: Harvard University Press.

CHAPTER 2

CULTURE AND CONTENT INSTRUCTION

CULTURE AND THE PROCESS OF CONTENT INSTRUCTION

Teachers occasionally find themselves puzzled by certain of their ELLs' classroom behaviors and responses. What they are seeing may well be the effects of a deeply ingrained culture transplanted to new environments.

Culture may be defined as "the sum of attitudes, customs, and beliefs that distinguishes one group of people from another. Culture is transmitted, through language, material objects, ritual, institutions, and art, from one generation to the next" (Hirsch, 2002, p. 431). Culture is shared by individuals within the group and is made up of many parts: values, beliefs, standards of beauty, ideas about celebrations, patterns of thinking, norms of behavior, and styles of communication. Among other things, culture determines how its group members interact with others. Culture goes beyond the sum of its parts: It is the eyes through which individuals view and interpret the world.

ELLs in U.S. schools strive to learn not only English but also the culture of American schools. They bring their culture with them, responding in ways that are appropriate and polite within their own groups. In their new classrooms, however, these patterns of behavior may be quite different from their teachers' expectations. The common parental admonishment to "behave in class," for example, may mean to sit silently, even when asked a direct question. Teachers, not realizing the cultural context of these responses, often mistakenly perceive these behaviors on an individual level as rudeness, disinterest, or lack of knowledge. Awareness of culture as a potential source of student behavior will help teachers depersonalize the behavior, moving it from the personal to the cultural level. The next sections examine areas of frequently misunderstood school behaviors.

Class Work Patterns

The typical classroom uses whole class, small group, and individual work formats. In American schools, effective instruction consists of balancing the three types. In cultures that place more value on group cooperation, however, misunderstandings of intent can occur when individual work is required, as in a testing situation. Some cultures, in contrast, view the teacher as the academic authority and, as such, the only appropriate source of learning. Students from this type of educational background may view group work as nonproductive and may be reluctant to participate in it.

> Yasmin's English skills were actually quite good, but she rarely participated in class. About halfway through the first semester, Ms. Dennis, her teacher, had a conference with her to talk about her lack of participation. Yasmin had a ready answer because it was a problem that she, too, was worried about.
>
> Yasmin explained that each night she read and memorized all the information in the textbook. But the next day in class, the teacher asked "other" questions—not questions about the facts in the book.
>
> It was a "lighbulb moment" for Ms. Dennis. Yasmin was 100% correct in her assessment of the situation. Ms. Dennis viewed the information in the textbook as a knowledge base and used class time to build upon that knowledge. Her questions guided students to extend their conceptual understandings by engaging them in critical thinking and problem solving tasks based on the textbook readings. Yasmin's prior academic experience had not prepared her for this approach to instruction.

Figure 2.1   A True Tale of Cross-Cultural Misunderstanding

Instructional Patterns

Critical thinking, problem solving, and discovery learning are considered the gold standards of American instructional approaches. School programs in other countries, on the other hand, often put greater emphasis on techniques of rote memorization and recitation for learning. ELLs from these cultures may experience difficulty in understanding and participating in the instructional processes in which they find themselves immersed. The incident described in Figure 2.1 is an example of this type of misunderstanding.

Questioning Patterns

American classrooms encourage and reward active student participation. Many school cultures in other countries, however, do not.

Teachers often lead discussions by calling on students who raise their hands. But students from cultures that deeply value humility may not volunteer answers because displaying knowledge is considered a form of showing off.

Also preventing some ELLs from freely participating in class is a cultural view of adults as figures of authority. Children who are taught not to speak until they are spoken to will not volunteer information, request clarification, or seek additional information. Moreover, calling on a student who doesn't volunteer may produce an unintended effect. Students from cultures in which being correct is prized may feel they have brought shame on themselves, their families, even their communities, by giving a wrong answer.

Additionally, students may not ask questions or seek clarification because they feel it might cause the teacher embarrassment since their not understanding would reflect poorly on the teacher's knowledge and ability to teach. Others who believe that questioning an adult is rude and disrespectful may view teachers who invite this type of interaction as lacking authority in their own classrooms.

Expressing Opinions

Students from some cultures may not be willing to participate in discussions that involve expressing opposing opinions or beliefs. For students whose culture teaches them that it is rude and disrespectful to disagree with an authority figure, offering an opinion that differs from that of the teacher is simply not an option. Even disagreeing with peers may feel impolite.

Response Time Patterns

Americans, in general, value conversation and are uncomfortable with silence. Every culture has its own rules of conversation—rules for when to speak, how and when to interrupt, and how many people can speak at the same time. Those who follow the rules are considered polite. Interestingly, rules vary not only across cultures but also regionally across the United States.

In cultures that value silence, children learn that taking time before responding shows courtesy, respect, and wisdom. Other cultures, in contrast, value responses that are loud and quick. Those who jump right in to answer a question are seen as smart, interested, involved, and even strong.

Variations in culturally determined response patterns may cause teachers to misinterpret student behaviors during class discussions. Teachers may characterize students who don't immediately reply to questions as slow or lacking knowledge and those who jump right in as rude, domineering, or overanxious. Teachers who can depersonalize these behaviors by repositioning them in a cultural context will be able to view these students more positively and to help them adjust to more appropriate behaviors for the American classroom.

Attention Patterns

In mainstream American culture, listeners in social and academic situations indicate that they are paying attention to the speaker through eye contact and head nods. Most teachers like to see every student looking directly at them while they teach and view lack of eye contact as a sign of disrespect or disinterest. In other cultures, however, downcast eyes denote respect for the speaker, particularly when the speaker is a figure of authority. Direct eye contact with an adult, especially a teacher, would be considered overt boldness or defiant behavior.

Teachers also feel understood and appreciated when students nod their heads during periods of instruction. In many cultures, however, head nods indicate neither understanding nor agreement. Head nods may simply show that the speaker is being heard. Still other cultures value emotional control, discouraging any show of enthusiasm or change in facial features.

Feedback Patterns

U.S. teachers are generous in their use of praise, doling out intrinsic and extrinsic rewards as reinforcement for achievement and behavior. They use praise to encourage students' efforts to learn. Positive reinforcement theory advocates finding even small successes to praise.

Praise in other cultures, however, is reserved for only true excellence and outstanding performance. Too much praise is seen as insincere. Teachers who praise generously may even be viewed as inadequate: If students are so praiseworthy, perhaps the teacher just doesn't know all that much more than the students. Alternatively, effusive praise offered in front of the whole class may bring feelings of discomfort to students whose culture values humility.

Misunderstandings also can occur in the area of error correction. Some cultures strive for academic perfection to a greater degree than U.S. school culture does. To those students, a teacher's lack of constant correction may be viewed, like too much praise, as a sign of inadequacy.

Even grading symbols may be misunderstood. Not all countries use the common notations of ✓ for right and ✗ for wrong. It is possible that such marks may also be subject to misinterpretation.

Patterns of Address

It is traditional in American schools to address teachers by using Mr. or Ms. and the last name. Teachers are often irritated to hear themselves called simply "Teacher" by their ELLs. It may come as a surprise to learn that ELLs are according their teachers great respect with this form of address. To them, it is the equivalent of the U.S. practice of addressing a physician as "Doctor" and the university instructor as "Professor." The next time a student calls you "Teacher," smile and enjoy the respect and admiration being offered you and your profession.

A Shift in Perception

Awareness of areas of potential cross-cultural misunderstanding allows teachers to develop multicultural competency and to see their ELL students in a clearer light. Reactively, thinking about culture as the source of a student's behavior will help to refocus the way you perceive what is happening in your classroom. Proactively, here are some of the things you can do to ease cultural adjustment issues for ELLs:

- Vary class work formats and explain the purpose of each type.
- Model and discuss commonly practiced classroom behaviors, such as asking and answering questions, offering an opinion or point of view, and taking turns.
- Praise something specific in a student's response rather than repeating the generic "Very good."
- Allow extended wait time for students whose culture values it.
- Explain the meaning of your written correction symbols.
- Learn about the cultures represented in your classroom by talking to adults familiar with those cultures or by doing Internet research on websites sponsored by unbiased sources.
- Talk about American cultural mores and behaviors to raise awareness for all students in your classes.

In addition to these specific proactive suggestions, it is valuable to involve ELLs' parents whenever possible; they, too, are making a cultural adjustment. You can overcome language barriers in a number of different ways. Did you know that there are free Internet translation sites? These are listed in the *References and Resources* section at the end of this chapter. Another strategy is to identify bilingual contacts and liaisons who may be willing to serve as volunteers. Foreign language instructors at high schools or local colleges may also be able to help. These last two resources work particularly well when coordinated as a whole school effort.

One final suggestion to ease cultural adjustment for ELLs is to find opportunities to promote friendships between them and their native-speaking peers. Students of every age and nationality share a need to belong and to contribute. ELLs who form a friendship with even one schoolmate are more likely to make successful adjustments to academic life. Teachers can encourage this by assigning new students a buddy, a work partner, even a lunch partner. It's amazing what a big difference this one small step can make.

Slow Change in Cultural Behaviors

Changes in culturally ingrained behavior take time. Students who become familiar with the variations in cultural expectations will probably not be able to put those new behaviors into immediate effect. Understanding that American students who volunteer

Mr. Elkind thought he had a great idea for his advanced class of young adult ESL students. Learning about American humor, he reasoned, would provide an enjoyable forum for his students' language development through class discussion and, at the same time, expose them to deeper understanding of their new culture. He had a great sense of humor himself and couldn't wait to get right into the fun of it.

But Mr. Elkind was wrong, and the unit fell completely flat. He discovered that understanding the culture behind a joke doesn't make it funny to someone whose culture doesn't share the same beliefs. Jokes about dogs having more creature comforts than a husband held no humor for those who believed that dogs are dirty and should never be allowed inside a home. Similarly, jokes about husbands' and wives' relationships with their mothers-in-law brought no smiles to those whose cultures elevate mothers-in-law to positions of great respect, esteem, even power.

In this unit, Mr. Elkind learned as much about culture as did his students. His students gathered new information about American cultural icons and beliefs, and Mr. Elkind learned that acquiring new cultural knowledge doesn't automatically result in deeper understandings. The unit on humor didn't turn out to be as funny as he had anticipated, but it was undeniably a great learning experience for everyone involved.

Figure 2.2 It's Just Not Funny

answers, for example, are not showing off will not make ELLs want to behave in that manner themselves, as the instructor in Figure 2.2 found out. In matters like these, emotional responses lag far behind rational understanding. The roots of culture run strong and deep.

CULTURE AND THE PRODUCT OF CONTENT LEARNING

Culture may also influence comprehension of specific content. Unlike notations of dates and time (see Figure 2.3), which cross all content areas, many content-specific cultural issues exist in math, science, social studies, and language arts. Teacher awareness of areas of potential confusion may avert cultural misunderstandings.

Figure 2.3 Differences in Writing Dates and Times

U.S. Notation	Foreign Notation
DATES	
month/day/year	day/month/year
7/22/04	22/7/04
TIME	
12-hour clock + a.m. or p.m.	24-hour clock with period
hour:minute	hour.minute
8:40 a.m.	08.40
1:30 p.m.	13.30
8:40 p.m.	20.40

1 2 3 4 5 6 7 8 9 0

Figure 2.4 European Notation of Numerals

Special Considerations for Teachers of Math

On the most basic level, students from foreign countries may form numerals differently from American notation. Figure 2.4 shows the numerals as a typical European-schooled student would write them. Additionally, some areas teach writing a zero with a line through it, so it looks like this: Ø.

Numbers are highly ingrained in students' native languages. Counting in English is particularly difficult, even for ELLs with well-developed English language skills. The fact that fully bilingual speakers can determine their dominant language by monitoring the language they count in illustrates how deeply rooted numbers and counting really are. Reading large numbers correctly and understanding large numbers aurally are skills that improve slowly with a great deal of practice.

Mathematical usage of decimal points and commas in written notation is another area of potential confusion. Many foreign countries use a system that is the opposite of U.S. notation: Periods replace commas to mark off hundreds in large numbers, and commas are used in place of periods to mark off decimal places, as shown in Figure 2.5.

Additionally, in some countries, the meaning of *billion* varies from the U.S. concept of billion as one thousand million. In those places, 1 billion is equal to 1 million million.

Most of the world's countries use the metric system to measure weight, volume, and distance. Students schooled outside the United States will be accustomed to calculating measurements in meters, liters, kilograms, and kilometers. They will need practice to become comfortable with the U.S. system of feet, quarts, pounds, and miles. And since "knowing metric" is a real plus in the world economy, ELLs and native-speaking students could engage in reciprocal teaching to everyone's advantage.

Another area of possible cultural difference is in the focus on process so prevalent in American schools. In some cultures, the final answer is more valued than the process of finding the answer. The teacher's request to "show your work" may not feel right to ELLs as their grades would have been lowered for doing so in their native countries.

Even the paper used for computation may seem unusual to ELLs. In some countries, students use graph paper for all math work to ensure that numerals are evenly spaced within the grid lines. When presented with blank paper, these students may experience difficulties arising from the lack of structure.

Teachers of math also must be aware that culturally unfamiliar vocabulary in math word problems may prevent students from demonstrating their true mathematical competency. Word problems built around certain situations—such as a circus, a county fair, or American-style football—may not be solvable by ELLs, not because of their computational ability but because of the unfamiliar vocabulary involved. Awareness will allow you to substitute a more familiar situation so that students can focus on the math.

	U.S. Notation	Foreign Notation
Grouping Hundreds	7,234,567	7,234.567
Marking Decimal Places	98.6	98,6
Showing Prices	$12.89	€12,89 (euro)
		£12,89 (pounds sterling)

Figure 2.5 Opposite Usage of Commas and Periods in Numeric Notation

Schools in foreign countries may also teach different algorithms for computation. Figure 2.6 through Figure 2.8 illustrate several alternative techniques for computation. If students in your classes are accustomed to using these approaches, it is wise to let them continue such practices. Ask them to demonstrate their particular techniques to the whole class. You and your students will be fascinated by their means of deriving an answer, and your ELLs may, in the process, earn some extra esteem and respect.

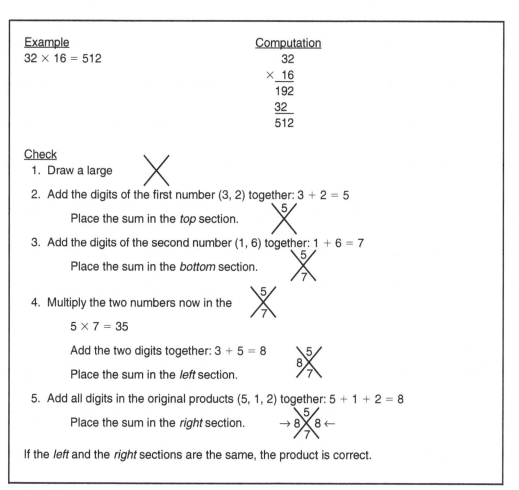

Figure 2.6 Alternative Division Algorithms

Figure 2.7 An Alternative Technique for Checking Multiplication Problems

Example	Computation
$89 \times 47 = 4183$	89

$$\begin{array}{r} 89 \\ 47 \\ \hline 623 \\ 356 \\ \hline 4183 \end{array}$$

Note: Only a single digit can be placed in the four sections of the $\times$

When the sum of any set of digits is more than a single digit, as in this example, add the second sum of digits together *again* to produce a single digit.

Check

1. Add the digits of the first number (8, 9) together: $8 + 9 = 17$

    Add the digits (1, 7) together again: $1 + 7 = 8$

    Place the sum in the *top* section.

2. Add the digits of the second number (4, 7) together: $4 + 7 = 11$

    Add the digits (1, 1) together again: $1 + 1 = 2$

    Place the sum in the *bottom* section.

3. Multiply the two numbers now in the

    $8 \times 2 = 16$

    Add the two digits together: $1 + 6 = 7$

    Place the sum in the *left* section.

4. Add all digits in the original products (4, 1, 8, 3) together: $4 + 1 + 8 + 3 = 16$

    Add the digits (1, 6) together again: $1 + 6 = 7$

    Place the sum in the *right* section.

If the *left* and the *right* sections are the same, the product is correct.
It *always* works!

Figure 2.8 It Always Works!

Special Considerations for Teachers of Science

Teachers of science should be aware that students from other parts of the world may perceive science as a foreign, even disturbing, subject. Fundamental differences between Western science and students' native cultures may act as an impediment to school learning.

Students from rural cultures in developing countries may have a more mystical, almost magical, view of nature. In U.S. classrooms, students learn that rainbows result when droplets of water refract light rays. In some African cultures, a rainbow signifies a python crossing a river or the death of a chief. Additionally, students whose parents did not have modern schooling may be steeped in traditional beliefs and explanations of phenomena that conflict with specific teachings in biology, chemistry, and physics. Finally, there may be cultural taboos that affect the study of science. Activities such as dissecting animals and handling human bones may be forbidden.

Like math teachers, teachers of science are unquestionably aware of the differences between U.S. measurement systems and those used in most other countries. Students from countries using the metric system will be unfamiliar with our measurements of ounces, pounds, tons, cups, pints, quarts, gallons, inches, feet, yards, and miles. And in terms of heat measurements, the centigrade scale is more widely used than the

Fahrenheit scale. It will take some practice for these students to feel comfortable using U.S. measurement systems.

Special Considerations for Teachers of Social Studies

Social studies is a nationalistic subject: Students everywhere learn about the people, places, and events that comprise the tapestry of world history from a nation-centered standpoint. The picture is global, but the focus is local. Wars, conquests, alliances, power shifts, and leaders are subject to local interpretation. Inhabitants of neighboring countries as well as distant ones may see the same historical events in a very different light. The particular understanding of history that ELLs are familiar with may differ from the one that U.S.-schooled students have learned. What, for example, might the World War II term "the Allies" mean to someone from Italy or Germany?

Another issue for teachers of social studies is that history in many parts of the world is rewritten as new rulers come into power. Current national, regional, ethnic, and religious perspectives color the way the past is seen. In his novel *1984,* George Orwell wrote, "Who controls the past controls the future: who controls the present controls the past." It is important that teachers recognize these potential disparities.

Special Considerations for Teachers of Language Arts, Reading, and Literature

As a teacher of language skills and literature, you know more about the English language than you probably realize. You know about grammar and vocabulary and choose words and phrases appropriate to situations and people. You use the idioms, proverbs, and common cultural references of the language. You understand intended meaning based on intonation. The messages of single words—*really, oh,* and *interesting,* for example— change entirely depending on how they are voiced. Few native speakers would confuse the meanings of "Really?" and "Really!"

You intuitively know how to order a series of adjectives that modify a noun. You would never say, for example, "the brick big red house." You also recognize that certain words go together because of common usage. You say "heavy smoker" but "weighty matter"—and never "weighty smoker" or "heavy matter" (unless, of course, you're talking science).

You understand the subtle differences in meaning of very close synonyms. Your description of an acquaintance's appearance as "slim," "thin," or "skinny" or someone's behavior as "childlike" instead of "childish" has everything to do with your feelings of approval or disapproval.

You recognize that certain words are group nouns that cannot be counted individually. Consequently, you say "three suitcases" but never "three luggages." You know that prepositions can change the meaning of a phrase and would never confuse a sign that said *On Sale* with one that said *For Sale.*

Amazing, isn't it? You, as a fluent speaker of English, possess an enormous amount of language knowledge. When you learn English as a first language or early in childhood, you acquire all this knowledge without giving much thought to its subtleties and nuances. It would not be unusual for you now, as a teacher, to intuitively use all the rules of the English language correctly but be unable to explain exactly what those rules are.

The good news is that many teacher resources are available to you. A rules-based grammar book designed for ELLs will address questions about ordering adjectives or using group nouns. And a student dictionary can define and explain shades of meaning and usage. Certain books explain and address common difficulties (called *language interference*) that speakers of a specific native language have when learning English. These reference materials are listed in the *References and Resources* section at the end of this chapter.

An additional area of potential difficulty for ELLs involves the use of common cultural references that virtually all native speakers know. These include not only idioms, proverbs, and adages, but also iconic references to historic American people, events, and places; to English language literature; and even to nursery rhymes and children's stories. Examples of each of these are shown in Figure 2.9.

Idiomatic Speech

Let the cat out of the bag

Bite the bullet

Keeping up with the Joneses

Tongue in cheek

Pop the question

Take the cake

Four-letter words

Beat around the bush

See eye to eye

Brain trust

By the book

Read between the lines

Pay lip service

Eleventh hour

Proverbs and Adages

Nothing succeeds like success.

The wish is the father of the deed.

Any port in a storm.

A word to the wise is sufficient.

Curiosity killed the cat.

Too many cooks spoil the broth.

Forewarned is forearmed.

Necessity is the mother of invention.

When it rains, it pours.

A stitch in time saves nine.

Make haste slowly.

Out of the frying pan, into the fire.

Once bitten, twice shy.

Iconic References to American People, Events, and Places

George Washington and the cherry tree

The Blue and the Gray

The father of our country

Uncle Sam

First Amendment rights

Paul Revere's ride

Underground railroad

Big stick diplomacy

Ellis Island

Prohibition and the Roaring Twenties

Watergate

Iconic References to Literature in English

She seems always to have an albatross around her neck. (Coleridge)

His ambition is matched only by Captain Ahab's. (Melville)

They were smiling like Cheshire cats. (Carroll)

Those two are like Tweedledum and Tweedledee. (Carroll)

You found it! Well aren't you a regular Sherlock Holmes! (Doyle)

My boss is a real Simon Legree. (Stowe)

I'm just starting out in my profession. I've got miles to go before I sleep. (Frost)

She should be wearing the scarlet letter. (Hawthorne)

Iconic References to Nursery Rhymes and Children's Stories

Be like the tortoise, not like the hare.

It was like trying to fix Humpty Dumpty.

His personality was a match for the Grinch.

They're killing the goose that lays the golden eggs.

She reacted to the spider like Little Miss Muffet.

He thinks he's Peter Pan.

It's a case of the boy who cried "Wolf."

Look at her now—a real ugly duckling.

Figure 2.9   Culturally Familiar References

References of these types are troublesome for ELLs in several ways. Teachers may be unaware of the need to explain them because they appear so commonly in print and speech. And even if explained, there may still be confusion if the symbolism or usage is not the same. Tuesday the 13th, for example, is the unlucky day in Greece and Spain; and for some Native Americans, the owl is a portent of death rather than a symbol of wisdom.

Not only ELLs, but also many young native-English speakers, are unfamiliar with some proverbs or iconic references. Teaching these expressions to both native and non-native English-speaking students can be as enjoyable as it is educational. A cultural-literacy dictionary in your classroom can serve as an excellent resource for you to help ELLs gain understanding of important cultural referents.

A final area of potential difficulty for ELLs in language arts and literature classes lies in the use of dialectic speech in novels that students may read in class. Conversations between characters in novels, such as Mark Twain's *The Adventures of Huckleberry Finn* and Zora Neale Hurston's *Their Eyes Were Watching God*, will tax ELLs' reading skills to the limit. A useful strategy for scaffolding such novels is to offer CliffsNotes or an ELL-simplified version as a supplement to the actual novel. Indeed, this may also help native-speaking struggling readers.

As a final note to this chapter, it is worth repeating that human beings are products of their culture. Culture and cultural beliefs are deeply ingrained, and culturally ingrained behaviors are not easily changed or discarded. Teachers of all subjects must develop an awareness of potential cultural determinants of behavior and cultural impediments to learning in American classrooms.

QUESTIONS FOR DISCUSSION

1. What qualities, characteristics, and behaviors are valued by the American culture?

2. What personal behaviors and beliefs do you feel have been shaped by the culture of your own family, religion, and/or ethnicity?

3. Have you ever visited a foreign country where you felt out of place because expectations of behavior were different from those you were accustomed to? Please explain.

4. Sometimes a move to a new area of the United States involves a cultural adjustment, even though it doesn't involve learning a new language. Have you ever had any experiences of this type?

5. Do you know people who immigrated to the United States from a foreign country? If so, interview them or their first-generation American children to find out about the cultural difficulties they experienced as they adjusted to life in their new country.

6. Use the Internet or personal resources to research proverbs, adages, animal symbolism, and cultural icons of a country or ethnicity of your own or your instructor's choice. Compare them with U.S. cultural references.

7. For one hour, listen either to a pair or group of people in conversation or to people talking on television. Create a list of the adages, idioms, and cultural references that you hear. Are there any that are unfamiliar to you?

REFERENCES AND RESOURCES

Diaz-Rico, L. T., & Weed, K. Z. (2005). *The cross cultural, language, and academic development handbook: A complete K–12 reference guide* (3rd ed.). Boston: Allyn & Bacon.

Firsten, R., with Killian, P. (2002). *The ELT grammar book: A teacher-friendly reference guide.* Burlingame, CA: Alta Book Center.

Helmer, S., & Eddy, C. (2003). *Look at me when I talk to you: ESL learners in non-ESL classrooms* (2nd ed.). Portsmouth, NH: Heinemann.

Hirsch, E. D., Jr. (2002). *The new dictionary of cultural literacy: What every American needs to know*. New York: Houghton Mifflin.

Igoa, C. (1995). *The inner world of the immigrant child*. New York: St. Martin's Press.

Longman Language Activator (thesaurus, 2nd ed.). (2002). White Plains, NY: Pearson Education.

Scarcella, R. (1992). Providing culturally sensitive feedback. In P. A. Richard-Amato & M. A. Snow (Eds.), *The multicultural classroom* (pp. 126–141). Reading, MA: Addison-Wesley.

Stewart, E. C., & Bennett, M. (1991). *American cultural patterns: A cross-cultural perspective*. Boston: Intercultural Press.

Swan, M., & Smith, B. (Eds.). (2001). *Learner English: A teacher's guide to interference and other problems*. Cambridge, England: Cambridge University Press.

Watkins-Goffman, L. (2001). *Lives in two languages: An exploration of identity and culture*. Ann Arbor: University of Michigan Press.

The Tech Connection

Free Internet Translation Sites

www.babelfish.altavista.com
http://translation.babylon.com/
http://tradukka.com

Culture-Specific Information

www.culturalorientation.net/
www.culturegrams.com
www.interculturalpress.com

STRATEGIES FOR CLASSROOM PRACTICE: INSTRUCTION

CHAPTER 3

MEETING STATE OBJECTIVES AND STANDARDS: MAKING GOOD CHOICES

State academic standards serve as rigorous goals for teaching and learning. They specify what students should know and be able to do in designated core areas of instruction as a result of their K–12 schooling. Standards promote consistency in classroom instruction and establish a content base for statewide assessment.

State standards are drawn from a detailed web of topics, concepts, and skills essential for each grade, as determined by professional organizations in each of the major content areas. States use this information to develop their own sets of standards and grade-level curricula. Classroom content teachers often know these standards better than the standards relating to the ELLs in their classrooms.

STANDARDS FOR ENGLISH LANGUAGE LEARNERS

In 1997, the organization Teachers of English to Speakers of Other Languages (TESOL) created a set of English as a second language (ESL) standards designed to complement the content area standards created by other professional associations. In 2006, TESOL extended and refocused those standards in a new document, *PreK–12 English Language Proficiency (ELP) Standards in the Core Content Areas*, which reflects trends relating to standards, content-based instruction, ELLs, and the provisions of the No Child Left Behind (NCLB) Act of 2001.

Five new standards acknowledge the central role of language in the achievement of content. The first standard deals with learning English for social, intercultural, and instructional purposes within the school setting. Standards 2 through 5 involve communicating information, ideas, and concepts necessary for academic success in the separate content areas of English language arts, mathematics, science, and social studies. These standards form the bridge between language learning and national standards in the core curriculum areas. They set high expectations for achievement in the realms of English language and general academics.

A matrix outlining model performance indicators for specific topics within each of the four core content areas delineates expectations by grade level cluster, language proficiency level, and language domain (see Figure 3.1). By aligning academic content standards with language domain and proficiency levels, TESOL has produced a framework that can serve teachers, schools, and districts in establishing realistic expectations and

Grade Level Clusters	Language Domains	Language Proficiency Levels
PreK–K: The Early Years	Listening	Level 1: Starting Up
Grades 1–3: Primary Grades	Speaking	Level 2: Beginning
Grades 4–5: Middle Elementary	Reading	Level 3: Developing
Grades 6–8: Middle School	Writing	Level 4: Expanding
Grades 9–12: High School		Level 5: Bridging Over

Figure 3.1   Differentiated Areas of TESOL's 2006 PreK–12 English Language Proficiency Standards

meaningful instruction for their ELL populations. The clear standards and model performance indicators define concrete goals for student achievement at each level of language proficiency and help to ensure that all students reach their full potential for academic success.

THE DILEMMA OF STANDARDS

Academic standards, whether discipline specific or ELP, specify what students should know and be able to do at each grade level and in each of the core content areas. They establish common yardsticks of instruction and curriculum. The dilemma they present to classroom teachers is one of curricular depth versus breadth: Should students spend a longer time learning fewer topics or a shorter time on more topics?

Teachers have long felt torn between conflicting beliefs. On the one hand, covering fewer curricular objectives and topics in greater depth allows opportunities to approach subject material in creative ways that can increase students' interest and motivation. On the other hand, teachers believe that they have a responsibility to expose their students to all curricular objectives and topics to prepare them, at least minimally, for future learning.

The issue of depth versus breadth has become even more serious for teachers in light of high-stakes testing. Because state accountability tests are directly linked to the standards, teachers feel themselves under intense pressure to cover these standards in the course of a school year. And if this is a challenge with the native English-speaking students in their classes, can teachers possibly meet those standards with their ELLs? If not, then what?

SELECTING STANDARDS, TOPICS, AND OBJECTIVES

The Objective: Analyze Standards, Topics, and Objectives to Make Sound Choices

The Rationale: The preceding questions must be addressed realistically. ELLs, simply because they are in the process of learning English, may not be able to master the complete curriculum, but they will be able to learn a great deal of it. Although the 2006 ELP Standards serve as a valuable guide, it is ultimately teachers' responsibility to select the standards, concepts, topics, and skills they believe are most essential for their ELLs. Those chosen should present reasonable expectations and be core concepts that are individually interesting and cognitively challenging.

STRATEGY 1   CREATE A SERIES OF TWO-TIERED PLANNERS

IN CONCEPT

A *two-tiered planner* is a means of systematically prioritizing instructional objectives for students in today's diverse classrooms. It allows teachers to selectively focus on essentials and set reasonable expectations for learning, with basic requirements for all students and more advanced requirements for many. Often, a third tier can be added with select advanced material to challenge a few at the top.

A thoughtful overview of the standards, objectives, topics, and subtopics in your curriculum will reveal valuable information for planning. Upon examination, you will see that some standards encompass high-level thinking skills and broad concepts whereas others are more narrowly based on separate, discrete skills and information. Some may seem more intrinsically important or basic than others.

IN PRACTICE

For each new unit, begin with the question "Of all these standards, benchmarks, and objectives, which ones must all my students *absolutely* know?" These are the ones that form the first tier, the minimum of learning for every student in your classroom. In the second tier are those that most students, with varying degrees of effort, can and should master.

What guidelines can you use to select the objectives that will constitute these basics for learning? The next three strategies will help to inform your decisions.

STRATEGY 2   SELECT CORE CONCEPTS

IN CONCEPT

Core concepts are those that most benefit students' future learning. They reappear in successive years of schooling in conceptually expanded forms. Because core concepts such as those shown in Figure 3.2 form the foundation of knowledge upon which more advanced and complex information, ideas, and relationships will be built, they should be given high instructional priority.

Math	Science	Social Studies
equality	adaptation	culture
operations	energy	liberty
equivalence	force	change
symmetry	matter	exploration
number systems	properties	rights/responsibilities

Figure 3.2 Some Core Concepts in Math, Science, and Social Studies

IN PRACTICE

You can best help the ELLs in your classroom today by concentrating first on the core concepts that they will be expected to know and demonstrate in the academic years that follow. Start by examining the content standards, benchmarks, topics, and skills for your grade or grade grouping, and then compare them to those at the next higher level.

The Sunshine (Florida) State Science Standards, for example, are delineated by strands and by grade level groupings. Figure 3.3 shows the standards and benchmarks of the Earth and Space strand for Grades 6–8 and 9–12. A middle school science teacher, after examining the corresponding high school standards, will recognize that the single benchmark in Standard 2 for Grades 6–8 is more critical than it might at first seem. It forms the foundation of understanding for the seven benchmarks at the next level. Its importance as the key to future benchmarks makes it a core topic.

Keep in mind that ELLs are learning a new language at the same time they are trying to learn content. Focusing on core concepts for your ELLs does not lower your expectations—it simply repositions them at a more realistic level.

STRATEGY 3   SELECT INTERESTING TOPICS

IN CONCEPT

Inherent interest in a topic is a natural motivator to learning. Students learn better—more quickly and in greater depth—when they are motivated. Developing a great deal of knowledge about a single topic, rather than a little bit of knowledge about many topics, also promotes long-term retention of learning.

In general, students are interested in topics that relate to previous personal experiences, prior learning, and/or real-world connections. Linking standards, topics, and skills to students' individual interests makes learning meaningful to them; meaningful content is understood more easily and retained longer.

IN PRACTICE

There is no doubt that you will have to make some content choices for the ELLs in your classroom. You can facilitate their learning by offering them a degree of choice in selecting topics that appeal to them.

The four benchmarks in Grades 6–8 Standard 1 (see Figure 3.3) cover a range of topics: the planets, their moons, satellite probes, the sun, the stars. ELLs may find a particular fascination with one of these topics. Encourage them to select that one for in-depth study. Their motivation and personal interest may lead them toward expanding their knowledge of science and building their English language skills as well.

STRATEGY 4   SELECT CHALLENGING TOPICS

IN CONCEPT

Any topic selected for study must maintain a high level of academic challenge. ELLs will not benefit in the long or short run from a watered-down curriculum or from lowered

Grades 6–8 Earth and Space

Standard 1: The student understands the interaction and organization of the Solar System and the universe and how this affects life on Earth.

1. understands the vast size of our Solar System and the relationship of the planets and their satellites.
2. knows that available data from various satellite probes show the similarities and differences among planets and their moons in the Solar System.
3. understands that our sun is one of many stars in our galaxy.
4. knows that stars appear to be made of similar chemical elements, although they differ in age, size, temperature, and distance.

Standard 2: The student recognizes the vastness of the universe and the Earth's place in it

1. knows that thousands of other galaxies appear to have the same elements, forces, and forms of energy found in our Solar System.

Grades 9–12 Earth and Space

Standard 1: The student understands the interaction and organization of the Solar System and the universe and how this affects life on Earth.

1. understands the relationships between events on Earth and the movements of the Earth, its moon, the other planets, and the sun.
2. knows how the characteristics of other planets and satellites are similar to and different from those of the Earth.
3. knows the various reasons that Earth is the only planet in our solar system that appears to be capable of supporting life as we know it.

Standard 2: The student recognizes the vastness of the universe and the Earth's place in it.

1. knows that the stages in the development of three categories of stars are based on mass: stars that have the approximate mass of our sun, stars that are two-to-three stellar masses and develop into neutron stars, and stars that are five-to-six stellar masses and develop into black holes.
2. identifies the arrangement of bodies found within and outside our galaxy.
3. knows astronomical distance and time.
4. understands stellar equilibrium.
5. knows various scientific theories on how the universe was formed.
6. knows the various ways in which scientists collect and generate data about our universe (e.g., X-ray telescopes, computer simulations of gravitational systems, nuclear reactions, space probes, and supercollider simulations).
7. knows that mathematical models and computer simulations are used in studying evidence from many sources to form a scientific account of the universe.

Figure 3.3   Sunshine State Science Standards: Earth and Space Strands for Grades 6–8 and Grades 9–12

Florida Department of Education. (2005). *Sunshine State Standards for Science, Grades 6–8.* Retrieved April 26, 2006, from *http://www.firn.edu/doe/curric/prek12/pdf/science6.pdf.*

Florida Department of Education. (2005). *Sunshine State Standard for Science, Grades 9–12.* Retrieved April 26, 2006, from *http://www.firn.edu/doe/curric/prek12/pdf/science9.pdf.*

Class	Unit	Expert Focus
Earth Science	Freshwater resources Ocean motions Weather factors Energy resources	Water pollution Currents Precipitation Fossil fuels
Life Science	Human anatomy Human physiology systems The sense organs Mammals	The skeletal system Circulatory system The sense of sight Mammal habitats

Figure 3.4   Topics for Class Specialists in Science

expectations. Thoughtful selection of content involves combining cognitively demanding topics and concepts with activities that require the use of higher level thinking skills.

IN PRACTICE

ELLs should focus on content depth rather than breadth. They can become the class *specialists* by concentrating their study on a narrow section of content. Figure 3.4 offers samples of subtopics for your ELL specialists to study. Figure 3.5 details possible assignments, discussed further in Chapter 10.

Choosing an area of expertise will feel empowering and motivating to ELLs. They can work on their expert topics at their own pace independently, in pairs, or in small groups, producing an example such as the graphic shown in Figure 3.6, while you continue your lessons with the class.

ELLs can share individual assignments with others in a group information exchange. All aspects of a topic can be covered—the five senses, for example—but with each student assuming a workable language/academic load. Through this type of cooperative or shared activity, ELLs learn a great deal about content, concept, and language. This approach also creates the opportunity to show your ELLs in a positive light when you call on "the experts" to share their knowledge as their topics arise during class discussion.

Inviting ELL students to become specialists in a narrow field of study is also a pedagogically sound approach to learning. Long-term retention of knowledge is dramatically increased when learning follows the principle of *learn more about less*. Students who merely memorize facts for a test usually retain the information only until the test is over, whereas information that has been learned in depth becomes part of their knowledge base.

Combining depth of study with choice based on interest will give your ELLs a solid chance to learn challenging material. You will have offered them the best possible means of becoming actively and effectively involved in their own learning.

STRATEGY 5   SELECT PRACTICAL TOPICS

IN CONCEPT

Certain topics, concepts, and objectives are more concrete and demonstrable in content and process. They are linguistically easier for ELLs to understand because they lend themselves to graphic representation and/or direct inquiry learning.

Unit	Expert Focus	Assignment Type
The Constitution	Amendments	Timeline
	The seven articles	Graphic representation
	Separation of powers	Graphic representation
	U.S. government vs. systems of government in ELLs' native countries	Venn diagram
The Civil War	Life in the North vs. life in the South	Venn diagram
	One battle: Antietam	Map, outcome graphic
	One general: Lee or Grant	Timeline
	The two generals compared	Venn diagram
Growth of the West	Railroads	Timeline, map
	Mining	Map, products
	Effects on Native American tribes	Graphic representation
The Progressive Era	The rise of unions	Timeline
	Reforms for women	Timeline
The Great Depression	Causes of the Depression	Graphic representation
	New Deal program summary	Graphic representation

Figure 3.5 Topics for Class Specialists in American History

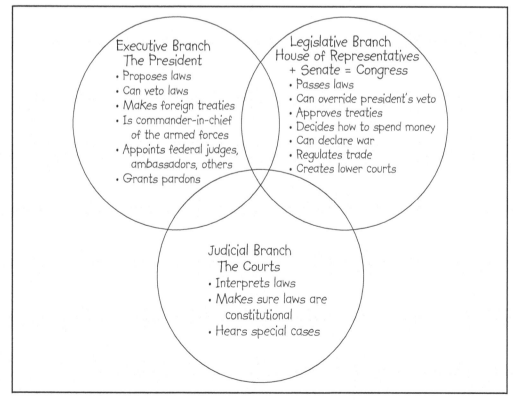

Figure 3.6 A Specialist's Report—The Three Branches of Government

IN PRACTICE

If you are deliberating among several topics that appear to offer equal challenge and long-term importance, such as those in the Grades 6–8 benchmarks of Standard 1 (see Figure 3.3), use *practicality* as a criterion of selection. The first benchmark about the solar system and the relationship of the planets and their satellites contains content that is practical because it can be broken into small, concrete chunks of information and then slowly built into the whole through demonstration, discovery learning, and multimedia graphics. Practical content offers you more ready access to the variety of strategies to scaffold instruction.

IN SUMMARY: SELECTING STANDARDS, TOPICS, AND OBJECTIVES

State standards are, at their best, a means to raise expectations for all students by improving the quality of learning in classrooms. At their worst, when too closely tied to high-stakes tests, state standards narrow curricula into little more than test preparation. Realistically, in the broad middle range of their potential, state standards maintain content integrity and use assessment to inform instruction. For better or worse, state standards are here to stay, and teachers have to work with them.

It would be wonderful if all students could meet all standards and learn everything in your curriculum. In an ideal world they could, but in the real world of your classroom, some of your students will accomplish it all, and some will not. Many ELLs, because they are learning the language while they are learning the content, will be in the group that will *not* accomplish it all. The medium of instruction is, for them, as challenging as the instruction itself.

The reality is that you must make curricular choices. Your most sincere attempts to cover the entire range of requirements with your ELLs—that is, to meet all the standards—may well result in little real learning and a great deal of frustration. You can help ELLs so much more by maintaining high expectations that focus on topics, concepts, and standards that are important, foundational, cognitively challenging, interesting, and practical. You will be giving them the gift of academic success.

QUESTIONS FOR DISCUSSION

1. Investigate the accommodations made for ELLs in your state accountability systems. Do they reflect the *12 Guidelines for Practice* outlined in Chapter 1? In what ways do you believe they should be modified?
2. Cite and summarize additional research and articles that give theoretical or experiential support to the strategies presented in this chapter.
3. Research the state standards for the grade(s) and content area(s) you are now teaching or will soon teach. Then research the state standards for ELLs. To what degree are the two sets of standards related to each other? If they are less than fully interrelated, propose a plan or outline for improvement.
4. What is the relationship between your state's standards and its accountability system? What advantages and disadvantages do you see in this arrangement? If you are not yet teaching, interview a teacher in your field about this, and report the results.

REFERENCES AND RESOURCES

Echevarria, J., & Graves, A. (2005). Curriculum adaptations. In P. Richard-Amato & M. A. Snow (Eds.), *Academic success for English language learners: Strategies for K–12 mainstream teachers* (pp. 224–247). White Plains, NY: Pearson Education.

Echevarria, J., Short, D., & Powers, K. (2003). *School reform and standards-based education: How do teachers help English language learners?* [Technical report]. Santa Cruz, CA: Center for Research on Education, Diversity, and Excellence.

Falk, B. (2005). Possibilities and problems of a standards-based approach: The good, the bad, and the ugly. In P. Richard-Amato & M. A. Snow (Eds.), *Academic success for English language learners: Strategies for K–12 mainstream teachers* (pp. 342–362). White Plains, NY: Pearson Education.

Freeman, Y. S., Freeman, D. E., & Mercuri, S. (2002). *Closing the achievement gap: How to reach limited-formal schooling and long-term English learners.* Portsmouth, NH: Heinemann.

Lachat, M. (2004). *Standards-based instruction and assessment for English language learners.* Thousand Oaks, CA: Corwin Press.

Schumm, J. S., Vaughn, S., & Leavell, S. G. (1994). Planning pyramid: A framework for planning for diverse student needs during content instruction. *The Reading Teacher, 47*(8), 608–615.

Teachers of English to Speakers of Other Languages (TESOL). (2006). *PreK–12 English language proficiency standards.* Alexandria, VA: TESOL.

Professional Organizations

The following professional organization websites contain a wealth of information on standards and topics that students should master at each grade level. Those relating to ELLs are listed first, followed by the national organizations for the core content areas.

www.bilingualeducation.org
California Association for Bilingual Education (CABE)

www.nabe.org
National Association for Bilingual Education (NABE)

www.tesol.org
Teachers of English to Speakers of Other Languages, Inc. (TESOL)

www.ncte.org
National Council of Teachers of English

www.nctm.org
National Council of Teachers of Mathematics

www.nsta.org
National Science Teachers Association

www.socialstudies.org
National Council for the Social Studies

Information and Research Centers

These websites offer extensive information relating to the education of ELLs, including answers to questions, research findings, databases of education literature, and links to additional Internet resources.

www.eric.ed.gov
Education Resources Information Center (ERIC)

www.cal.org
Center for Applied Linguistics (CAL)

www.ncela.gwu.edu
National Clearinghouse for English Language Acquisition (NCELA) and Language Instruction Educational Programs

www.crede.org
Center for Research on Education, Diversity, and Excellence (CREDE)

CHAPTER 4

LEARNING STRATEGIES FOR ENGLISH LANGUAGE LEARNERS

L earning strategies are the keys to academic success for all students. Effective learners in all subject areas are those who have developed a repertoire of learning techniques and know which to select to meet their immediate learning needs. They have acquired the tools for successful academic learning.

All students need to use learning strategies, but not all students develop them intuitively. It is surprising that many students believe that those who achieve high grades do so because they are "smart," not because they work hard and study effectively.

All students benefit from direct instruction in choosing and using learning strategies. ELLs, even more so, need this guidance to overcome the challenge of learning a new language while trying to use that language to learn new content.

LEARNING STRATEGIES DEFINED

Learning strategies are techniques that facilitate the process of understanding, retaining, and applying knowledge. They are the "specific actions taken by the learner to make learning easier, faster, more enjoyable, more self-directed, and more transferable to new situations" (Oxford, 1990, p. 8). These strategies are really the *tricks of the learning trade*. They come in many varieties, but not all strategies work equally well for all learners, nor do they work equally well in all learning situations. Exposure to different types allows students to develop their own personal menu of strategies—a repertoire of techniques that work well for *them*. Students can then choose appropriate strategies that, in combination with their personal learning styles, fit the type of knowledge they need to learn. For ELLs in content classrooms, learning strategies take on extra importance and value.

LEARNING STRATEGIES AND TEACHING STRATEGIES: SAME OR DIFFERENT?

Learning strategies and teaching strategies are often thought of interchangeably, but they are definitely *not* the same. Learning strategies are used *by the student* to understand, retain, and apply new knowledge. They are not readily visible or immediately identifiable.

Teaching strategies are used *by the teacher* to facilitate understanding for students and to make content more accessible to them. These are the techniques, approaches, activities, and assignments that teachers use to help students process new information and apply prior learning. Teaching strategies are immediately visible and identifiable. They are what administrators evaluate when they do classroom observations. The subset of teaching strategies used for ELLs is part of scaffolded instruction. Teaching strategies are concerned with how teachers *send* the message; learning strategies deal with how the message is *received*, and that is the focus of this chapter.

LEARNING STRATEGIES AND LEARNING STYLES: SAME OR DIFFERENT?

Again, learning strategies and learning styles are *not* the same thing. Learning styles involve individual preferences for particular work patterns. Learning styles are personal, enduring, and often unconscious choices of ways to learn, such as individual or group work, auditory or visual input, a quiet environment or background noise, and single-task or multitask focus. Learning strategies, in contrast, are learned, changeable from task to task, and often consciously chosen.

Although learning styles are individual, teachers should be aware that education systems around the world value and reward different learning styles. As discussed in Chapter 2, ELLs may prefer styles of learning that have been shaped by their cultures.

TYPES OF LEARNING STRATEGIES

Much has been written about how students learn and what strategies they use in the process. The classification of strategy types that is used in this text is built largely upon the research and writings of O'Malley and Chamot (1990) and Oxford (1990). Learning strategies for ELLs fall into four broad types—metacognitive, cognitive, social, and compensation strategies. It is important to understand how each of these strategy types helps students learn.

Metacognitive Strategies

Metacognitive strategies are those that involve *thinking* about learning. These can be divided into two subtypes: those that deal with *organizing* and *planning* for learning, and those that deal with *self-monitoring* and *self-evaluating* learning.

Examples of Metacognitive Strategies Dealing with Organizing and Planning for Learning
- Using a homework notebook to write down assignments
- Keeping a calendar/organizer to write down long-term assignments
- Dividing long-term assignments into shorter segments and tasks
- Setting deadlines for completion of each segment or task
- Determining the most efficient strategies to learn specific content
- Planning how to study for a test

Examples of Metacognitive Strategies Dealing with Self-Monitoring and Self-Evaluation of Learning
- Recognizing your own knowledge gaps or weaknesses
- Discovering strategies that work best for you (and those that don't)
- Monitoring your own progress in learning by asking yourself, "How am I doing?" and "Am I understanding this?"
- Seeking a new strategy if the one you're using isn't working

Cognitive Strategies

Cognitive strategies are those that involve any type of *practice activity*. These are techniques that promote deeper understanding, better retention, and/or increased ability to apply new knowledge. Successful learners regularly use a varied set of cognitive strategies.

Examples of Cognitive Strategies

- Making specific connections between new and old learning
- Making specific connections between English and your native language
- Highlighting important information while you're reading
- Dividing a large body of information into smaller units
- Note taking (even in your native language)
- Condensing your notes to study for a test
- Making and using flash cards to test yourself
- Making visual associations to aid in retention
- Making categories and classifications
- Creating graphic organizers, maps, charts, diagrams, timelines, and flowcharts to organize information

Cognitive strategies form the core of learning techniques. They fall into the general category that students call *studying*. Cognitive strategies that are creative, interesting, even gamelike in nature put a positive spin on studying, making it more motivating and productive for all students.

Memory Strategies

Memory strategies are a subtype of cognitive strategies. Their purpose is to *trigger the recall* of specific groups of items or ideas that have been learned through other cognitive techniques. Memory strategies promote rote recitation of elements without any attempt to understand those elements more completely.

A simple example of a memory strategy is the alphabet song learned by young children, often long before they have any concept of letters. It is strictly a rote memory device—a *mnemonic*. However, it is so effective that children often use the song to remind themselves of alphabetic order when they have learned to recognize and write the letters.

Mnemonics in academia are created, often by individual students, to help remember rules, key words, lists, and categories. Memory strategies such as poems, songs, acronyms, sentences (e.g., with the first letter of each word in the sentence being the same as the first letter of an item in an ordered list), and word patterns are very effective in recalling much larger bodies of information that have been learned through other cognitive approaches. ELLs can even use their native languages to create their own memory devices.

Examples of Familiar Mnemonics

- The "I before E" poem to recall spelling rules
- The poem and the knuckle technique for remembering which months have fewer than 31 days (see Figure 4.1)
- The made-up word to recall the correct order of the color spectrum (see Figure 4.2)
- The silly sentence to remember the notes on a treble staff (see Figure 4.2)
- The tricks of the multiplication tables (see Figure 4.3)

As students recognize the efficiency of mnemonics as a recall tool and feel comfortable using them, you can make the creation of a mnemonic a creative homework assignment, as described in Figure 4.4.

You May Know This Poem:

Thirty days hath September

April, June, and November

All the rest have thirty-one

Excepting February alone

It has twenty-eight days time

And each leap year twenty-nine

But Do You Know The Knuckle Technique?

Hold your hand forward, palm down, and make a fist.

Starting with the knuckle above the index finger, count off the months, naming a month as you touch *each knuckle and the spaces* between.

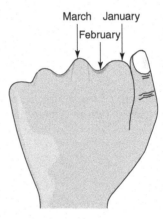

March   January

February

When you get to July at the pinky knuckle, touch that knuckle again for August and reverse direction.

Have you noticed that all the months that fall into the spaces have fewer than thirty-one days?

Figure 4.1   Two Mnemonics to Remember the Number of Days in the Months

Figure 4.2   More Mnemonics

For the Color Spectrum

"Roy-G-Biv" = **r**ed, **o**range, **y**ellow, **g**reen, **b**lue, **i**ndigo, **v**iolet

For the Notes on a Treble Staff
E, G, B, D, F = **E**very **g**ood **b**oy **d**oes **f**ine.
                         Every **g**ood **b**oy **d**eserves **f**udge.

Social Strategies

Social strategies are of two types. In the first type, language learners attempt to learn English by attending to and interacting with English in their immediate environment.

The second type more closely relates to the classroom. Here language learners work with one or more other students to learn information or to complete a task. Group work and cooperative learning are social learning strategies. Because social strategies are, as the name states, social, they are often less stressful and may occasionally even feel like fun.

Figure 4.3 Multiplication Mnemonics

The 9 Times Trick

Hold both hands in front of you with your fingers spread out.

For 9 × 3, bend your third finger on your left hand down.

  (9 × 4 would be the fourth finger, and so on.)

You have 2 fingers in front of the bent finger and 7 after the bent

  finger. And there's the answer: 27.

This technique works for the 9 times tables up to 10.

The 4 Times Trick

For this one, you only need to know how to double a number.

Simply, double a number and then double It again!

The 11 Times Trick

To multiply 11 by any two-digit numbers:

Example 1

Multiply 11 by 18. Jot down 1 and 8 with a space between:

    1   8

Add the 1 and the 8 and put that number in the middle: 198.

    11 × 18 = 198

Example 2

When the digits of the multiplier add up to 10 or more, do it this

way: Multiply 11 by 39. Jot down 3 and 9 with a space between:

    3   9

Add the 3 and the 9 to get 12.

Put the 2 in the middle between the 3 and the 9, then add the 1

  to the 3:

    4

    3 2 9   11 × 39 = 429

Figure 4.4 Assigning a Mnemonic for Homework: Challenging, Fun, and Effective

Ask students to create a mnemonic designed to recall the elements in a set of information. The mnemonic can be an acronym that sounds good or a silly sentence that works.

  Students will have to process the content under study to complete this assignment, but they'll hardly know they're doing itl

Examples of Social Strategies

- Working in groups to clarify content, solve problems, or complete projects
- Using buddy reading, literature circles, and writing partners
- Playing teacher-made or professionally designed games to sharpen skills
- Doing homework with a friend
- Studying with a partner for a test
- Watching select television programs
- Observing peers to learn more about culture and language
- Asking questions and making requests (see Figure 4.5)

Compensation Strategies

Compensation strategies are techniques used to make up for something that is either un-known or not immediately accessible from memory. Proficient speakers of English regularly

Figure 4.5 Questions and Requests: A Social Strategy for English Language Learners

Please say that again.
Would you write that word on the board, please?
Could you speak more slowly, please?
Can you give more examples, please?
Would you please explain what _____ means?
Can you say the directions again, please?

use this type of strategy in conversations when they use words or phrases such as "whatchamacallit," "thingamajiggy," or just "that thing—you know what I mean" to replace the language they have momentarily lost.

Examples of Compensation Strategies

- Stalling for time while thinking of an appropriate response
- Making an educated guess that extends and generalizes what we know to what we don't know
- Using a circumlocution, that is, a substitute phrase to avoid the word we don't know or the word we can't spell

Figure 4.6 gives specific examples of each of these compensation strategies. Explaining the concept of compensation strategies to your ELLs and encouraging them to use them may go a long way toward making ELLs feel more willing to participate in class.

Figure 4.6 Examples of Compensation Strategies

Stalling for Time
- Repeating the question or statement
- Using fillers like *Well . . . or Hmmm . . .*
- Using expressions such as *"That's a tough question"* or *"That's a complicated issue"*
- Coughing or clearing your throat
- Any combination of the above

Making Educated Guesses
- Using airplane driver as an extension of known expressions, such as truck driver and taxi driver, when the word *pilot* is not known

Using Circumlocutions
- Using the descriptive phrase the man who drives the airplane instead of the unknown word *pilot*
- Using the phrase the machine that cooks the bread dark in place of the unknown word *toaster*

WORKING WITH LEARNING STRATEGIES

The Objective: Combine Strategies and Strategy Types

The Rationale: Even though all students need to use a variety of strategy types, ELLs, in particular, will benefit from using varied strategies *in combination*. More varied approaches to learning and more opportunities to hear and use authentic academic English will support the process of developing conceptual understanding.

STRATEGY 6   USE TWO OR MORE COGNITIVE STRATEGIES TOGETHER

IN CONCEPT

Trying to learn by using the same cognitive strategy repeatedly, as in reading and rereading a textbook chapter, often results in little knowledge acquisition. Using several techniques in combination strengthens the effectiveness of each and reinforces student learning.

IN PRACTICE

Show students how powerful learning strategies can be when they are combined sequentially, as in a guided whole class activity that takes students through a series of cognitive learning strategies to learn information and concepts presented in a reading passage. Using a photocopied reading passage, guide students as they read, and highlight important information and concepts for them. As the next step, have students write up a set of notes based on the highlighted sections. Then have them condense their notes and make flash cards to study in preparation for a quiz. The grades on the quiz should speak well for this combined strategic approach.

You can underscore the effectiveness of combining strategies by doing another guided whole class activity, either prior to or following this activity, in which your students use only one cognitive strategy to learn the elements of a similar reading passage. Comparing the two approaches to learning should bring about a lively class discussion.

STRATEGY 7   USE SOCIAL AND COGNITIVE STRATEGIES TOGETHER

IN CONCEPT

ELLs increase their opportunities for academic success when they interact with native English-speaking peers to negotiate the meaning of both language and content. Working in pairs or small groups serves to widen the language learner's zone of proximal development (Vygotsky's theory, discussed in Chapter 1).

IN PRACTICE

Successful students spontaneously create their own strategy combinations. You may remember making flash cards to help you learn large sets of information. Then you used them to check yourself to see how much you really knew. Finally, you and a friend or classmate quizzed each other. Intuitively, you paired a cognitive technique with a social one, which is an excellent way to learn.

ELLs face daily challenges to learning that are similar to the scenario described in Figure 4.7. Combining cognitive and social learning strategies in the multistep approach called *streamlining*, which is detailed in Figure 4.8, offers a systematic structure for ELLs to isolate important math data from the English language knowledge that is impeding them.

Figure 4.7 Math Class or English Class?

Wei looks at the assigned word problems in his math book and knows that there is no way he can possibly figure out any of the answers. It's not that Wei's math skills are weak—in fact, he knows he's really pretty good at computation. He also knows that, once again, It's all those words in the problem that will bar his way to success. Wei is an English language learner.

Figure 4.8 Streamlining: A Multistep Approach for Math Word Problems

Step 1: Make language substitutions.

In pairs or small groups, students look for words or phrases that can be eliminated or replaced with more simple language. They use a bilingual dictionary or a student dictionary as needed.

Step 2: Determine the information presented.

Students, still in pairs or groups, reread the now-simplified wording of the problem. They search out and write down all information given in the problem.

Step 3: Determine the information needed for solution.

Students now look for words that offer clues to the information needed in the solution. They first eliminate extraneous words and information and then write out the words and phrases that tell how to process the information in the problem.

Step 4: Determine the process needed for solution.

Using the words or phrases from Step 3, students figure out the process needed to find the solution.

Step 5: Solve the problem.

Students individually perform the necessary computations and compare results.

WORKING WITH LEARNING STRATEGIES

The Objective: Actively Teach Learning Strategies

The Rationale: Strategy training should not be subtle. It needs to be taught explicitly and overtly. For students to recognize the usefulness of learning strategies in general, new strategies, as they are taught, must be directly tied to learning specific content.

STRATEGY 8   USE THE SIX-STEP APPROACH TO TEACH LEARNING STRATEGIES

IN CONCEPT

Strategy teaching is a six-step process. First, *introduce* the strategy to your students, and label it as a new learning strategy. Next, *identify* it with a name, and explain how it is

1. *Introduce* it and label it as a new strategy.
2. *Identify* it by name and explain its use.
3. *Demonstrate* how to use it.
4. Give students time and opportunity for *practice*.
5. *Discuss* effectiveness and application to other tasks.
6. *Display* strategy name and example in a prominent place in your classroom.

Figure 4.9   Strategy Teaching in Six Steps

used. Then, *demonstrate* how to apply it directly to learning specific content. Next, give students the time and opportunity to *practice* using it with that content. Then, *discuss* with your students how effective they found this strategy to be, and ask them to think of other types of learning tasks for which this new strategy might be helpful. Finally, in a prominent place in your classroom, *display* each new strategy with an example of usage. Figure 4.9 summarizes these steps.

IN PRACTICE

The clearest way to understand the six-step approach is to examine an actual example of a strategy lesson. The teacher in this example has observed when he teaches that few of the students are able to distinguish major concepts and ideas from supporting details. The lesson he has planned will give students a strategy for listening for key pieces of information during class lessons and discussions.

For Step 1—*introduce and label the new strategy*—he opens the lesson with a question: "Do you have trouble knowing what's really important when I teach? Today we're going to learn a new strategy that will help you with this."

He moves immediately to Step 2—*identify it by name and explain its use*—by saying, "We're going to call this strategy 'Listening for Key Words.'* [The asterisk symbolizes words that the teacher writes on the board as he speaks them.] Here's how it works."

> LISTENING FOR KEY WORDS

"When I teach, I often use phrases like 'This is really important,'* and 'Here's the important part,'* and 'This is a key point.'* Have you ever heard me say any of those things? Or have you heard me repeat words or phrases* or say something several times? I do that because I want you to know it's really important."

> LISTENING FOR KEY WORDS
>
> "This is really important."
> "Here's the important part."
> "This is a key point."
> REPEAT words or phrases.

"So look at what I've written on the board. Let's call these 'listening cues.'* They're like flags that wave at you to tell you to listen and remember."

LISTENING FOR KEY WORDS

"This is the important part."
"Here's the important part."   LISTENING CUES
"This is a key point."
REPEAT words or phrases.

Continuing to Step *3—demonstrate how to use it*—the teacher says, "OK, let's try it. For the next five minutes, while I teach, I want you to raise your hand every time you hear me say one of these phrases. [He points to and repeats the phrases on the board.] Then we'll talk about how they tell you that something important is coming up next."

After the five-minute segment, he moves to Step 4—*give students time and opportunity for practice*—explaining to the students that they are to listen carefully for these phrases for the rest of the instructional period. Any time they hear one, they are to write down the information that comes immediately after the phrase.

In Step 5—*discuss its effectiveness and application to other tasks*—the students share the information they have written down. They discuss whether they found the strategy helpful as a means of recognizing important facts and concepts during oral instruction, as well as where else they think this strategy might be useful.

In Step 6—*display the strategy name and example in a prominent place*—the teacher adds to the strategy bulletin board "Use listening cues to know what's important" and the example "For class lessons and discussions."

These students have now completed the six-step process for learning a strategy to recognize critical pieces of information during class lessons. As reinforcement, the teacher will point to the strategy on the bulletin board and will remind students to use it during subsequent lessons and class discussions.

STRATEGY 9   USE THINK-ALOUDS AND MODELING

IN CONCEPT

Think-alouds and modeling demonstrate the step-by-step process involved in completing many types of activities. In think-alouds, you, the teacher, explain how your brain is working at each step as you try to figure something out. Modeling does the same thing but uses actual samples and examples of steps along the way. The two techniques work most effectively when used together.

IN PRACTICE

Technique I
When students are faced with a complicated learning task, you might say something like this: "If I had to learn this, I would probably . . . ," giving a detailed, step-by-step description of the *process* you would use. You are, in effect, explaining the how-to of learning.

Your student correctly infers information from the text.

ASK: Where did you find the information that helped you with that answer?

Your student solves a complex problem.

ASK: How did you figure out that answer?

Your student presents an informed opinion on a topic.

ASK: What information led you to this opinion?

Your student gets a good grade on a test.

ASK: How exactly did you study for this test?

Figure 4.10 Think-Aloud Applications for Strategy Training

Technique II

Students themselves can be a good source for think-aloud strategy training. Use guided questions such as those in Figure 4.10 to allow students to hear about strategies successfully used by their peers and to learn directly from them. If a student describes a way of learning that has not yet been discussed in class, label it with the name of the student who contributed it. Imagine how empowering it is to have a strategy named for you!

STRATEGY 10   BRAINSTORM LEARNING STRATEGIES

IN CONCEPT

Some students easily organize their plans for learning; others find it a daunting task. Using a class discussion to brainstorm ideas for learning can be a productive strategy.

IN PRACTICE

When students face a difficult learning task—memorizing the table of periodic elements in chemistry, for example—you can conduct an open-ended discussion about which learning strategies they could use to accomplish this feat. Discuss with them any specific strategies they've used in the past that might help them to learn the type of content they're facing now. It is equally valuable to include in the discussion strategies that will probably *not* be particularly helpful.

STRATEGY 11   IDENTIFY STUDENTS' PERSONAL PREFERRED STRATEGIES

IN CONCEPT

Because not all learning strategies work for all students in all situations, it is important that students understand that strategy usage is personal and individual.

IN PRACTICE

Teachers can help students identify their preferred learning strategies through questions and discussion. Ask students regularly *how* they learned required material. Keep learning strategies at the forefront of students' thinking by referring frequently to the display of strategy names and examples. Students can also keep personal learning strategy logs or journals. In either case, display or journal, students will have a ready reference or guide from which to draw.

STRATEGY 12 INTEGRATE LEARNING STRATEGY TRAINING INTO DAILY INSTRUCTION

IN CONCEPT

The more seamlessly you integrate learning strategy training into your instruction, the more students will incorporate learning strategies into their thinking about learning. Making conscious decisions about which learning strategies to use for which tasks will become a deeply ingrained pattern for lifelong learning.

IN PRACTICE

Technique I

Give students frequent tips—strategies to help them manage their time, take notes, classify and categorize information, and study for tests. Before students begin a class or homework assignment, ask them which learning strategies they think might be most effective and efficient to achieve a successful outcome. Make sure the students remember to use the wall display as a resource.

Technique II

Students of every age love to hear about the lives of their teachers. They will listen in rapt attention when you talk about your own personal learning experiences. Tell them about the successful and not-so-successful strategies you have used to learn things. Talk about how you learn now. Take advantage of every possible opportunity to bring learning strategies into class lessons and discussion.

IN SUMMARY: WORKING WITH LEARNING STRATEGIES

Teachers who recognize the value of learning strategies and the potential of each strategy type, alone and in combination, understand the importance of making strategy training an ongoing part of their classroom instruction. Their students will develop a repertoire of effective learning strategies and will know how to make task-appropriate choices. Actively teaching and reinforcing learning strategies offers students the means to meet with academic success.

QUESTIONS FOR DISCUSSION

1. Which of the *12 Guidelines for Practice* presented at the end of Chapter 1 inform the strategies in this chapter?
2. Cite and summarize additional research that gives theoretical and/or experiential support to the strategies discussed in this chapter.

3. Label each of the following examples of learning strategies according to type—metacognitive (organizational or self-monitoring), cognitive, memory, social, or compensation:

a. Helping friends with homework

b. Making flash cards and using them to study

c. Substituting a synonym for a word you can't pronounce or spell

d. Breaking an assignment into its component parts, ordering the parts, and setting timelines for completion

e. Taking notes from highlighted text sections

f. Reading the questions at the end of a passage before reading the text

g. Using "the next day" instead of "tomorrow" in writing

h. Testing your understanding by making up your own quizzes

i. Actively reading and interpreting street signs and billboards

j. Asking another student or a sibling to quiz you

k. Guessing at new words

l. Keeping a vocabulary journal

4. Create a mnemonic for remembering the types of learning strategies.

5. Think about the strategies you have used as a learner. Which ones have been successful for you? How did you learn to use them? Did you try any learning strategies that you discarded when you realized they didn't work well for you?

6. Analyze the learning strategies that you now use most frequently. Do you use different strategies for different types of tasks?

7. Prepare a think-aloud demonstration (Strategy 9) to present in class. Your colleagues will offer verbal feedback or a written critique.

REFERENCES AND RESOURCES

Chamot, A. U., Barnhardt, S., El-Dinary, P. B., & Robbins, J. (1999). *The learning strategies handbook*. White Plains, NY: Pearson Education.

O'Malley, J. M., & Chamot, A. U. (1990). *Learning strategies in second language acquisition*. New York: Cambridge University Press.

Oxford, R. (1990). *Language learning strategies: What every teacher should know*. New York: Newbury House.

Reid, J. (Ed.). (1998). *Understanding learning styles in the second language classroom*. Upper Saddle River, NJ: Prentice Hall Regents.

CHAPTER 5

A SOLID START: BUILDING AND ACTIVATING BACKGROUND KNOWLEDGE

What makes something easier or harder to learn? Most answers to this question would include two factors among other possibilities: motivation and preexisting knowledge.

MOTIVATION

People learn what they want or need to learn. They learn because it is important to some aspect of their lives, perhaps even to their very survival. How fast they learn depends on how valuable, interesting, or necessary they perceive the new knowledge to be: The greater the felt need or desire to learn, the easier and faster the learning. Motivation is a powerful influence on the learning process.

PREEXISTING KNOWLEDGE

The other factor influencing the learning process is the amount that is already known about the topic (Leinhardt, 1992). People learn most readily by adding new data to preexisting information. It is a far greater challenge to learn something from scratch.

Learning something new is like gathering individual grains of moist sand. At the start, it is hard to form a whole from the tiny disparate grains because each grain can stick to so few others. Eventually, enough sand accumulates to form a small mass, and then new grains have an easier time finding a spot to fit in.

So, too, it is with facts: Like sand, each new fact about an unknown topic is unrelated to any other fact and must be processed individually. In time, enough facts accumulate to form a small mass of knowledge. New facts then begin to relate more easily to what has already been learned, and at this point background knowledge enters the picture. Background knowledge is the mass that makes new facts meaningful. The larger the mass of background knowledge and the more it can be actively recalled, the easier it will be for new knowledge to find its place.

THE NEED FOR BACKGROUND KNOWLEDGE

A student's own background knowledge forms the building blocks upon which new learning is built. Why, then, is this a special issue for ELLs? A school curriculum is planned around a set of basic assumptions about students' common academic backgrounds and life experiences at each grade level. ELLs entering U.S. schools from other countries, however, have had differing sets of personal, cultural, and academic experiences and may lack background knowledge specific to learning classroom content. Their teachers must first assess what knowledge is there and build in what is missing before presenting new material.

WORKING WITH BACKGROUND KNOWLEDGE

The Objective: Use Varied Techniques to Activate and Build Background Knowledge

The Rationale: All students, not only language learners, learn more effectively when teachers make explicit connections between past and present learning and take time to build up weak foundational backgrounds. Indeed, a strong indicator of how well students will learn new content is the amount of relevant background knowledge or experience they already have. Activating students' prior knowledge is an essential teaching strategy.

Activating background knowledge not only makes learning easier; it also makes learning meaningful, awakens interest in the topic, and increases motivation. Students who can see the relevance of a topic to their own lives will be interested in learning about it. Teachers who understand the importance of background knowledge and motivation can facilitate their students' learning; finding the right connection pulls students directly into the material.

The aim of building background knowledge is to develop a connection between what students already know and what they will be learning. The strategies presented in this section simultaneously activate prior knowledge for students who have it and build new knowledge for those who need it.

STRATEGY 13   BEGIN WITH BRAINSTORMING

IN CONCEPT

Brainstorming (Osborn, 1953) is the strategy of asking students to think about and tell what they already know (or think they know) about a new topic before it is actually introduced. This strategy activates existing background knowledge in those students who have it, fills in gaps for those students who lack it, and engages student interest for all. For ELLs, brainstorming may be a first exposure to new vocabulary as they hear the pronunciation of a word and see it written at the same time. Teachers benefit, too, by being able to immediately assess whether or not students have enough background knowledge to move ahead.

IN PRACTICE
Technique I
To begin brainstorming, write a topic word on the board or on an overhead transparency. Accompany it with the open-ended question "What do you think of when I say the

Figure 5.1   Carousel Brainstorming

Tape sheets of chart paper on the walls at various locations around your classroom. At the top of each sheet, write a word or phrase pertaining to the new topic to be studied. For large groups and to save time, have several sets of the same words or phrases.

Following your signals, students walk around the room in small groups writing their associations with the word at the top of the paper. Allow no more than two minutes before signaling time to move to the next location.

word _____?" As students respond, write their words and phrases around the topic word to form a graphic display. Accept all answers, right or wrong. When you feel ready to move on with the lesson, tell students that you will return later to reexamine these ideas; say something like "Let's save these answers. We'll come back to them later to see what we've found out about them."

Technique II

A variation of this strategy is called *carousel brainstorming*, described in Figure 5.1. This technique gets students up and physically moving and involves all students simultaneously. You will enjoy watching students' faces as they generate new ideas by reading what others have written. The activity culminates in a single brainstorming graphic that you write on the board as groups read aloud the entries on the chart paper sheets.

Technique III

Use the brainstorming graphic for summary and review at the end of the lesson. Ask, as you point to each item, "Did we talk about this?" Students can review what they learned in the lesson, adding new words and phrases and correcting misconceptions.

Technique IV

Save the initial brainstorming graphic on an overhead transparency or chart paper, and use it the next day to activate the previous day's learning. You can update it daily as students add new pieces of information.

STRATEGY 14   USE THINK–WRITE–PAIR–SHARE

IN CONCEPT

Think–Write–Pair–Share is a technique that encourages participation at the same time that it activates students' prior knowledge. It is a way of getting students actively and immediately involved in learning new concepts and topics.

IN PRACTICE

Start with the same open-ended question as in the brainstorming activity, but this time, before students share their oral responses, give them a short time—30 to 90 seconds—to think about and jot down any relevant words or phrases. For the next minute or two, pair students with partners to discuss and expand their individual lists. Finally, invite students to share their ideas with the rest of the class. You will lower learner anxiety and increase participation by asking students to tell you an idea they either *had* or *heard*.

STRATEGY 15   USE K–W–L CHARTS

IN CONCEPT

A graphic organizer that complements the Think-Write-Pair-Share activity is the K–W–L (Ogle, 1986) chart shown in Figure 5.2. This strategy works best when completed in small groups. Talking about the topic helps students generate the ideas and vocabulary needed to complete the columns.

IN PRACTICE

Technique I

Students are asked to write what they already *know* (or think they know) about a topic in the *K* column. Then, with a partner or in a small group, they discuss what they *want* to know to complete the *W* column. The *L* column, listing what they *learned*, gets completed at the end of the lesson, again with students in pairs or small groups.

As topical information builds, daily entries in each column provide an ongoing means of activating students' prior knowledge and stimulating critical thinking. The completed K–W–L chart at the end of a unit serves as an excellent source of summary information from which to study for tests.

Technique II

You may want to include two additional columns on K–W–L charts, as shown in Figure 5.3. The first adds an *H* column for students to write *how* they learned the information in the *L* section. The *H* column is effective in focusing awareness on learning strategies.

A second variation is to add a *Q* column, "What *questions* do I still have?" At first, the *Q* section may seem repetitive of the *W* section, but it is not. The *W* column—"*What* do I want to know?"—is anticipatory; it is designed to get students thinking in advance of the topic. In contrast, the *Q* column deals with questions about information they have just

What do I KNOW?	What do I WANT to know?	What have I LEARNED?

Figure 5.2   K–W–L Chart

What do I KNOW?	What do I WANT to know?	What have I LEARNED?	HOW did I learn it?

What do I KNOW?	What do I WANT to know?	What have I LEARNED?	What QUESTIONS do I still have?

Figure 5.3   Additions to the K–W–L Chart

learned and have added to the *L* column. These questions can cover concepts, vocabulary, even how to go about learning the material. Student-generated items in the *L* and *Q* sections are a good way to open the next day's lesson: They activate background knowledge and serve as an immediate connection between past and present learning.

STRATEGY 16   PERSONALIZE THE LESSON

IN CONCEPT

Students often enjoy sharing their own personal stories and hearing about the experiences of others, *especially* those of their teacher. Personalizing a lesson is an attention-getting way to begin a new topic. Students who have lived in other states, countries, or cultures may have had personal experiences that relate to some aspect of the content being introduced. Hearing about these experiences activates and builds background knowledge for all students. It also increases motivation by stimulating student interest in the topic and demonstrating its relatedness to the real world.

IN PRACTICE

ELLs may be able to contribute unusual items of topical knowledge and life experience. An introduction to a unit on the Civil War, for example, often includes a discussion of how differences among individuals and groups can lead to conflict. Students who have lived outside the United States may lack background knowledge about the U.S. Civil War, but they may have lived through times of conflict—political, ethnic, or religious—in their native countries. Students may also have heard family stories about life in times of war or conflict. On a more personal level, some students, including the native English speakers, may want to share stories about family feuds.

In science, some students may be familiar with terrain or weather that is uncommon to your area. Can any of your students talk about living in or near rainforests, mountains, deserts, oceans, or rivers or about experiencing a tornado, hurricane, or earthquake? Some may have lived in or near areas with visible air or water pollution. Sharing this type of knowledge awakens immediate personal interest and allows you to draw comparisons and make generalizations.

In math, ELLs often come from educational systems that introduce concepts and processes earlier in the curriculum than is common in the United States. Those students can show others unusual algorithms or can explain real-life applications. They can also serve as peer tutors for their classmates in an unusual role reversal that will raise their peers' respect for them and bolster their own self-confidence.

STRATEGY 17   MAKE ANALOGIES

IN CONCEPT

Making an analogy of something known or imagined in real life to a new academic concept can promote immediate interest in the topic. Before introducing the academic topic, create a parallel situation, either real or imagined, that students can relate to. Their interest will spread to the topic under consideration. Imagination motivates learning as it builds background knowledge.

IN PRACTICE

A unit on westward expansion might not engender spontaneous interest in a class of eighth graders, but early settlements on Mars might. Engage students in a discussion about why someone would want to move to Mars, how it would feel to leave familiar surroundings for a long journey to places unknown, what dangers might lie ahead, what might be gained, and what lost. Then make the connection to mid-19th-century settlers by pointing out that both groups were adventurers going off into new and potentially dangerous environments. Analogies like this create a natural bridge of interest for learning academic concepts.

STRATEGY 18   SPARK INTEREST

IN CONCEPT

Interest motivates learning. Activities that create an element of excitement will raise students' interest levels at the same time that they activate background knowledge.

IN PRACTICE

Graphics and visuals stimulate interest in and discussion about a new topic. Create novelty by thinking beyond typical introductory photos, videos, and short films. Display a series of objects on your desk, and ask students about them and how they may be tied together. Wear an unusual item of clothing, or carry a prop in class. Or start with an exciting science demonstration. Remember that "Wow!" sensation the first time you witnessed the effect of dry ice in water? Interest acts as a motivator that facilitates learning.

STRATEGY 19   CREATE CURIOSITY

IN CONCEPT

Curiosity is another means of motivating learning. Raising intriguing questions in your students' minds can lead them naturally down the path to new learning.

IN PRACTICE

You can raise student curiosity by engaging students in an activity that might be named Start Your Brain Engines! or Think About It! These anticipation activities—first introduced by Readence, Bean, and Baldwin (1981)—come in many variations, several of which are shown in Figures 5.4 through 5.7. In all forms, they serve as an ungraded pretest, designed

Figure 5.4   *What Do You Know About Speed?*

Rank these forms of transportation in order from slowest to fastest. Write number 1 next to the one you think is the slowest, up to number 10 next to the one you think is the fastest. When you finish numbering, write down a speed for each one.

_____ Motorcycle
_____ Train
_____ Skateboard
_____ Race car
_____ Tractor
_____ Bicycle
_____ Inline skates
_____ Rowboat
_____ Jet plane
_____ Ship

PART II • STRATEGIES FOR CLASSROOM PRACTICE: INSTRUCTION

Directions: Number these events in the order you think they occurred. Write the number 1 next to the first (or earliest) through number 7 for the last. Can you "smart-guess" how long ago each of these happened?

Number   **How long ago?**

_____ Humans acquire language.   _____

_____ Humans learn to grow crops.   _____

_____ Humans invent the wheel.   _____

_____ Humans make the first tools.   _____

_____ Humans invent writing.   _____

_____ Humans make tools from metals.   _____

_____ Humans discover fire.   _____

Figure 5.5 Wake Up Your Thinking About Prehistoric Times

Look at the pictures below. Read what is in each cup. Working with your partner, decide which cup is the lightest. Mark it number 1. Which cup is the heaviest? Mark it number 6. Mark the other four cups in order of their weight.

#_____   🫗   1 cup of water

#_____   🫗   1 cup of glass marbles

#_____   🫗   1 cup of cotton balls

#_____   🫗   1 cup of sand

#_____   🫗   1 cup of cooked rice

#_____   🫗   1 cup of flour

Figure 5.6 What Do You Know About Matter, Mass, and Molecules?

Source: Excerpt p. 67 from EARTH AND PHYSICAL SCIENCE by Mary Ann Christison and Sharron Bassano. Copyright © 1992 by Addison-Wesley Publishing Company. Reprinted by permission of Pearson Education, Inc.

to start students thinking in advance of a new topic. Ideas will flow more productively when the activities are completed in pairs or small groups. And be sure to tell students that it's OK to be wrong—that's what a guess is.

Anticipation activities are inherently motivating because students like to see how close they come to the right answers. Those who do better than expected may be even more motivated by discovering that they already know more than they thought they did about a new topic. Class discussion to check and compare students' answers serves as a seamless introduction to the new topic.

Is what you "know" really true? For each of the following statements, decide whether or not it is true. If it is true, write FACT, and if it is not true, write FICTION.

_____ Sound travels in waves.
_____ Sound is caused by vibrations.
_____ Sound travels through the air.
_____ Sound travels through water.
_____ Sound travels through steel.
_____ Sound always travels at the same speed.
_____ Sound travels faster than light.
_____ Sound is measured in amperes.
_____ Technically, there is no real difference between music and noise.
_____ When people have excellent hearing, they can hear every sound that is made.
_____ Sound can be unhealthy for people.

Figure 5.7 Fact or Fiction?

STRATEGY 20   LINK LESSONS

IN CONCEPT

Lessons benefit from reviving students' past learning, linking it to concepts about to be presented. Explicit linking serves as a form of reinforcement and review and demonstrates the interrelatedness of information as it exists in the real world. The more frequently you revisit conceptually important pieces of information, the more opportunity students have for learning. By regularly stimulating background knowledge, you facilitate students' continuing conceptual development and increase the potential for new learning and enhanced retention.

IN PRACTICE

Technique I

Simple questions form effective links to prior knowledge. Start your daily instruction by activating previous learning with questions like these:

"What did we talk about yesterday when we were discussing the _____?"

"Who remembers the reasons for _____?"

"What did we learn about _____?"

"Who remembers some examples of _____?"

"What were some new words we used yesterday when we discussed _____?"

Technique II

Another type of linking attempts to reactivate previously taught concepts that may serve as background knowledge for new learning. Review questions at the ends of chapters provide excellent material for creating this type of linking activity, an example of which is shown in Figure 5.8. You can also revive topics using questionnaires similar to those illustrated in Figures 5.4 through 5.7.

Figure 5.8   How Much Do You
Remember About Clouds?

Before we learn more about meteorology, check yourself to see
what you remember about clouds. Next to each statement, put a
T for TRUE or an F for FALSE. If you think the statement is false,
rewrite it to make it true.

_____ Clouds are masses of water droplets and ice crystals.
_____ Clouds change shape because of wind and sunlight.
_____ Clouds are grouped into classes according to their size.
_____ Certain clouds are formed entirely of ice crystals.
_____ High, thin clouds cause thunderstorms.
_____ Clouds cause tornadoes and hurricanes.
_____ Clouds at night lower ground temperature.

STRATEGY 21   PREVIEW THE MATERIAL

IN CONCEPT

Previews create a framework for understanding a challenging reading on a new topic at
the same time that they supply critical pieces of background information. Previews make
a new undertaking appear more learnable and facilitate students' comprehension.

IN PRACTICE

Technique I
Before beginning a new topic, "walk" your students through the chapter in their textbook. Start your guided tour with the visuals, asking, "What can you learn about the
topic from this picture?" Move on to the headers, subheaders, and highlighted information such as text boxes, graphs, and bullets, asking, "What do you know now?" at
appropriate points along the way (see also Strategy 70 in Chapter 9). Helping your students
get the big picture of upcoming themes, people, issues, and events builds background
knowledge.

Technique II
When you recognize that a reading passage may present difficulties for students, give
them a written introduction that outlines important information they will need for comprehension. Include explanations of vocabulary, concepts, people, and events along with
supporting visuals (graphics, maps, tables, charts, photos) to aid understanding. Think of
previewing as the CliffsNotes of background knowledge.

   For example, previewing is an excellent strategy to use at the start of a long and detailed work of fiction. Previews might include a list of major characters with details about
their personalities and relationships to others in the book; brief notes about historical
events and cultural understandings that are important to the plot; and maps showing
routes of journeys or places of significance in the story. Previews provide students with
background knowledge through initial discussion and will continue to guide them as
they read.

STRATEGY 22   MAKE NEW LEARNING FEEL LEARNABLE

IN CONCEPT

Many ELLs feel daunted by the amount of information they are expected to learn. New topics often feel overwhelming in their breadth and depth. Strategies that make new learning feel *learnable* help students build confidence in themselves as learners. The previewing strategy just described, for example, helps students build self-confidence in their ability to learn at the same time that it builds background knowledge.

IN PRACTICE

Technique I

For some students, thinking about the new information they must learn feels much like starting a 1,000-piece jigsaw puzzle—just too many little, indistinct pieces. You can explicitly tie new information to previously learned topics through *spiraling*, reactivating previously learned concepts that relate to a new topic. Students will have a more positive attitude when they realize that they already have some pieces of the puzzle in place. This technique has the dual purpose of building self-confidence as it builds background knowledge.

Technique II

When you announce that students will be learning a completely new topic, start by acknowledging that it *is* complex. Then explain that *all* new topics appear complex before you learn them. Help students recall other topics they have learned that seemed difficult at the beginning but were, after all, quite learnable. Assure them that this new topic is no different. A positive mind-set motivates learning.

STRATEGY 23   COMBINE STRATEGIES TO INCREASE EFFECTIVENESS

IN CONCEPT

Each strategy in this chapter is effective in building and activating background knowledge for your students. However, pairing strategies often produces even better results. The more background knowledge students develop, the more easily they will process, retain, and apply new information.

IN PRACTICE

Using Think–Write–Pair–Share (Strategy 14) in combination with carousel brainstorming (Strategy 13), for example, offers an extra opportunity to hear ideas related to the new topic. Interest awakeners (Strategy 18) also lend themselves well to pairing with other background knowledge strategies. Figure 5.9 lists some possible pairings for mixing and matching strategies. Combinations are limited only by your own creativity and imagination.

Try	With
Think–Write–Pair–Share (Strategy 14) ⟶	Carousel brainstorming (Strategy 13)
Brainstorming (Strategy 13) ⟶	Previews (Strategy 21)
Interest awakeners (Strategy 18) ⟶	K-W-L charts (Strategy 15)
Make analogies (Strategy 17) ⟶	Numbered heads (Strategy 48, Chapter 7)
Numbered heads (Strategy 48) ⟶	Brainstorming (Strategy 13)

Figure 5.9 Mix and Match Strategies

IN SUMMARY: WORKING WITH BACKGROUND KNOWLEDGE

It is worth repeating: How well students learn new content is directly related to the amount of relevant background knowledge and/or experience they already have. The minutes, even hours, you spend in class activating and building background knowledge will pay you and your students back many times over by facilitating their learning and maximizing their possibilities for academic success.

QUESTIONS FOR DISCUSSION

1. Which of the *12 Guidelines for Practice* presented at the end of Chapter 1 inform the strategies in this chapter?

2. Cite and summarize additional research that gives theoretical and/or experiential support to the strategies discussed in this chapter.

3. Think back to something you learned from scratch. How did you feel as you were starting? Did it feel learnable? overwhelming? Can you think of anything that would have made you feel better about starting on the new topic? At what point did you realize that you were finally "getting it"? Did your ability to learn and/or your feeling about learning change after that? If so, how?

4. If you are currently teaching, select a lesson you have taught that began with a particularly effective introduction to build and activate background knowledge. Describe the strategies you used and why you believe they were effective.

   If you are not currently teaching, work with a partner or a small group to plan interesting ways to build and activate background knowledge as an introduction to the following topics:

   Violent weather: Thunderstorms, tornadoes, earthquakes, and hurricanes

   Industrial Revolution: The rise of labor unions

   Human anatomy: Skin, muscles, and bones of the human body

REFERENCES AND RESOURCES

Chamot, A. U., & O'Malley, J. M. (1994). *The CALLA handbook: Implementing the cognitive academic language learning approach* (pp. 84–86, 199–200, 263–264, 283–284, 293–294). Reading, MA: Addison-Wesley.

Echevarria, J., & Graves, A. (2005). Curriculum adaptations. In P. A. Richard-Amato & M. A. Snow (Eds.), *Academic success for English language learners: Strategies for K–12 mainstream teachers* (pp. 224–247). White Plains, NY: Pearson Education.

Echevarria, J., Vogt, M., & Short, D. J. (2007). *Making content comprehensible for English learners: The SIOP model* (3rd ed.). Needham, MA: Allyn & Bacon.

Leinhardt, G. (1992). What research on learning tells us about teaching. *Educational Leadership, 49*(7), 20–25.

Ogle, D. M. (1986). K–W–L: A teaching model that develops active reading of expository text. *Reading Teacher, 39*, 564–570.

Osborn, A. (1953). *Applied imagination: Principles and procedures of creative problem solving.* New York: Charles Scribner's Sons.

Readence, J. E., Bean, T. W., & Baldwin, R. S. (1981). *Content area reading: An integrated approach* (2nd ed.). Dubuque, IA: Kendall/Hunt.

CHAPTER 6

PRESENTING NEW MATERIAL: TEACHING THE LESSON

You've introduced the new topic to your students and sparked their interest. You've activated your students' prior knowledge and built a foundational background. You've motivated your students by demonstrating real-life applications. Your students are now ready to learn the material that you've planned to teach. The strategies in this chapter will help you present the information in ways that will make it easier for the ELLs in your class to understand it.

ORAL ACADEMIC LANGUAGE

Have you ever tried to talk to someone in a foreign language? You may have visited a country whose people speak a language you studied in school. Or perhaps you learned a few useful phrases in preparation for your trip. You were delighted to be understood when you asked, "*Où est la gare?*" or "*¿Dónde está la playa?*" Then you got the answer, and poof!—the bubble of satisfaction burst. You didn't have the faintest idea where that train station or beach really was. The words were coming at you so fast that you couldn't make sense of them at all.

Why do speakers of foreign languages seem to speak so fast? The answer lies not with the rate of speech but rather with the rate of listening. Nonnative speakers are *slow listeners*. They need extra time to bring meaning to what they're hearing, to actively process the incoming language. That is not easy to do, especially while trying to pay attention to the new words that continue to be spoken.

Imagine now that these foreign words are not about something as simple as the price of a souvenir or the location of the restroom. Imagine instead that they deal with complex academic concepts in math, science, and social studies. That is the challenge that ELLs face in content classes.

THE DIFFICULTIES OF ORAL ACADEMIC LANGUAGE

The spoken language of academic instruction is difficult for language learners for several reasons. First, oral language is ephemeral in nature. Words, once spoken, are gone; you cannot rehear them for review.

Second, language learners need more time to process the incoming words than the speaker takes to deliver them. Concentrating on the meaning of one spoken sentence interferes with the ability to attend to the next one. Listening is a complex task; even native speakers experience occasional difficulty processing spoken language—for example, while listening to TV news or radio traffic reports.

Third, English, the language students are trying to learn, is the medium through which academic content is delivered. For ELLs, the language itself adds an additional burden of complexity to the content. Understanding academic concepts depends not just on what the teacher says but also on how the teacher says it. For ELLs, the *how* can help bring meaning to the *what*.

TEACHER TALK

The Objective: Pace Your Speech

The Rationale: Oral instruction becomes more comprehensible for ELLs when the speaker focuses on how the words of instruction are delivered. Teachers, of course, speak clearly enough for native English-speaking students, but ELLs benefit when those teachers use strategies to enhance the clarity and reduce the complexity of the language used to present new information. Language-sensitive instruction eases the challenge of academic listening for ELLs.

STRATEGY 24   SLOW DOWN!

IN CONCEPT

The simplest and most helpful strategy to modify the way you speak is to slow down. The goal is to speak at a slightly slower pace—but not so slow that it feels or sounds unnatural. A good way to slow down speech is to *pause* for an extra beat or two at natural breaks between phrases or sentences.

IN PRACTICE

Examine in Figure 6.1 the pausing the teacher uses in delivering this overview of the eighth-grade American history curriculum on the first day of school. The dots between phrases represent the pause time, two dots for shorter pauses and four dots for longer ones. Each pause offers ELLs valuable extra time to process the language of the incoming content.

Figure 6.1 Slowing Down Speech with Pauses

> What are we going to study this year? . . . . This year . . we'll be studying the significant . . historical . . events . . . . that led to the development . . of our nation's traditions. . . . We'll survey American history . . . . with a special emphasis . . on the 19th century . . . . First, . . we'll examine in detail . . the Declaration of Independence. . . . and the Constitution . . . . because they're fundamental . . to the history of the United States . . . . Then . . we'll study topics such as slavery, ... the Civil War, ... reconstruction, ... industrialization, ... and the United States as a world power.

STRATEGY 25   ENHANCE THE INTONATION OF YOUR WORDS

IN CONCEPT

Enhanced intonation helps you enunciate the words you speak. You can highlight important words by raising or lowering your voice level and your pitch. Giving special intonation to key content words is the equivalent of underlining, bolding, or italicizing words in writing. Clearly enunciated, well-paced speech with interesting and varied tonal patterns is more enjoyable and easier to understand than speech that is rapid or monotonal or, even worse, both.

IN PRACTICE

Return now to the social studies course overview in Figure 6.1. Even with the pausing, it is a heavy dose of language for ELLs. Using rising and falling intonation to emphasize important content words signifies to ELLs which words to focus on at the same time that it slows the pacing of speech even further. Read aloud the overview in Figure 6.2, giving special emphasis to the boldfaced words. You should be able to hear the difference that pausing and intonation can make for your ELLs.

   To demonstrate how effective this strategy is, look at the list of words in Figure 6.3. These are the boldfaced words designated for enhanced intonation in Figure 6.2. Reading

What are we going to study this year? . . . . This year . . we'll be studying the significant . . **historical . . events** . . . . that led to the development . . of our **nation's traditions** . . . . We'll survey **American history** . . . . with a special emphasis . . on the **19th century** . . . . **First**, . . we'll examine in detail . . the **Declaration of Independence** . . . . and the **Constitution** . . . . because they're **fundamental** . . to the history of the United States . . . . **Then** . . we'll study topics such as **slavery**, ... **the Civil War**, ... **reconstruction**, ... **Industrialization**, ... and the United States as a **world power**.

Figure 6.2   Slowing Speech Even More with Enhanced Intonation

historical events
nation's traditions
American history
19th century
First
Declaration of Independence
Constitution
fundamental
Then
slavery
the Civil War
reconstruction
industrialization
world power

Figure 6.3   Getting the Message from the Boldfaced Words Alone

through the list of just those words *alone* gives you a pretty good idea of the message. Your oral instruction will be more easily understood by your ELLs if you speak with enhanced pausing and intonation.

TEACHER TALK

The Objective: Simplify Your Speech

The Rationale: Oral language patterns differ greatly from patterns used in writing. Speakers tend to use familiar words in short, simple sentences. Often they use phrases instead of complete sentences. Speakers lose their place and backtrack, or they repeat themselves, or they correct themselves. They make false starts and use extraneous words as fillers or spacers. They regularly use contractions and merge words together. Teachers can facilitate comprehension of spoken academic language by making minor adaptations to their normal speech patterns.

STRATEGY 26   LIMIT USE OF CONTRACTIONS

IN CONCEPT

All fluent English speakers contract words when speaking. Contractions are one of the normal differences between spoken and written English, as well as a salient difference between language learners and native speakers.

For ELLs, contractions are a source of misunderstanding. Words like *they're* and *it's* are easily confused with their other forms: *there/their* and *its*. Another issue is the two ways of contracting the phrase *it is not*; do *it isn't* and *it's not* really mean the same thing? In addition, many ELLs do not connect the spoken *should've*, which sounds like *should of*, with its written form, *should have*. And almost every listener has sought clarification, at some time, of *can* and *can't*.

IN PRACTICE

You can help your ELLs by using the full form of these and other contracted words—*they are, there are, they have, it is, it is not,* and *cannot*—as often as you can. The uncontracted forms help ELLs not only by making the meaning more apparent but also by slowing down your rate of speech.

STRATEGY 27   USE FEWER PRONOUNS

IN CONCEPT

ELLs can bring meaning to spoken language more readily when they hear more nouns and fewer pronouns. Pronouns involve an extra level of language processing that slows down comprehension.

IN PRACTICE

Although it may sound a bit strange or stilted to you, try to repeat names and other nouns more frequently than you might normally. Look at the nouns in the following sentence:

> The colonists who participated in the Boston Tea Party were willing to risk deprivation, even their lives, for the principle of no taxation without representation.

For ELLs, any pronoun that might follow in the next sentence would require a great deal of grammatical processing to determine its antecedent noun. Instead of *they*, repeat *the colonists*; instead of *it*, repeat *the Boston Tea Party* or *no taxation without representation*. Even native speakers occasionally become confused when pronouns like *it* or *they* are used too many times.

STRATEGY 28 SIMPLIFY YOUR SENTENCE STRUCTURE

IN CONCEPT

Teachers often read aloud articles or book segments to supplement their lessons or students' textbooks. These written passages are composed of long, complex sentences intended for silent reading and slow processing. They are difficult to process orally.

IN PRACTICE

Modify the text materials you read aloud during oral instruction by shortening the sentences and simplifying the structure. Consider the following textbook sentence:

> The Civil War, which took more American lives than any other war in our history, divided the people of the United States, so that in many families, brother fought against brother.

You could facilitate the listening comprehension of this passage for your ELLs by subdividing the sentences and paraphrasing the wording like this:

> The Civil War divided the people of the United States. It even divided families. In many families, brother fought against brother. More Americans died in the Civil War than in any other war in American history.

STRATEGY 29 USE FAMILIAR WORDS AND BE CONSISTENT

IN CONCEPT

Using synonyms and colorful words undoubtedly makes speech sound more interesting, but for ELLs it adds another source of confusion. Your language of instruction should make consistent use of high-frequency words and phrases to allow ELLs to focus on content and concepts. Their vocabulary growth will not be limited if you incorporate the techniques that follow.

IN PRACTICE

Technique I

All students benefit from exposure to a wide range of interesting vocabulary presented by association. Every time you use low-frequency words, pair them immediately with their more familiar synonym, such as *autonomy* with *independence* and *emancipation* with *freedom* (also see Strategy 65 in Chapter 8). Frequent repetition of the pair solidifies the association, and the unfamiliar word soon becomes readily recognized.

Technique II

Be consistent in the words you use to give oral directions for assignments and activities. Teachers are often unaware that they are using different words to give the same set of directions, as in the following:

Circle the word that best describes _____.

Draw a circle around the best word choice for _____.

Find the word that best answers each question, and then circle it.

Using consistent word patterns to communicate directions simplifies oral input for ELLs.

Technique III

The words you speak in class should also be consistent with the words and phrases used in the students' textbooks. A brief examination of the words used in the textbook to give directions or to discuss a topic can help you decide which words and phrases to use in presenting and discussing the material. When you believe that directions written in the text seem overly complicated, like those in Figure 6.4, explain them through paraphrase and discussion. For ELLs, maintaining the consistency of the words used in class and frequently associating those words with the ones used in their textbooks will help facilitate comprehension.

Technique IV

"Translate" the current pedagogical jargon used in your school district by pairing such terminology with more traditional forms of expression. Some widely used examples are shown in Figure 6.5. Use jargon if you must, but be sure that all your students know what the new phrases really mean.

Figure 6.4 Simplify Unclear Directions in the Textbook

If the textbook says:
Evaluate the following expression for the given value of the variable.

$$A + 5 = \qquad \text{For } A = 2; A = 6.$$

Paraphrase to:

(Good) Find A + 5 when A = 2.
Find A + 5 when A = 6.

(Better) If A = 2, then A + 5 = ?
If A = 6, then A + 5 = ?

Figure 6.5 The Challenge of Current Terminology

Today's Terminology	Traditional Terminology
an extended constructed response	an essay
a brief constructed response	a paragraph
selected response questions	multiple-choice questions
making text-to-text connections	comparing books

STRATEGY 30   BECOME AWARE OF IDIOMATIC LANGUAGE

IN CONCEPT

Idioms and figurative speech add color to speech. Language learners feel they are learning the "real English" when they learn idioms, and perhaps they are. Native speakers use them liberally in speech. However, idioms and figurative speech often puzzle ELLs because the meaning of the individual words, even when each word is known, does not reflect the actual meaning of the message.

IN PRACTICE

Teachers use figurative language to get their students' attention. A teacher might begin a question session with something like "OK, I'm going to pitch some practice questions. Let's see who can hit a home run here!" Although this definitely adds an element of fun, the ELLs in this classroom are likely to respond by looking around the room for a baseball and bat.

It is not possible or desirable to avoid using idioms and figurative speech. Such language flavors speech and often injects interest and humor. However, developing an awareness of the idioms and figurative speech you use as you speak allows you the opportunity to paraphrase or explain your language choices in a simple way.

STRATEGY 31   AUDIOTAPE AND ANALYZE YOUR SPEECH

IN CONCEPT

It is difficult to know your own particular speech patterns. One way to help you develop awareness is to audiotape several lessons that you teach and then analyze what you hear.

IN PRACTICE

Using the checklist shown in Figure 6.6, replay your recording several times, noting your rate of speech, complexity of sentence structure, pauses and intonation, repetition and

Rate of Speech	Fast	Moderate	Slow
Pausing	Infrequent	Adequate	Often
Sentence Structure	Complex	Mixed	Simple
Enunciation	Often unclear	Sometimes unclear	Clear
Intonation	Monotonal	Adequate	Enhanced
Repetition/Redundancy	Infrequent	Adequate	Frequent
Pronoun Usage	Unclear referents		Clear referents
Synonym Frequency	Few used		Many used
Synonym Clarity	Used but no explanation		Used with explanation
Idiom Frequency	Few used		Many used
Idiom Clarity	Used with no explanation		Used with explanation

Speech areas for improvement:

Figure 6.6   Speech Analysis Checklist

redundancy (more is better), transparency of pronoun usage, and frequency and clarification of synonyms and idioms. It will help you to jot down words and phrases you use. Then follow up by noting the elements of your speech pattern you would like to improve.

TEACHER TALK

The Objective: Enhance Your Words

The Rationale: Why is the radio no longer a source of family entertainment? Why are music videos so popular? The answer is that television and computers enhance spoken words and music in ways that engage people. Enhancing words of instruction in the classroom will engage your students, too.

Adding visual elements to speech embeds it in context and facilitates comprehension of the oral language of instruction. Using strategies that move oral instruction from Cummins's Quadrant IV to Quadrant III (see again Figure 1.3 in Chapter 1) makes it easier for ELLs to understand concepts and content.

STRATEGY 32   ANIMATE YOUR WORDS

IN CONCEPT

A video-recorded lecture is much easier to process than one that is audio only. So, too, do the visual components of hand gestures, facial expressions, and body language make oral language easier to process by embedding it in context.

IN PRACTICE

In classroom instruction, ELLs will become more involved if you make oral language a visually engaging experience. Make ample use of natural gestures and facial expressions. When you tell your students, "There are three important things to remember," hold up three fingers for your students to see. Then continue using one, two, or three fingers as you explain each piece of information. Point again to your first finger when you review by asking, "What was the first thing we discussed?" Students form a visual picture that helps them retain the information.

Also, take advantage of any pictures or objects in the classroom that you can use to illustrate a particular word. In addition, using pantomime to help explain a new or difficult term is a surefire way of getting the attention of all your students.

STRATEGY 33   USE VISUALS AND GRAPHICS

IN CONCEPT

Support your words with graphic representation. Seeing words and phrases in written form reinforces oral language and facilitates content comprehension.

sovereignty	epitome	tough
pneumatic	psychology	though
phlegm	posthumous	through
mnemonic	hegemony	thorough
choir	conscience	thought

Figure 6.7 Pronunciation Puzzlers

IN PRACTICE

Technique I

Use the chalk–talk approach. As you speak, write key vocabulary words and phrases on the board or on an overhead transparency. Often, ELLs do not associate words in their spoken and written forms because the pronunciation is so unlike the spelling, as illustrated in Figure 6.7. It may be that a word is confusing orally because its spelling is close to that of many others, such as those in the last column in Figure 6.7. Or perhaps a word previously encountered only in print differs from a student's mental pronunciation. Seeing a word in writing as you speak it facilitates comprehension for ELLs students.

Technique II

Extend the chalk–talk approach to include graphic organizers as a regular part of your teaching. Graphic organizers (discussed at length in Chapter 10) contextually embed oral language. They help ELLs see relationships and understand vocabulary and concepts in a linguistically simplified way.

Technique III

Incorporate pictures, photos, maps, graphs, tables, and anything else you may have on hand to help illustrate the meaning of your words. Draw a picture of an object—even stick figures and rough sketches are helpful. Refer to them as you talk. Remember the adage "One picture is worth a thousand words." For language learners, this is a primary principle.

Technique IV

Complement class lectures and discussions with filmstrips, slides, videotapes, CDs, and DVDs. ELLs will learn visually from them, although they may find the soundtracks challenging. You can remedy this by finding some class time for ELLs to see a preview without sound, or you can give students an outline or a list of key words and phrases to guide them as they watch.

Technique V

Encourage students to find and share content-appropriate websites on the Internet. You might maintain space on a bulletin board or chalkboard for students to write in discoveries of new and interesting URLs that support class content.

Technique VI

Bring in *realia* to engage your students. Realia are authentic, real-world objects that illustrate a concept by making meaningful connections to students' lives and to the world outside the classroom. Teachers of math, for example, can spark interest and motivate learning with real bank deposit slips and check registers to support a unit on banking, big store sales brochures to calculate percentage, copies of actual floor plans to calculate square footage. Students can also be encouraged to share realia from their homes for everyone to enjoy.

STRATEGY 34   DEMONSTRATE YOUR WORDS

IN CONCEPT

Demonstration and modeling are effective ways to facilitate comprehension of the words of oral instruction. Students can "see" how to find an answer or solve a problem.

IN PRACTICE

Take your students through a step-by-step process to explain how to reach an end result. For each step, do a think-aloud to demonstrate why you are choosing to do it in a certain way and *not* in other ways. Vocalize the questions you would normally ask yourself silently to show the steps you are taking. For example, in a lesson about classifying objects, after asking the question, you might say something like "Now how can I decide whether this is A or B? I have to think about . . . . I'll start by looking for . . . ."

It is important *not* to make the process seem too simple. Students need to realize that thinking, adjusting, rethinking, and readjusting are a natural part of the learning process. Figure 6.8 shows some appropriate classroom applications of this strategy.

Figure 6.8   Use Think-Aloud
Demonstrations to Show Process

How to classify information
How to sequence information
How to summarize information
How to locate information to answer a question
How to highlight important information
How to select the main idea and supporting details

STRATEGY 35   BE DRAMATIC

IN CONCEPT

Dramatic lessons are memorable lessons. Make your lessons memorable by hamming them up.

IN PRACTICE

Dramatize, emote, role-play, pantomime. Have a good time! Greet your class wearing a costume or unusual piece of clothing or holding an unusual prop. Bring a magnifying glass to "look more closely" into something. Doing such things gives your students tacit permission to be dramatic, too. Groups of students might enjoy staging mini-reenactments of events or acting out imaginary dialogues between historical or scientific figures. Students will remember the material and probably you, too.

CLASSROOM ROUTINE AND REVIEW

Routines create patterns of consistency, and review creates patterns of opportunity. Both lower levels of anxiety for the students in your classroom. Routines lessen the need for wordy explanations that create confusion and raise anxiety levels for ELLs. Review offers students multiple opportunities for reinforcement of instructional information. Automating routines will free up valuable extra minutes for review.

The Objective: Create Classroom Routines

The Rationale: Students often enter the classroom over a period of several minutes. Of course you're not going to start until everyone is seated and ready. How many minutes does it actually take until you are doing something instructional? (Hint: Students stall as long as possible.) Routines will remedy this situation.

STRATEGY 36   MAXIMIZE THE FIRST 5 MINUTES

IN CONCEPT

Students should know what to do immediately upon arrival. Think about the ways you take attendance and correct homework. Streamline the process so it starts immediately and automatically to save valuable time at the beginning of each class period.

IN PRACTICE

Technique I
Designate a group captain (either on a regular rotation basis or as an academic reward) whose job is to take attendance and visually check completed homework assignments as soon as the students enter the room.

Technique II
Captains can discuss and compare homework answers within their groups. They can then report to you any items that appear problematic for the group or for which group members' answers differed. This gives you the option of spending valuable class time on only those items that need review, reinforcement, or possibly even reteaching. Students' homework should be on their desks, clearly visible as you walk around the room to supervise and offer help during the homework discussion time. Captains can also collect the papers for you if you want to see them every day.

Technique III
Teachers engage in an ongoing debate about whether and how often to collect homework. Collecting and correcting it daily adds another burden to teachers' already-heavy workloads, but some teachers feel it may be the only way to ensure that all the students actually complete their assignments.

An effective technique to resolve this situation is to do a homework check on random days of the week, anywhere from two to six days apart. The idea is to give the students just enough time to copy down the answers from the particular assignments you have listed on the board. If they've done the work, it is an easy task to simply locate

1. Students fold a blank sheet of paper into four or six sections.
2. Students number each box 1 through 4 or 1 through 6.
3. Teacher writes on the board four or six items to transfer to the appropriate box.

    Examples:
        Box 1. Tuesday, Question 5, page 138.
        Box 2. Wednesday, Question 2, page 151.

1. Tuesday, Q 5, P 138	2. Wednesday, Q 2, P 151
3. Thursday, Q 1, P 167	4. Friday, Q 3, P 189

4. Teacher allots only enough time to copy answers, not to respond or compute them.
5. Teacher collects and corrects the papers.

Figure 6.9   Homework Check

and rewrite the items you request. If they have not done the assignment, they will not have enough time to complete the task. The details of this technique are illustrated in Figure 6.9.

STRATEGY 37   DISPLAY THE CLASS PLAN

IN CONCEPT

Lesson objectives, clearly stating what students should know and be able to do, focus students' attention on work to be accomplished.

IN PRACTICE

Display lesson objectives, topics, and activities for the day or for the week in a prominent place in your classroom. Read them aloud at the beginning of each day's lesson, and evaluate at the end which were achieved. For ELLs, seeing what they will be doing next in class decreases reliance on oral language, lowers anxiety, and increases ability to focus on classroom tasks.

STRATEGY 38   POST THE HOMEWORK

IN CONCEPT

Teachers often run out of time at the end of a lesson, and homework assignments get delivered in a hurried burst of words as students are packing up books and getting ready to leave. For ELLs, this can be a confusing and difficult situation.

IN PRACTICE

Homework assignments—by day, week, or unit—should be written out before class begins and should appear in a consistent place—on a section of the board, on chart paper, on an overhead transparency, or on your class webpage. The goal is to avoid rushing through it orally as the bell is ringing. Make sure students know that homework information will appear in the same place every day. Then your students can never use the excuse that they didn't hear you.

CLASSROOM ROUTINE AND REVIEW

The Objective: Get into the Routine of Review

The Rationale: If background knowledge forms the building blocks of learning, then review is the cement that holds those blocks together. Mini-reviews during a lesson and a final review at the end benefit all students. Those who know will shine, and those who don't know will get another opportunity for learning. In addition, you will get the opportunity to hear and correct any misconceptions. It's a win–win situation for everyone. Frequent review during and at the end of every class period reinforces learning; it far exceeds in value the minutes devoted to it.

STRATEGY 39   REVIEW WHILE YOU TEACH

IN CONCEPT

All students benefit from quick and frequent review of key content and vocabulary as a lesson progresses. Multiple mini-reviews focus students' attention and concentration throughout class time. For ELLs, in particular, repetition and review offer extra opportunities for language input to reinforce their conceptual understanding.

IN PRACTICE

As you teach, stop every 5 or 10 minutes to ask appropriate questions so that students can repeat, review, paraphrase, and summarize:

"Who can repeat what I just said?"

"Who can use different words to explain what I just said?"

"Who remembers the reasons for _____?"

"Who remembers what _____ means?"

"What synonym did we use for _____?"

A good challenge is to ask simple yes/no questions that contain misinformation, such as "Vinegar is an acid, right?" Misinformation questions promote critical listening and encourage students to think before answering. You may also find that your students like the idea of correcting your misstatements.

One middle school teacher treated review questions as a gamelike challenge. At any point in the lesson, she would announce, "Quick check!" Her students became instantly alert in anticipation of the question and the opportunity to score bonus points. They loved it—perhaps your students will, too.

STRATEGY 40   END EACH LESSON WITH ORAL AND WRITTEN REVIEW

IN CONCEPT

Teachers aim to use every minute of class time for learning and often run out of time to review. With all good intentions, those who do this nonetheless lose a critically important teaching tool. All students benefit from spending the last three to five minutes of class time in review. Every lesson needs closure, even those that will be continued the next day. Oral review is good, written review is better, and the combination of the two is best.

IN PRACTICE

Technique I
Shortly before class ends, ask the simple question, "So, what did we talk about today?" If you opened your lesson with a brainstorming graphic, return to it for review. For important information that has not been recalled, use questions like "What about _____? What did we say about that?"

Technique II
In Elbow Buddy Review, you ask your paired students to turn to their partners—their "elbow buddies"—and tell them a specific piece of information that you call for. Ideas for this type of review are listed in Figure 6.10.

Figure 6.10   Elbow Buddy Review

"Turn to your elbow buddy and tell him or her . . . "

2 causes of _____

3 substances that _____

the definition of _____

3 reasons for _____

2 places that _____

2 people who _____

Figure 6.11 3–2–1 Review

```
3 facts I learned today are

     1. _____

     2. _____

     3. _____

2 words I want to remember are

     1. _____

     2. _____

1 thing I found very interesting is

     1. _____
```

Technique III

Partner Review pairs students who are then designated as Partner A or B. Using the same types of prompts as in Figure 6.10, ask Partner A to tell Partner B the review item you announce, alternating partners with each request for an additional review item. To ensure that the information being exchanged between partners is correct and complete, you can ask students to share with the class what they have just told their partners.

Technique IV

The 3–2–1 Review is fast, effective, and fun. At the end of a lesson, students write three facts they learned, two new words, and one item of particular interest, as shown in Figure 6.11. You can also add a zero line at the bottom of the review page that reads, "0: I still don't know anything about _____ and I would like to!"

All written forms of review are more productive when used *after* oral partnered review. However, if you must use only written review, allow students to complete it in pairs or small groups, structuring it with a Think-Pair-Share approach (see Strategy 49 in Chapter 7) for greater productivity.

Technique V

Working in pairs, students can use any of the graphic organizers discussed at length in Chapter 10 to summarize and review information. Graphic organizers are a linguistically simplified means of expressing conceptually complex concepts.

Technique VI

K–W–L charts (see Chapter 5, Figures 5.2 and 5.3) and learning logs (see Chapter 9, Figure 9.10) also can be used for review. After other forms of oral and/or written review have been completed, students can transfer items to the L section of their K–W–L charts or to their learning logs. For ELLs, this may be an appropriate homework task.

Technique VII

Students in groups can write a set of review questions for another group to answer. Students absorb a great deal of information in the process of formulating questions. Groups then exchange their questions and discuss their answers before class ends. The questions can be used again as the next day's lesson opener to activate prior knowledge. You can also add an extra incentive by announcing that you will use any really good questions on your next quiz or test.

Technique VIII

An AlphaBox Review, shown in Figure 6.12, consists of a 6 x 4 grid with boxes labeled A through Z. It is used as a cumulative review, with students daily adding key

Figure 6.12 AlphaBox Review

Adapted from Buehl, D. (2009). *Classroom Strategies for Interactive Learning* (3rd ed., p. 194). Originally published in *Classroom Strategies for Interactive Learning* (2001, 2nd ed.) and Ricci, G., & Wahlgren, C., (1998).

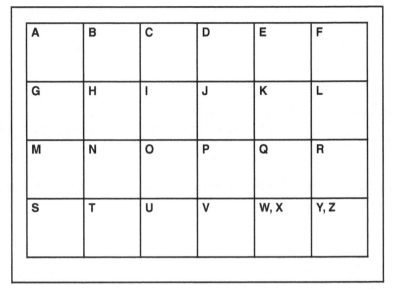

words—concepts, terms, vocabulary, attributes—in the letter-appropriate box. The fun and challenge here is to find some data for every box. As with most reviews, it works best in pairs or small groups and, because of its limited space, as an adjunct to other forms of written review.

STRATEGY 41   MAKE ACTIVE USE OF REVIEW NOTES

IN CONCEPT

Daily reviews reinforce and consolidate knowledge. They become an even more powerful learning tool when used in conjunction with a review notebook or learning log.

IN PRACTICE

Students can keep their daily written reviews in a review notebook or a separate notebook section titled WWLY (What We Learned Yesterday) or, more dramatically, This I Know. Yesterday's review notes can be used to activate prior knowledge as you begin the next day's lesson. And students can be encouraged to use their review notes to study for tests. Later in the semester, you can direct students to their notes to make direct connections between previously learned material and new information. There are many valid reasons to make review a regular part of your class routine.

IN SUMMARY: TEACHING THE LESSON

Good classroom instruction begins with speaking in a manner that facilitates comprehension for your ELLs. The challenge, however, lies in changing highly ingrained speech habits and mannerisms that may interfere with clarity. The first step in the process, and perhaps the hardest, is becoming aware of what you actually do orally. Once you have developed awareness, select one or two areas you would like to improve. Choose the strategies you think would help, and begin to incorporate them into your patterns of oral instruction. When those feel comfortable, try working on others, one or two at a time. Each modification you make fine-tunes the clarity of your oral instruction for your ELLs.

The second part of good instruction involves classroom routine and review. For ELLs, predictable classroom routines and frequent content review lower anxiety and support language development at the same time that they facilitate comprehension of content. For teachers, routines save time, effort, and energy. They are clearly good for everyone. Try getting into your own routines for arrival, homework, review, and dismissal. You're going to like what happens.

QUESTIONS FOR DISCUSSION

1. Which of the *12 Guidelines for Practice* presented at the end of Chapter 1 inform the strategies in this chapter?

2. Cite and summarize additional research that gives theoretical and/or experiential support to the strategies discussed in this chapter.

3. If you are currently teaching a class, audiotape a lesson in which you are actively teaching, and analyze it using the checklist in Figure 6.6. What advice would you give yourself to facilitate comprehension of your oral language by the English language learners in your classroom?

   If you are not currently teaching, get permission to audiotape a lesson in which a teacher is actively teaching. Analyze the recording as above.

4. In pairs, preferably including one who is currently teaching and one who is not, compare and critique each other's analyses of the recorded lessons.

5. Prepare a text passage to read aloud in a small group setting. After the reading, have your colleagues give you verbal feedback or a written critique.

6. Prepare a get-the-message-from-the-boldfaced-words activity (Strategy 25). Read it to your peers in class. Did they get the message?

7. If you are now teaching a class, what routines do you think you could create to lower language input for your ELLs and, at the same time, make your class period more time efficient?

   If you are not currently teaching a class, observe a teacher and keep a written record, minute to minute, of classroom activities—from the arrival of the first students through the final dismissal. In what ways do you think this teacher could benefit from creating routines?

REFERENCES AND RESOURCES

Buehl, D. (2009). *Classroom strategies for interactive teaching* (3rd ed.). Newark, DE: International Reading Association.

Fillmore, L. W., & Snow, C. E. (2005). What teachers need to know about language. In P. A. Richard-Amato & M. A. Snow (Eds.), *Academic success for English language learners: Strategies for K–12 mainstream teachers* (pp. 47–75). White Plains, NY: Pearson Education.

Ricci, G., & Wahlgren, C. (1998, May). *The key to know "PAINE" know gain.* Paper presented at the 43rd Annual Convention of the International Reading Association, Orlando, FL.

Richard-Amato, P. A., & Snow, M. A. (2005). Instructional strategies for K–12 mainstream teachers. In P. A. Richard-Amato and M. A. Snow (Eds.), *Academic success for English language learners: Strategies for K–12 mainstream teachers* (pp. 197–223). White Plains, NY: Pearson Education.

CHAPTER 7

DID THEY GET WHAT I TAUGHT? CHECKING COMPREHENSION

You've taught the lesson. Now it's time to check comprehension: Did your students understand what you taught? Teachers sincerely want to know that their instruction has been understood. They follow up their lessons with questions and answers that traditionally conform to this pattern: Teacher asks, teacher calls on student, student answers. If the response is incomplete, the teacher calls on more students to add information. If the response is adequate, the teacher moves on to the next question. The same students raise their hands to participate. The teacher's attempts to involve others in the class often result in uncomfortable silences.

The strategies in this chapter will expand student participation and increase the success of your question-and-answer sessions.

QUESTIONS, ANSWERS, AND PARTICIPATION IN THE CLASSROOM

The Objective: Formulate Questions in Ways That Encourage Participation

The Rationale: Students hesitate to participate in class for a number of reasons. Three common ones are that they didn't understand the question, they don't know the answer, or they know the answer but are fearful or shy. More students will willingly participate when you use strategies that involve selecting appropriate question types, offering assistance with answers, and lowering affective filters.

STRATEGY 42   DON'T FALL INTO THE "DOES EVERYONE UNDERSTAND?" TRAP

IN CONCEPT

Teachers sincerely want to make sure that students *really* understand new material that has just been taught. Consequently, they willingly seek to clarify, repeat, explain, give more examples, and correct misunderstandings before moving ahead. So at several points in the lesson, teachers stop to check student comprehension with questions such as these:

"Does everyone understand?"

"Does anyone have any questions?"

"Does anyone need me to repeat any part of this?"

"OK, so everyone gets it, yes?"

Why is it, then, that no matter how little students have understood—no matter how totally confused they are—they just don't raise their hands in response to these questions? The answer lies in the way the questions are phrased. In effect, what students hear is "Will the one really dumb person in this class who didn't get this please raise your hand and publicly identify yourself?" Why would anyone want to do such a thing? Better just to sit there and *feel* dumb rather than to raise your hand and remove all doubt! The unintended effect of these questions is exactly the opposite of the teacher's objective.

IN PRACTICE

How can you word a question that will actually achieve your desired goal? Try this:

"It's question time. Who's got a question for me?"

This wording makes it sound like questions are a normal part of every lesson. And indeed they are: No one ever learns without asking questions and making mistakes. You can underscore this attitude by assuring that your voice goes *down* at the end so it sounds like a statement rather than a question.

You can reinforce your accepting attitude toward questions even further when you respond to a student's question with something very positive:

"That's a great question!"

"Thank you for asking that!"

"Good question!"

Responses like these actually make students feel *rewarded* for seeking clarification instead of penalized. You, too, will be rewarded by your students' responses when you change "Does everyone understand?" to "Question time. Who's got a question for me?"

STRATEGY 43   SELECT EFFECTIVE QUESTION TYPES

IN CONCEPT

Teachers' questions vary in difficulty depending on their conceptual and/or linguistic complexity. Carefully selecting the types of questions you direct to your ELLs promotes their participation.

IN PRACTICE

Students, even in early stages of second-language acquisition, may be willing and able to respond with answers requiring only a minimum number of words, especially if they can refer to key words and phrases that you have previously written on the board. Pattern your questions to your linguistically less advanced ELLs to elicit nonverbal, yes/no, either/or, or one-word responses, as in the examples shown in Figure 7.1.

Point to . . .	Can you show us the location of Washington, DC on the map?
Yes/no	Do Bedouins live on grassy plains?
Either/or	Is the Ukraine east or west of the major part of Russia?
Add more information	Who can give me another example of a deciduous tree?

Figure 7.1   Select Questions for English Language Learners

However, these lower order questions elicit only simple recall of information and involve little thought processing. To become critical thinkers, students must engage in processing higher order questions that ask them to explain, analyze, synthesize, and evaluate information (review Bloom's taxonomy in Chapter 1). For ELLs, the challenge lies not in the cognitive level of these questions, but rather in the higher levels of language ability required to answer them. Questions that ask students to select, classify, or order information often offer a solution to this difficulty.

Directing follow-up questions to ELLs can also help to balance linguistic and cognitive demands. ELLs can engage in complex thought processing while answering the following types of questions with relatively simple English:

"Do you agree with Ilya's answer?"

"Why? Why not?"

"What can you add to Shihan's answer?"

STRATEGY 44   PLAN QUESTIONS IN ADVANCE

IN CONCEPT

In the course of a school day, teachers ask hundreds of questions, the vast majority of which, according to research spanning many decades, are lower level, convergent questions—simple fact questions with only one correct answer. Students, however, must develop critical-thinking skills by responding to higher order, divergent questions that require them to *use* the facts to analyze, apply, extend, and evaluate information.

IN PRACTICE

The best way to incorporate higher order, divergent questions into your teaching is to *plan* them as you plan your lesson. Select two or three points within the lesson that you believe would be enhanced by a series of thought-provoking questions. Consider writing them on a PowerPoint display or an overhead transparency so students can see and hear them at the same time.

Arrange your questions to follow a logical sequence—from general to specific, simple to complex, fact to opinion, and/or sequential according to content. To guide your creative thinking, consider the following question types:

- *Predictive:* "What do you think will happen when we combine these two substances?"
- *Inferential:* "What do you think she was feeling as she wrote the letter?" or "What do you know by looking at this picture [specimen, object, shape, etc.]?"

- *Reflective:* This asks students to think about the past with an eye toward the future. "What do you think ____ might have done to change the outcome?"
- *Hypothetical:* "What do you think would happen if . . . ?"
- *Evaluative:* This asks students to compare, contrast, prioritize, predict, justify.
- *Elaborative:* This asks students to expand their own or another's responses.

Questions of these types help students improve their reasoning skills, make insightful observations, and develop critical-thinking skills.

STRATEGY 45   PROMOTE ACTIVE LISTENING

IN CONCEPT

What happens immediately after the teacher calls on someone to give an answer? In most classes, the other students simply switch off their thinking and listening until the teacher asks the next question. Using this strategy, however, will encourage active listening among your students throughout the lesson.

IN PRACTICE

Promote active listening by following up on a student response with a request for another student to *paraphrase* or *evaluate* what was just said. Frequent follow-up questions, such as those in Figure 7.2, make students aware of other students' thinking and problem-solving strategies. Follow-up questions also keep students tuned in and ready to respond.

The easiest follow-up question is simply "Do you agree with that answer?" Teachers routinely ask this question when the answer is wrong. The first time you try it when the answer is *right*, you will witness a fascinating reaction. Students are so accustomed to hearing this question exclusively as a means of correcting misinformation that asking it as a follow-up to a *correct* question renders them virtually speechless! After the shock of the first such experience, remind students at the start of Q and A and discussion sessions that you will frequently ask them if they agree or disagree with other students' answers. That awareness promotes active listening *and* critical thinking: Because students may be called upon at any time to evaluate a response they just heard, in effect they are never "off the hook."

Figure 7.2   Follow-up Questions Encourage Active Listening

"Brahim, can you tell me in your own words what Raoul just said?"

"Rosalba, do you agree or disagree with what Raoul just said, and why?"

"Eunan, can you give me an example of the concept that Raoul just explained?"

"Irina, Raoul gave such a good answer. I think we all need to hear what he said again."

STRATEGY 46   VARY WHOLE CLASS RESPONSE TECHNIQUES

IN CONCEPT

Teachers often use whole class choral response to answer a question. But how can the teacher *really* know who answers correctly and who does not? The following techniques allow ELLs to participate in a linguistically simple and nonthreatening manner. The entire class is actively involved and you, the teacher, get immediate feedback about your students' level of understanding.

IN PRACTICE

Technique I

Students use *hand gestures* to answer—for example, the thumbs up/thumbs down response to a series of short yes/no questions. Thumbs in the mid-position can mean "sometimes" or "depending on circumstances" or even "I'm not sure."

Students can also hold up one to five fingers to indicate their responses to numbered choices you've written on the board. It's multiple-choice without the answer sheet. This works particularly well for classification activities. If you see more than one response, you have an immediate opportunity to clarify misunderstandings.

Using group response techniques like these allows ELLs to participate even when they're not sure of the answer. According to Lave and Wenger's (1991) theory of legitimate peripheral participation, even when ELLs merely mimic the responses they see, it helps them move toward becoming part of the collective.

Technique II

Students prepare for a question or review session by creating *response cards*. On index cards or small squares of paper, they write content-specific information—numbers, categories, identifying names, descriptive phrases, mathematical signs denoting processes, the words *yes* and *no*, or the symbols + for presence or − for absence of a quality. They then hold up a card or card combination in response to each question.

Technique III

Students use markers on *dry-erase boards* to write brief answers to questions. They can work individually or in pairs. At your signal, they then hold up the boards for you to see. They love this strategy because it feels like the TV show *Jeopardy*.

You can get the dry-erase boards from large hardware and home improvement stores. These stores willingly donate scrap ends from customers' custom cuttings to teachers who request them. The stores will save them up to make class sets and may even trim them to size.

STRATEGY 47   "PRE-PAIR" TO RESPOND

IN CONCEPT

Students dread looking foolish in front of peers and often avoid answering teachers' questions for this reason. You can lower students' anxiety by offering them the opportunity of testing out an answer with a partner before stating it in front of the whole class.

IN PRACTICE

With the *Pre-Pair* strategy, after you pose a question, student partners in prearranged pairs have 10 to 20 seconds to share their ideas with each other before you request a response. At the end of the partner conference time, you can invite students to share an idea they *had* or one they *heard*.

STRATEGY 48   TRY NUMBERED HEADS

IN CONCEPT

Numbered Heads is a structured strategy that promotes student participation by allowing small group discussion before anyone is required to respond. It offers extra linguistic support for ELLs and reinforces conceptual understanding for all students. It also lowers learner anxiety and builds students' self-confidence. In addition, it increases student–student interaction and becomes a source of authentic language input for language learners. And students even like it because it feels like a game.

IN PRACTICE

Students sit in groups of four. Each student has a designated number, 1 through 4, decided by the members of each group (see Figure 7.3). Following a question, the groups get a short time, from 20 to 90 seconds depending on the complexity of the question, to discuss their answers. When time is up, the teacher calls out a number—3, for example. All the number 3 students then raise their hands or stand up. The teacher chooses one to answer the question and continues calling on other number 3s until sufficient information has been offered. This procedure is repeated with each question.

A randomized process for choosing numbers works best here. Teachers can make a spinner with four quadrants; use numbered popsicle sticks, poker chips, or balls; or put numbered slips of paper in a box or paper bag. Psychologically, random drawings make students feel that no one number is being favored, neglected, or picked on. Even better, random drawings keep all students focused and on task for every question because they know they can be called on two or more times in a row.

Figure 7.3 Numbered Heads

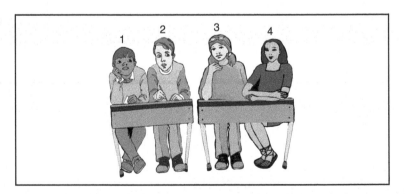

STRATEGY 49   USE THINK–PAIR–SHARE

IN CONCEPT

Think–Pair–Share (a modification of Strategy 14, Think–Write–Pair–Share, in Chapter 5) is another means to actively scaffold learning by offering ELLs the opportunity to negotiate their conceptual understandings through interaction with peers. ELLs will experience less participation anxiety when they are able to test their content knowledge and language usage in the shelter of a small group setting.

IN PRACTICE

Prepare students by informing them that they will be using the Think–Pair–Share strategy prior to raising their hands to answer questions. During your Q and A session, allot 10 to 20 seconds for students to think about an appropriate response after you ask a question. Follow this "think time" with another 20-second segment for students to discuss their ideas with a partner or small group. In whole class discussion, students should again be encouraged to share an idea they had or one they heard.

STRATEGY 50   ALLOW EXTRA WAIT TIME

IN CONCEPT

Wait time is the period of silence during which students think about an answer to a question. No doubt you encountered the concept of wait time early in your teacher training classes, and it is likely that you have not actively thought about it since then. Wait time is important because most students need time to process the content required to answer a question. It is even more essential for ELLs because of the additional time they require for language processing.

IN PRACTICE

Language learners benefit from wait times of from three to five seconds for simple questions, up to 10 or even 20 seconds for more complicated questions. One way to ensure adequate time is to count slowly to yourself. The sound of silence may initially feel uncomfortable to you, but wait times of up to 20 seconds help lower the anxiety that often comes from being called on to produce an answer in a new language. Interestingly, wait times beyond 20 seconds may feel punitive to students, ultimately raising anxiety and lowering participation.

STRATEGY 51   GIVE CREDIT FOR TRYING

IN CONCEPT

Teachers hear wrong answers every day. How they respond to them can make the difference between students who are willing to participate and those who are not.

Acknowledging incorrect answers with a pleasant, positive response takes at least some of the risk out of classroom participation.

IN PRACTICE

Try saying one of the following with sincerity and a smile when students offer misinformation:

"Good try."

"Almost."

"Thank you for trying."

"Not quite, but you're thinking."

"What an interesting [unusual] way to look at it!"

Such responses lessen the stigma and anxiety of wrong answers and encourage continued attempts at participation. Wrong answers thus become an acceptable and normal part of learning.

STRATEGY 52   OFFER FACE SAVERS

IN CONCEPT

Offering students a face-saving way to *not* answer a question also lowers anxiety levels. It lowers the affective filters of students and makes them more willing to take academic risks in the classroom.

IN PRACTICE

Technique I

Consider offering your students a *pass* option. Students who cannot answer a question simply say, "Pass," after which you can add, "Fine. We'll get back to you later." Be sure that you do.

You can hand out an actual pass token to each student using the pass option. The tokens are to remain in plain view on the students' desks until they can "return" them by answering a later question or by contributing to the review at the end of the class.

Technique II

A second technique is to allow students to call on another student for assistance. To make this an effective learning tool rather than merely an escape, the student you initially called on must paraphrase or repeat the information given by the student who assisted in answering the question.

STRATEGY 53   WATCH FOR STUDENT READINESS

IN CONCEPT

Sometimes you can sense that certain students would like to try to answer but can't quite bring themselves to raise their hands. This is a good time to *invite* their participation by

Teacher Question	Student Response	Teacher Expansion
What is the name of the courts directly under the Supreme Court?	Circ . . . circa . . . circle courts.	Yes, the *circuit* court of appeals. (Write the word *circuit* on the board.)
Why do objects in motion continue to move in a vacuum?	No fiction.	Exactly, a vacuum is a *frictionless* environment.
When would you use a bar graph and when a line graph?	Bar graph . . . to count . . . to put together . . . line for much change . . . long time.	Excellent! A bar graph shows data that can be counted and compared, and a line graph shows change over time.

Figure 7.4 Expanding Students' Responses

making friendly eye contact and smiling at them. Look closely at their faces when you direct a general question to the whole class. Call on them when you detect readiness, but ensure that they have positive early participation experiences; in other words, select appropriate questions, assist their efforts, and give them positive feedback.

IN PRACTICE

Technique I
Smile and nod as you encourage ELLs to use visual aids to support their words. Point to anything in the classroom that might help them respond, particularly key words and phrases written on the board or on a word wall. Look around the room for charts, pictures, or maps that might offer these students assistance in completing their response.

Technique II
Smile and nod as you expand the ELLs' few words into more complete thoughts. Use your words to augment theirs, as in Figure 7.4. Follow up a one-word student response with "Good—tell me more" or "True, but tell me why you think so." Affirming the correctness of the original answer gives students the confidence to continue.

Technique III
Smile and nod as you help by supplying the word or phrase a student is searching for or stumbling over. Providing that one missing word or phrase may be enough to allow the student to continue to respond.

STRATEGY 54   FOCUS ON CONTENT

IN CONCEPT

When ELLs attempt to answer questions, keep your attention on the message, not on the medium. Focus on the *content* of the response rather than on the language used to express it.

IN PRACTICE

ELLs will participate more readily if their language usage and pronunciation are not constantly and overtly corrected. Instead, you should model correct usage, as illustrated in Figure 7.4, by rephrasing student answers as complete sentences with correct grammar, vocabulary, and pronunciation. However, restructuring responses should be a *subtle* form of correction. Too much overt correction raises students' affective filters and decreases their willingness to participate.

STRATEGY 55   COMBINE QUESTIONING STRATEGIES FOR BEST RESULTS

IN CONCEPT

You will certainly improve the quality of your questioning techniques by instituting any of the strategies in this section. However, the best results come from using them in combination.

IN PRACTICE

What do best practices in questioning look like in your classroom? They start with pre-planned, higher order, divergent questions for your lessons. Then, during discussion, you allow appropriate wait time and vary the response pattern—calling on volunteers and nonvolunteers and using pair and small group prediscussion as well as whole class techniques. You thoughtfully direct questions to specific students that are appropriate to their language and ability levels. You routinely use follow-up questions to extend student thinking. You encourage and reward students for trying, and your praise is specifically and judiciously offered. Teachers who use this combination of questioning strategies will have students who are willing to think and ready to participate.

QUESTIONS, ANSWERS, AND PARTICIPATION IN THE CLASSROOM

The Objective: Fine-Tune Your Awareness of Student Participation

The Rationale: Successful learning takes place in classrooms that promote student participation. Teachers try to involve *every* student in class discussions, but few know if they actually succeed. The next two strategies will help you fine-tune your awareness of student participation in your classroom.

STRATEGY 56   MONITOR YOUR INTERACTION PATTERNS

IN CONCEPT

Many teachers have a distinct *action zone* (Richards & Lockhart, 1996, p. 139) a localized area of the classroom that they favor. In this section sit the students toward whom they direct their instruction and discussion. Unconsciously, they look at and call on the students in this zone much more than on the others.

IN PRACTICE

You can determine your action zone by video recording a class you teach. (The suggestions in Figure 7.5 will ensure that you do not violate any privacy laws.) Making the video is easy if your school can provide an audiovisual team member to operate the camera as you teach. Lacking that, you can set the camera, focused on you, on a tripod in the rear of the room.

Reviewing the videotape will help you determine whether you favor a particular section of the classroom and will allow you to observe your patterns of interaction. As you watch your videotape, imagine your classroom divided into four quadrants. Did you stand in one quadrant, or did you move around? Did you direct your attention to one section more than the others? And which students did you actually call on? Use a class seating chart to carefully note where you stand and who you look at as you teach. Note which students you call on and how many times. Your tallies may make you aware of an action zone and an interaction pattern you never knew you had.

Teachers have made many discoveries from viewing themselves teaching. Some were surprised that they had called on several of their students so many times. Others saw that they had neglected to call on several very quiet students in the class, even though they felt sure they had actively involved every single student. Still others realized that they might improve student participation by working on smiling more and moving around the room.

Schoolwide Permission

Many schools routinely send home forms requesting permission to video record for educational purposes. Parents sign and return the forms at the beginning of the school year. If your school does this, you are covered.

Individual Permission

If your school doesn't do this, you must request parental permission with a letter similar to this one:

Dear Parents,

In my ongoing pursuit of excellence in teaching, I would like your permission to video record *myself* as I teach a lesson in our classroom. The focus will be on me and my teaching, and only I will view the tape. I will be observing myself as I seek ways to improve the quality of my instruction. My goal is to become the very best teacher I can be for your children, who will be the beneficiaries of this experience.

Thank you very much.

(Your Signature)

I give permission to video record for this purpose only.

Parent's Signature _____

Student Name_____ Date _____

Figure 7.5 Getting Permission to Video Record

STRATEGY 57   LEARN FROM YOUR VIDEO

IN CONCEPT

If you like the participation patterns you see on your video, give yourself a pat on the back. If, however, you want to increase student participation, here are several ideas you might try.

IN PRACTICE

Technique I

The simplest way of assuring full class participation is to check off students' names as you call on them, using a preprinted class list or seating chart. Remember, of course, to be sensitive to ELLs by using the questioning strategies described in this chapter.

Technique II

Another approach is to write students' names on popsicle sticks, poker chips, or cards and place them in a container. Then randomly draw one after asking a question. Use your teacher prerogative with a question that may be too difficult for the name you drew; you might say, "Oops, I just called this name" or "Absent," or you might even substitute another student's name.

Technique III

Explain to your students your abiding belief that participation promotes active learning. Toward that goal, institute a rule in your class that students who don't participate during the class time will have to contribute to the review at the end. You may be amazed at the increase in voluntary class participation.

IN SUMMARY: CLASSROOM QUESTIONS, ANSWERS, AND PARTICIPATION

Teachers who strive to create a classroom environment that fosters participation invite students to become active learners, and active learners are better learners. Strategies that increase participation maximize the potential for students to show what they know and to begin to experience feelings of academic success.

QUESTIONS FOR DISCUSSION

1. Which of the *12 Guidelines for Practice* presented at the end of Chapter 1 inform the strategies in this chapter?
2. Cite and summarize additional research that gives theoretical and/or experiential support to the strategies discussed in this chapter.
3. Questions are categorized in many different ways. Bloom grouped them into lower and higher order questions. Research additional question types used in classrooms, and give examples of each question type. Discuss the effect of each type of question on student participation and student learning.
4. How does lowering the affective filter promote classroom participation? Give some specific examples.

5. Compare a class you took in which you participated with a class in which you did not. Evaluate what the instructor did or did not do to encourage/discourage participation.

6. Respond to the following scenario individually if you are currently teaching a class and with a partner if you are not:

You have just been assigned a student teacher, and you want to start him/her out right. Write a list of at least five practices that encourage classroom participation and five practices that are sure to discourage participation.

REFERENCES AND RESOURCES

Brown, H. D. (1994). *Teaching by principles: An interactive approach to language pedagogy* (pp. 157–169). Englewood Cliffs, NJ: Prentice Hall Regents.

Freeman, Y. S., & Freeman, D. E. (1998). *ESL/EFL teaching: Principles for success.* Portsmouth, NH: Heinemann.

Lave, J., & Wenger, E. (1991). *Situated learning: Legitimate peripheral participation.* Cambridge, England: Cambridge University Press.

Richards, J. C., & Lockhart, C. (1996). *Reflective teaching in second language classrooms.* Cambridge, England: Cambridge University Press.

Rowe, M. (1987). Wait-time: Slowing down may be a way of speeding up. *American Educator, 11,* 38–43.

CHAPTER 8

EXTENDING COMPREHENSION: TEXTBOOK VOCABULARY STRATEGIES

If ELLs could tell you what part of their content classes they found the most challenging, the majority would say their textbooks. The language of textbooks combines the twin difficulties of highly abstract, cognitively demanding concepts with content-specific words and advanced academic vocabulary, written in language appropriate to the grade for which they are intended. Fortunately, textbooks can be made more comprehensible to ELLs—and to struggling readers—through the creative application of scaffolding strategies. This chapter focuses on vocabulary strategies that facilitate comprehension of textbooks, and the next will focus on reading strategies.

NEW VOCABULARY: WHICH WORDS TO TEACH?

Many ELLs believe that the key to understanding English lies in the vocabulary. It is difficult to argue against this point of view: Knowing what words mean is unquestionably critical to comprehension.

Textbooks and their accompanying teacher's editions do a creditable job of identifying and defining new vocabulary that appears in each chapter. These words are content specific or technical in nature, words that students must learn if they are to understand the concepts that follow. If it were only these words that needed explanation, teachers and students would have an easy task. Four other categories of words, however, may be unknown or misunderstood by ELLs: (a) synonyms, (b) idioms, (c) new usage of familiar words, and (d) just plain new words.

Synonyms

All writers use synonyms to add interest and variety to text. Indeed, it would be boring to read the same nouns, adjectives, or verbs repeatedly in a passage. Although synonyms have the positive effect of adding flavor to writing, they also have the unintended negative effect of burdening ELLs with more unknown vocabulary. Consider the number of synonymous phrases we use to talk about the following simple arithmetic problem:

$$\begin{array}{r} 8 \\ -5 \\ \hline \end{array}$$

Subtract 5 from 8.

5 from 8 equals _____.

8 minus 5 equals _____.

Take 5 away from 8.

How much is 8 less 5?

How much less is 5 than 8?

How many fewer is 5 than 8?

What is the difference between 8 and 5?

Amazing, isn't it? At a more advanced level, think about the many words and phrases that are used to represent the concept of *freedom* in written texts. A search through several high school social studies textbooks produced this list:

liberty	self-determination	autonomy
sovereignty	self-government	emancipation
independence	self-sufficiency	home rule

Adding another layer of confusion for ELLs are words and phrases used in class that differ significantly from the wording used in the textbook. Vocabulary is a real challenge.

Idioms

As mentioned in an earlier chapter, ELLs love to learn idioms because they feel that if they understand idioms, they *really* know English. Idioms are phrases with meanings that are more than the sum of their parts. Analyzing them on a word-by-word basis often produces some odd mental images. Visualize the literal meanings of these:

She really put her foot in her mouth.   I'm all ears.

It's raining cats and dogs.   He's got two left feet.

Idiomatic expressions also appear in academic writing. The phrases in Figure 8.1 are common idiomatic references in American history textbooks. Language learners would undoubtedly be confused by these expressions, which are so widely understood by native English speakers.

New Usage of Familiar Words

Consider the word *strike*. In what context might ELLs be familiar with this word? Did you think of baseball or bowling or fishing? Students will know these uses of the word *strike* from watching or participating in these activities or having parents who do.

Apart from sports, *strike*, as used in everyday conversation, has multiple meanings depending on the context in which it appears. Here are some of them:

Police thought the murderer would *strike* again.

He hoped a brilliant idea would *strike* him.

She tried unsuccessfully to *strike* up a conversation.

He tried again to *strike* the match.

She tried to *strike* a bargain. [Did she light it on fire?]

The dog was *struck* by a car.

Figure 8.1   Idiomatic References in Social Studies

About the Civil War	About the American Flag
a house divided fighting under the Confederate flag on the home front loss of lives	the Stars and Stripes Old Glory the Red, White, and Blue

He was *struck* by the beauty of the sunset. [Did it hurt him?]

We heard the clock *striking* midnight.

The similarity was *striking*. [And loud, too?]

In textbooks, however, the word *strike* appears in wholly different contexts. Think now of how it relates to these topics:

Industry: The workers went on *strike*.

Mining: The prospectors were hoping to *strike* gold.

Weather: Lightning can *strike* before a storm.

Military: The air *strike* was considered successful.

All subject domains have their own set of concept words, many of which fall into the category of familiar words used in new ways. Figure 8.2 lists examples from science, math, social studies, and language arts. Imagine ELLs' mental images of a river bed and a river bank. And who got invited to those political parties? Now add the further complication of certain words that represent unrelated concepts in two or more academic domains, some of which are shown in Figure 8.3. It's easy to see why familiar words with new academic meanings create confusion for ELLs. Figure 8.4 is a true story of a near-perfect misunderstanding resulting from students knowing only the common usage of a word.

Just Plain New Words

This is the catchall category—the least well-defined, the most individualized, and the most challenging for a teacher. Words in this category are usually high-incidence academic words that cross all disciplines—for example, *caption, explicit, excerpt, factor, preface, relevant, selection, section, segment*—and are not widely used in conversation. They are omitted from content vocabulary lists because they are not topic specific, but these are the very words that ELLs need to make a part of their academic toolkit. The strategies in this chapter offer ideas to help make academic vocabulary more comprehensible and meaningful to your students.

Science	energy, mass, matter, force, kingdom, iron, eye, trunk, current, depression
Math	table, round, root, mean, power, expression, gross, yard, volume, face, plane, odd, even
Social Studies	river bed, river bank, interest rates, counter, left wing, right wing, (political) parties, (Gettysburg) address
Language Arts	play, state, article, novel, idiomatic expressions in literature (e.g., stalk a victim)

Figure 8.2 Domain-Specific Usage of Familiar Words

root	science, math, language arts
state	science, language arts, social studies
depression	science, math, social studies
radical	math, social studies
article	social studies, language arts

Figure 8.3 Domain-Crossing Usage of Familiar Words

Figure 8.4 A True Tale of
Misunderstanding

A second-grade teacher of a self-contained ESL class was teaching about how Christopher Columbus explored the Caribbean Islands and conquered the native Indian populations living there. She asked her class why they thought that Columbus, with so few men, was able to conquer the many thousands of native Indians who lived there. When none of them answered, she explained: "It's because Christopher Columbus and his men had arms, and the native Indians didn't have any."

Not yet realizing any misunderstanding, she continued the discussion by asking about the kind of life the Caribbean Indians had before being conquered by Columbus. One student answered, "Very hard," as all the others nodded their heads in agreement.

Surprised by this response, she asked, "How could it have been a hard life? They had beautiful warm weather, lots of food to eat—especially fruits and vegetables. They didn't need to wear a lot of clothing or build strong houses to keep out the cold. Why do you think they had a hard life?"

One student timidly offered an explanation: "Because they had no arms! How could they do anything?"

TEACHING AND LEARNING VOCABULARY

The Objective: Use Meaningful Strategies for Teaching and Learning Vocabulary

The Rationale: Knowing which words to teach is not the same as knowing how to teach them. Methodologies for teaching and learning vocabulary are often old-fashioned, uncreative, and unproductive. The most widely used strategies for teaching vocabulary result in little long-term retention because they teach words in isolation. "Look the words up in a dictionary, and use each in an original sentence" is rarely an effective assignment. Students memorize the words and remember them only as long as they must to pass a test. Activities such as word searches, scrambled words, matching tasks, or crossword puzzles also do little to add to students' long-term retention and usage of new words, again because the words are used in isolation. Vocabulary teaching and learning strategies that approach words as they are used in context and are meaningful to students will result in more authentic and effective learning.

STRATEGY 58   LOOK BEYOND CONTENT-SPECIFIC WORDS

IN CONCEPT

Teachers can help their ELLs by making students aware of the four areas of potential vocabulary confusion. Students can also help teachers become aware of potential vocabulary confusion.

IN PRACTICE

Monitor your spoken words and phrases for synonyms, idioms, and new meanings of familiar words. Scan your students' facial expressions for looks of confusion, and be ready to offer an explanation. If you see smiles or perhaps smirks, you may have unknowingly used an expression that has a meaning to these students that you are unaware of. Actively attending to student reaction will guide you in facilitating comprehension of new vocabulary for ELLs.

STRATEGY 59   SELECT STUDENTS TO BE YOUR VOCABULARY HELPERS

IN CONCEPT

Teachers can engage more advanced students in the task of previewing text chapters for ELLs, looking for potentially confusing words and phrases.

IN PRACTICE

Designated or volunteer students can be asked to scan text looking for words and phrases used synonymously to refer to one or several central concepts or ideas, as well as for idiomatic usages and references. The resulting lists can help to lighten the vocabulary load for ELLs as they read the chapter. Additionally, the students making the lists reinforce their vocabulary knowledge and can receive extra credit or bonus points for their efforts.

Although this strategy may at first seem to limit ELLs' vocabulary development, bear in mind that scaffolding strategies are used only until learners no longer need them. In this case, easing the language load allows ELLs greater access to textbook content. During class instruction and discussion, however, you can feel comfortable using synonyms and idioms freely, pairing them with the more widely known words (see Strategy 65, later in this chapter).

STRATEGY 60   TURN YOUR STUDENTS INTO "LANGUAGE DETECTIVES"

IN CONCEPT

This is a wonderful strategy for students whose native language is Spanish or one of the other Latin-root languages. This strategy works because of an event that took place in the year 1066. In that year, the Normans from France conquered the Angles and Saxons living in what is now England. The conquerors' language, an early version of today's French, became the language of position and power. It also became the language of academia and the educated. But the conquered Anglo-Saxons continued using their own language in everyday life, and a duality was created that still exists in the English that we use today.

Many academic words in English—words that cut across all academic disciplines—come from the old Norman French, which has its roots in ancient Greek and Latin. However, common words used in social, spoken English derive from Anglo-Saxon roots. So we often speak and hear different words in conversation than we read and write in school, as illustrated in Figure 8.5. High-frequency words in Spanish—*frecuencia* and *rápido*, for example—are low-frequency, academic words (*frequency, rapid*) in English. These common root words, called *cognates*, can help your ELLs who speak Spanish and other Latin- or Greek-root languages.

Conversational English	Academic English
Did you *meet* anyone at the store today?	The troops *encountered* no resistance.
Get in *line*.	Arrange the numbers in *sequence*.
Let's *build* a castle.	The troops planned to *construct* a bridge.
The vacation *lasted* two full weeks.	The people *endured* two centuries of tyranny.
The salad was *enough* for two people.	The supplies were *sufficient* for only a week.

Figure 8.5 Comparing Conversational and Academic English

Figure 8.6 Turning Spanish Speakers into Language Detectives

Academic Word	Spanish Word	Common Word
encounter	*encontrar*	meet
observe	*observar*	watch
maintain	*mantener*	keep
ultimate	*último*	last
equal	*igual*	same
entire	*entero*	whole
quantity	*cantidad*	amount

IN PRACTICE

Spanish speakers can become *language detectives* by scanning textbooks for academic words with Spanish cognates, some examples of which are shown in Figure 8.6. Be sure to advise them of the existence of occasional *false* cognates, as in words like *rope/ropa* ("clothes") and *embarrassed/embarazada* ("pregnant"). All the students may be interested in the discoveries the ELLs have made about cognates, false and true. It's a fun way to keep the focus on vocabulary and a win–win situation for all.

STRATEGY 61 HAVE STUDENTS DEVELOP A PERSONAL DICTIONARY

IN CONCEPT

Personal dictionaries benefit all students. These valuable, easy-to-use tools for building vocabulary can be formatted in a variety of ways. No matter their form, they help students remember new words and phrases that are academically useful and/or personally meaningful or interesting.

IN PRACTICE

With your students, select an organizing principle: alphabetical, subject specific, general/technical, or social/academic. Additional sections can be devoted to idioms, academic usage of familiar words, and synonym lists. Entries can be written in English only or can

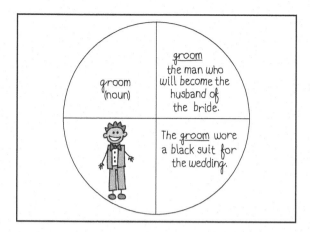

Figure 8.7 Vocabulary Circle

Figure 8.8 Examples of Collocations

New Word	Goes with . . .	But not . . .
bargain	fair bargain hard bargain	balanced, just firm, stiff, rigid
trick	clever trick dirty trick	bright, smart, intelligent dishonest, crooked
truce	uneasy truce	worried, nervous
rhetoric	empty rhetoric	vacant, blank, unoccupied
famine	severe famine	rigid, stern, strict, heavy
oath	solemn oath	serious, grave, somber

include notations in students' native languages. ELLs at the beginner's level can use the format shown in Figure 8.7, the Vocabulary Circle. Other items that may be included in the circle or as a column entry in personal dictionaries are native-language translations, synonyms, and antonyms.

It may also be helpful to include collocations: words that commonly appear in combination with the entry word. ELLs must learn these high-frequency word associations that come so naturally to native speakers, who know, for example, that air can be *heavy* with humidity but *thick* with smoke and *thin*, never *slim* or *skinny*, at high altitudes. Figure 8.8 offers additional examples of collocated usage in a format suitable for students to use.

STRATEGY 62   USE CONCEPT-DEFINITION MAPS

IN CONCEPT

A single word often represents a complex concept that is difficult to define in the traditional way. Using a concept-definition map (Schwartz & Raphael, 1985) for words such as *nomad, quadrilateral,* or *biome* offers students deeper conceptual understandings in a linguistically simplified format.

IN PRACTICE

A concept-definition map is a graphic that asks three questions about the central concept word: What is it? What is it like? What are some examples? Students, in small group discussion, use their textbooks, other resource books, dictionaries, glossaries, and Internet websites to create the type of explanatory graphic shown in Figure 8.9.

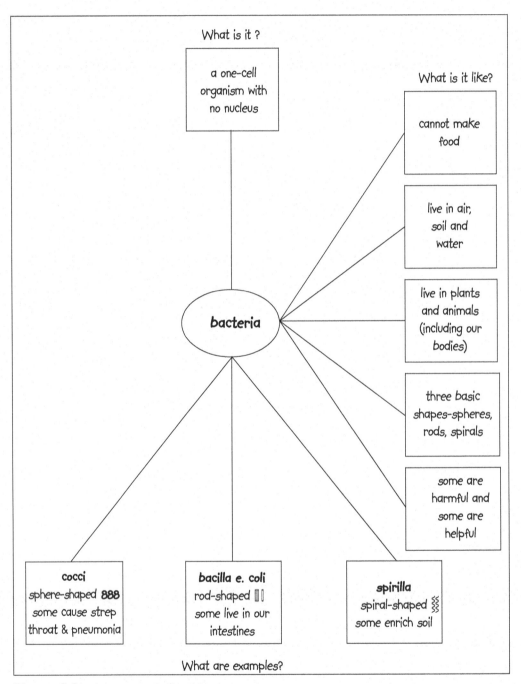

Figure 8.9 Concept-Definition Map

Adapted from Buehl, D. (2009). *Classroom Strategies for Interactive Learning* (3rd ed., p. 199). Originally published in Schwartz, R. M., & Raphael, T. E. (1985), *The Reading Teacher, 39*(2), 198–205. http://www.reading.org/general/publications/books/bK686.aspx

STRATEGY 63 DEMONSTRATE THE VALUE OF A STUDENT-FRIENDLY DICTIONARY

IN CONCEPT

Have you ever looked up a word in the dictionary and, after reading the definition, found you still had no idea of what the word meant? If that happens to an educated native English-language speaker, imagine what a challenge it is for an ELL! A student dictionary is designed to remedy this problem.

In the Longman series of student dictionaries—available at beginner, intermediate, and advanced levels—the vocabulary used in the definitions is based on the 2,000 most commonly used words in the English language. A side-by-side comparison of the definitions shown in Figure 8.10 leaves little doubt about which one is easier to understand.

Unlike regular dictionaries, student dictionaries are designed to make using them a more productive experience. They list multiple meanings of words as separate entries. They use words in sentences and offer usage notes, synonyms, antonyms, examples, illustrations, and photographs. At the advanced level, they label words as approving or disapproving—think about the subtle differences among the words *thin/slim/skinny* or

Longman's Basic Dictionary	*Merriam-Webster's Collegiate Dictionary*
landlady	**landlady**
a woman who owns a building and rents it to others	a woman who is a landlord
landlord	**landlord**
someone who owns a building and rents it to others	**1:** the owner of property (as land, houses, or apartments) that is leased or rented to another **2:** the master of an inn or lodging house: INNKEEPER

Longman's Advanced American Dictionary	*Merriam-Webster's Collegiate Dictionary*
spurious 1 not based on facts or good reasoning and not genuine or true (SYN) false: *a spurious claim* **2** insincere: *spurious sympathy*	**spurious 1:** of illegitimate birth: BASTARD **2:** outwardly similar or corresponding to something without having its genuine qualities: FALSE <the ~ eminence of the pop celebrity> **3a:** of falsified or erroneously attributed origin: FORGED <a ~ signature> **b:** of a deceitful nature or quality <~ excuses>

Figure 8.10 A Comparison of Dictionary Definitions

Longman's Advanced American Dictionary (2nd ed., p. 1539), 2009, Essex, England: Pearson Education Limited. Used by permission.

Longman Basic Dictionary of American English (2nd ed., p. 162), 1999, Essex, England: Pearson Education Limited. Used by permission.

By permission. From *Merriam-Webster's Collegiate® Dictionary*, 11th Edition © 2010 by Merriam-Webster, Incorporated (http://www.merriam-webster.com/>).

Figure 8.11 The Dictionary Game: Find It Fast!

Find synonyms for the word _____.

Find the first and last word in the dictionary _____.

Find a word on page _____ that means _____.

Find the first adjective on page _____.

Find an informal word on page _____.

Find the third word on the page with the guide words _____ and _____.

Find a word with more than one meaning on page _____.

childish/childlike, for example—as well as formal, literary or old-fashioned, informal, humorous, slang or nonstandard, even offensive or taboo, and they include idiomatic expressions and collocations. At every level, student dictionaries aim to make the task of understanding word meanings less formidable. They are wonderful resources, but only if students feel confident enough to use them.

IN PRACTICE

Technique I

Play dictionary games to accustom your students to working with a dictionary. Figure 8.11 gives examples of items that might be included in this type of activity. Make it feel like a game by setting it up as a timed competition among small groups of students, or set one half of the room against the other. Activities that are gamelike get students instantly involved and motivated.

Technique II

Student dictionaries are valuable to students, but they are perhaps even more valuable to *teachers*. Use a student dictionary to make your vocabulary teaching clearer and more complete.

In teaching, a word often comes up that requires some explanation. Take advantage of that teachable moment by reaching for the student dictionary that you keep on your desk. You will give better definitions—clearer, with examples and synonyms—and each time you use that dictionary, you are modeling an effective vocabulary strategy.

Every classroom should have at least one student dictionary. You and your students will seek it out on a regular basis.

STRATEGY 64   USE AN INTERNET WEBSITE TO DETERMINE WHICH WORDS TO TEACH

IN CONCEPT

A text-analysis website can help you decide which words, of all the many in a text passage, you really need to teach. It is an awesome tool.

One such website, *The Compleat Lexical Tutor*, has been developed by the Université de Québec à Montréal. It is designed to create a vocabulary profile of any text you input. You can find it at *www.lextutor.ca/vp/eng*. You can also use a search engine to find *The Compleat Lexical Tutor* by name.

The Lexical Tutor website presents you with a box in which to type or paste the desired text. When you have completed inputting the text, click the SUBMIT tab, and in a matter of seconds a color-coded vocabulary profile of the text appears on your computer screen. The color coding represents words of four different frequency types:

K1 (blue): the most frequent 1,000 word families

K2 (green): the second 1,000 most frequent word families

AWL (yellow): Academic Word List, words that appear in all subject domains

Off-List Words (red): topic-specific, technical, and/or infrequently used words; also dates, place names, and names of people

IN PRACTICE

The easiest way to understand the wonders of this web tool is to look at an actual example from a middle school social studies textbook, *World Explorer: People, Places, and Cultures* (Kracht, 2003, p. 35). Figure 8.12 shows the original passage as it appears in the textbook. After typing or pasting it into the webpage's textbox, the passage reappears, color coded with a complete analysis of word counts and other linguistic data. Accompanying the passage is a vocabulary profile listing the words in each of the four

Figure 8.12   Original Text Passage

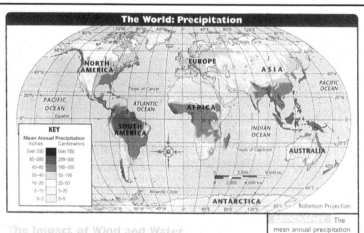

The World: Precipitation

KEY
Mean Annual Precipitation

Inches	Centimeters
Over 200	Over 500
80–200	200–500
40–80	100–200
20–40	50–100
10–20	25–50
2–10	5–25
0–2	0–5

Robinson Projection

The mean annual precipitation is the amount of rain or snow that falls in a region in an average year. **Map Study** Which areas get the most precipitation? Which get the least?

The Impact of Wind and Water

Without wind and water, the Earth would overheat. Together, wind and water moderate the effect of the sun's heat. Heat causes air to rise, especially near the Equator and over warm ocean water. Cold air sinks towards the surface away from the Equator. Wind blows from places where air is sinking towards places where air is rising. The Earth's rotation bends this flow to create circular wind patterns. So, depending on where you are in a circling weather system, the wind may be blowing north, south, east, or west.

The Earth's rotation also creates ocean currents, which are like rivers in the oceans. Some currents carry warm water from near the Equator toward the north and the south. Other currents carry cold water from the poles toward the Equator. Oceans also moderate the climate of nearby land just by their presence. Water takes longer to heat and cool than land. As a result, when the land has warmed during the summer, the nearby ocean remains cooler. Air blowing over the ocean becomes cool and then cools the land. In the winter, the opposite occurs.

Raging Storms   Wind and water can make climates milder, but they also create storms. Hurricanes are storms that form over the ocean in the tropics. Hurricanes rotate in a counter-clockwise direction around an "eye." They have winds of at least 74 miles (124 km) per hour and usually involve heavy rainfall. Tornadoes are just as dangerous, but they affect smaller areas. Their wind can range from 40 miles (67 km) per hour to over 300 miles (501 km) per hour and wreck anything in their path.

LINKS TO

Normally, air is cooler at higher altitudes. During a temperature inversion, however, a layer of warm air sits on top of the cooler air. The warm air traps pollution near the ground. This mixture of dangerous smoke and fog is called smog. The brown air seen in cities such as Los Angeles and Denver is smog caused by car exhaust.

Category	Word Families	Tokens (Words)	Percentage (%)
K1 Words (1–1,000)	81	184	77.99
K2 Words (1,001–2,000)	13	28	11.72
AWL Words (academic)	4	6	2.51
Off-List Words	12	21	8.79
TOTALS	98	239	100.00

Figure 8.13 Vocabulary Profile Summary

frequency categories. This profile, summarized in Figure 8.13, is the key to helping you locate the words your ELLs may find difficult.

The first piece of valuable information is that almost 78% of the words (184 of the 239) are in the K1 category. You can reasonably assume that these words are currently part of your ELLs' working vocabularies.

Examine next the words that fall into the other three categories, as listed in Figure 8.14. Of the 13 words listed in the K2 category, students may already know some of them, such as *bend, cool, during, especially, ocean, storm, warm,* and *weather.* Just 5 words remain in this category.

The Off-List category contains 12 words. This list, too, can be reduced by removing words such as *climate, Equator, hurricane, km,* and *tropics,* which will have been either included in the preselected vocabulary for the chapter or previously learned. With the 7 words remaining in the Off-List category, the five K2 word families, and the four AWL families, the grand total of potentially unknown words for your ELLs is 16 (see Figure 8.15), or less than 7% of the original 239 words in the passage.

It should be a comforting thought to know that your ELLs can handle over 90% of the words in this passage. Only the small number of remaining words are the ones you and your students need to focus on to increase their understanding. A vocabulary profile tool such as this can help you, the content teacher, narrow the challenge of "so many words, so little time." Try it—it's amazing.

Figure 8.14 K2, Academic, and Off-List Words

K2 Words	Academic Words	Off-List Words
bends	create	climate
cool	impact	clockwise
during	involve	counter
especially	occurs	currents
milder		Equator
moderate		hurricanes
ocean		km
opposite		overheat
patterns		poles
sinking		raging
storms		rotate/rotation
warm		tropics
weather		

K2 Words	Academic Words (AWL)	Off-List Words
Teach: 　milder 　moderate 　opposite 　patterns 　sink Review: 　bends	Teach: 　create 　impact 　involve 　occur	Teach: 　clockwise 　counter 　currents 　overheat 　poles 　raging 　rotate/rotation Review: 　climate 　Equator 　hurricanes 　km 　tropics

Figure 8.15 Which Words to Teach?

TEACHING AND LEARNING VOCABULARY

The Objective: Integrate Vocabulary Development into Daily Instruction

The Rationale: Just as words do not appear in isolation in the environment, so too should it be with vocabulary development. Teachers should replace the classic vocabulary drill with strategies that integrate vocabulary into every lesson taught. Learning words in context and using them repeatedly in authentic applications aid long-term retention.

STRATEGY 65   GET INTO A PAIR–DEFINE–EXPLAIN ROUTINE

IN CONCEPT

Young children acquire words from the environment at a staggering rate. Classroom strategies to expand vocabulary in ways similar to the natural acquisition of children are effective for long-term retention.

IN PRACTICE

As you teach, advance students' vocabulary development by sprinkling your instruction with interesting words and phrases, but *pair* each word or phrase with a high-frequency synonym, a definition or explanation, or a visual depiction. Students will learn new words naturally if you repeat them frequently, pairing them every time with a brief form of

Figure 8.16 Extending Students'
Vocabulary Through the
Pair–Define–Explain Routine

"He committed an egregious error—a very bad mistake—an
    egregious error."

"The liquid becomes effervescent—bubbly, full of bubbles—
    effervescent when we stir it."

"The Pilgrims embarked on a long journey. They began . . . they
    started out . . . they embarked on a long trip."

"She was motivated by vengeance—she wanted to punish him, sort
    of get back or get even with him. She wanted vengeance. "

explanation. After you've repeated a specific pairing a number of times, try saying only the target word and asking, "What does that mean?" The association will be there. And the more naturally you can work this pairing into your speech patterns, as in the examples in Figure 8.16, the more effective this technique will be.

STRATEGY 66   USE ONLINE RESOURCES FOR VOCABULARY GROWTH

IN CONCEPT

Most students feel that working on the Internet is fun. Most also feel that learning vocabulary is not. Students who can use online resources for vocabulary development may be more motivated to learn.

IN PRACTICE

Educational websites for vocabulary development include general and content-specific dictionaries, vocabulary quiz questions that speak the target words, listings and definitions of American idioms and adages, and synonyms and antonyms of student-specified words. Students can also access listings and translations of true and false cognates in English and many other languages by searching *cognates English* + [the native language]. The *TechConnection* section at the end of this chapter offers web addresses of some interesting sites, and you can challenge your students to come up with new ones.

STRATEGY 67   SET UP A WORD OF THE WEEK PROGRAM

IN CONCEPT

Learning new words involves more than just knowing their meaning; students also must be able to use words appropriately in authentic contexts. This is a fun strategy that promotes natural usage as it extends students' knowledge of vocabulary.

IN PRACTICE

Technique I

An entire school can make vocabulary growth a long-term goal. Each Monday morning, a word, along with its definition and several examples of usage, is announced as the *Word of the Week.* Words selected for this honor should be academic words that cross all disciplines. Students receive bonus points for using the word appropriately in any of their classes. Teachers, too, use the word daily in natural and meaningful academic contexts. Students can also show by a designated nonverbal signal that they recognize the word.

Technique II
As an individual class strategy, teachers can institute a *Word of the Day*, choosing new, academically interesting words or recycling previously used words for reinforcement. Students try to write or speak the day's word in class discussions, activities, and assignments. Daily or weekly, students record the words in their personal dictionaries. You can also give extra bonus points when students recycle a past Word of the Day in current class times.

STRATEGY 68   MAKE YOUR STUDENTS WORD WIZARDS

IN CONCEPT
You can make vocabulary growth an ongoing objective in your classroom by developing practices that encourage your students to become Word Wizards who use interesting words in class.

IN PRACTICE
Technique I
Create a word wall, a space to write new words that students come across in any form of media. Motivate students by making an ongoing game of it: Students win points for adding a new word and/or using it orally or in writing. Be ready to verbally recognize unusual vocabulary during class Q and A sessions, discussions, and conversations. Show your appreciation of uncommon or interesting words by praising their usage. Ask students how they know the given word. Make vocabulary one-upmanship work to everyone's advantage.

Technique II
As you teach, use synonyms or descriptive phrases as a substitute for a word on the word wall. Then ask students which word on the word wall means the same thing. It's another way to keep the focus on vocabulary in your classroom.

STRATEGY 69   PLAY VOCABULARY BINGO

IN CONCEPT
Bingo is a game that has been enjoyed by generations of children and most adults. You can make learning new vocabulary fun with a strategy that gives bingo a twist.

IN PRACTICE
After handing out preprinted blank bingo grids, tell your students to fill in the week's vocabulary words in any pattern on their papers. As the caller, you randomly select words,

but instead of saying the word, you pantomime, show or draw a visual, or give a verbal description, example, synonym, antonym, or—occasionally—the definition. By using their own grids, nonwinning students cannot blame bad card choices or an unfair caller.

You will enhance Vocabulary Bingo even more by requiring the winner to use the winning words in sentences. And if you use a team approach that invites team members to create the sentences, you will increase motivation and participation as well.

IN SUMMARY: TEACHING AND LEARNING VOCABULARY

True vocabulary growth is a long-term process. Students need a variety of approaches to develop the vocabulary that they need for academic success. Students don't have to know the meaning of every word *before* they read a text passage. A great deal of vocabulary learning occurs as students engage in the reading process and afterward in discussion and assignments, especially when teachers make vocabulary learning a routine part of their classrooms.

QUESTIONS FOR DISCUSSION

1. Which of the *12 Guidelines for Practice* presented at the end of Chapter 1 inform the strategies in this chapter?
2. Research the strategies for teaching vocabulary that are most commonly practiced in today's classrooms. Evaluate their effectiveness.
3. Prepare a list of additional examples of domain-specific and domain-crossing usage of familiar words, similar to the examples illustrated in Figures 8.2 and 8.3.
4. What strategies did you use in your years of schooling to learn vocabulary? How would you evaluate them? Do you believe you might have benefitted from any of the vocabulary strategies discussed in this chapter?
5. What do you currently do when you find an unfamiliar word in a book you are reading? How often do you look it up in a dictionary? Do you remember the word and its meaning after you have looked it up? What strategies could you use if you really wanted to remember the word?
6. How often have you used a thesaurus? When was the last time you referred to one? What are the advantages and disadvantages of using a thesaurus?
7. For a delightful way to better understand idioms, read one of the books in the *Amelia Bedelia* series written by Peggy Parish. Amelia is a very literal-minded person.

REFERENCES AND RESOURCES

Cobb, T. (n. d.). Why & how to use frequency lists to learn words. Retrieved March 4, 2010, from *www.lextutor.ca/research/rationale.htm*

Folse, K. (2004). *Vocabulary myths: Applying second language research to classroom teaching.* Ann Arbor: University of Michigan Press.

Kracht, J. B. (2003). *Prentice Hall world explorer: People, places, and cultures.* Upper Saddle River, NJ: Pearson Education.

Nation, P. (2001). *Learning vocabulary in another language.* New York: Cambridge University Press.

Schwartz, R. M., & Raphael, T. (1985). Concept of definition: A key to improving students' vocabulary. *Reading Teacher, 39*(2), 198–205.

English Language Resources for Students and Teachers

For Beginners

Student Dictionaries

Oxford picture dictionary for the content areas (2nd ed.). (2010). Oxford, England: Oxford University Press.

    Also available in English/Spanish version.

Vox Spanish and English student dictionary. (1999). Columbus, OH: McGraw-Hill. *Word by word basic picture dictionary: International* (2nd ed). (2006). White Plains, NY: Pearson Longman.

    Also available in eight bilingual versions: English + Chinese, Haitian Kreyol, Japanese, Korean, Portuguese, Russian, Spanish, Vietnamese.

For High Beginners and Low Intermediates

Student Dictionary

Longman basic dictionary of American English. (1999). White Plains, NY: Pearson Longman.

    All three levels of the Longman Student Dictionary series use the Longman Defining Vocabulary, the 2,000 most common English words, to facilitate comprehension of definitions and sentence examples.

Merriam Webster's visual dictionary. (2006). Springfield, MA: Merriam Webster.

Ultimate visual dictionary. (2006). New York: DK.

Ultimate visual dictionary of science. (2006). New York: DK.

For Intermediates

Student Dictionary

Longman dictionary of American English (4th ed.). (2008). White Plains, NY: Pearson Longman.

Thesaurus

Longman essential activator (2nd ed.). (2006). White Plains, NY: Pearson Longman.

Dictionary of Idioms

Longman pocket idioms dictionary. (2002). White Plains, NY: Pearson Longman.

For High Intermediates and Advanced

Student Dictionary

Longman advanced American dictionary (2nd ed.). (2007). White Plains, NY: Pearson Longman.

Thesaurus

Longman language activator. (2002). White Plains, NY: Pearson Longman.

Dictionaries of Idioms

Longman American idioms dictionary. (2000). White Plains, NY: Pearson Longman.

Oxford idioms: Dictionary for learners of English. (2007). Oxford, England: Oxford University Press.

Collocation Dictionaries

BBI dictionary of English word combinations. (1997). Amsterdam, The Netherlands: John Benjamins.

LTP dictionary of selected collocations. (1999). Hove, England: Language Teaching Publications.

Oxford collocations dictionary for students of English (2nd ed.). (2009). Oxford, England: Oxford University Press.

The TechConnection

http://www.wordcentral.com
Online all-purpose dictionary.

http://www.math.com/students/references.html#dictionaries
Online reference for math words and more.

http://www.clichesite.com/index.asp
Online source for idioms, sayings, and proverbs, organized topically.

http://lexipedia.com
Online source of synonyms, antonyms, and definitions.

http://freerice.org
Gamelike questions about English vocabulary (also English grammar, world geography, chemistry, and more). For each correct response, 10 grains of rice are collected for distribution through the UN World Food Programme to help feed the hungry.

CHAPTER 9

EXTENDING COMPREHENSION: TEXTBOOK READING STRATEGIES

Classroom teachers generally agree that today's textbooks and ancillary materials are designed to be user-friendly and engaging for students. ELLs, however, may view them quite differently. For them, content-area textbooks challenge their English reading skills. The time and effort spent trying to make the texts understandable often bring ELLs few rewards and little satisfaction. Even the textbook size and amount of information can appear overwhelming. The strategies that follow will help make textbook reading more comprehensible for ELLs and other struggling readers in your classroom.

WORKING WITH YOUR TEXTBOOK

The Objective: Show Students How to Get the Most Out of Their Textbooks

The Rationale: The shift from learning to read to reading to learn occurs in third grade. From that point on, teachers focus student learning on the *information* in their textbooks but rarely on ways of *using* those texts to make learning easier. Yet few students intuitively develop the skills to use textbooks in ways that would serve to facilitate their comprehension.

STRATEGY 70   TEACH TEXTBOOK AIDS

IN CONCEPT

Textbook aids are designed to embed the written word in context, but amazingly, students neither realize that intent nor utilize the support. One student, in mid-January, told her teacher, "Our textbook has a bilingual dictionary in the back! Did you know that?" This student surely would have benefitted from this resource during the first half of the year.

Teachers must make students aware that textbook aids are included not to make the page look pretty (or, as one student suggested, so the author didn't have to write so many words) but to support students' efforts to understand the concepts the printed words convey.

IN PRACTICE

Using textbook aids to facilitate comprehension is an important learning strategy and should be taught actively and explicitly at the beginning of the school year or whenever

Figure 9.1   An Activity to Demonstrate
the Value of Textbook Aids

Write:	chapter title, headings, and subheadings on board
Ask:	"What is this chapter about?"
Make:	brainstorming graphic
Tell:	students to open textbook to that chapter
Allot:	3 minutes to look over other textbook aids
Add:	more ideas to graphic
Use:	graphic as review at end of reading

a new textbook is introduced. Use a class session to do a "book walk"—to teach about the aids that your particular textbook offers (types of aids and their uses are described soon). Give explicit instruction, or try a discovery approach: Prepare a list of aids, and have the students work in groups to identify and locate examples of each item in their textbooks. In either case, explain the purpose of each aid and how it supports students' understanding of the text. You can use the activity described in Figure 9.1 as an introduction to the lesson and, later, at the beginning of each new chapter. Figure 9.2 tells of a more radical approach that one teacher used.

Remind students frequently to use textbook aids as a *prereading* activity each time they are assigned a textbook reading. The more students use textbook aids, the more they will recognize how valuable the aids are to comprehension.

The ***table of contents*** and ***index*** serve as shortcuts for locating specific information contained in a text. To demonstrate their usefulness, give students a list of topics. Working in groups, students should note the page number(s) on which these topics appear and indicate whether they used the index or the table of contents to locate the information. Or try turning this practice activity into a game: Give it an intriguing name, like *Textbook Sleuths*, add a time limit, and make it a competition.

On the first day of school, Ms. Molvick, a middle school science teacher, spent the period talking about the course that lay ahead. The class ended with a homework assignment to "familiarize yourselves with your textbook." What the students heard, of course, was "No homework."

The next day as class began, Ms. Molvick told the students to clear their desks, take out a piece of paper, write their names at the top, and number a list 1 through 10. The students gave each other puzzled looks. A quiz? How could they have a quiz when they hadn't had any homework?

The first question on the quiz was "What is the name of your textbook?" Other questions followed:

What information is given at the beginning of each chapter?

What information is given at the end of each chapter?

How is new vocabulary presented in the text?

Does the text use margin notes or footnotes?

Does your textbook have a glossary?

Are any appendices included?

Ms. Molvick created the opportunity to teach a lesson on textbook aids when she corrected the quiz with the class. It was her way of ensuring that the students became well acquainted with their textbooks. The students in this science class learned a valuable lesson in class that day—about their textbook and about their teacher.

Figure 9.2   True Tale: One Way to Teach Textbook Aids

Chapter titles, section headings, and ***subsection headings*** contain key words and phrases that highlight important facts or concepts that can help students organize their thinking about the information to follow. Teach students to scan headings and make associations as a regular *prereading* activity.

Outlines and ***focus questions*** at the beginning of each chapter highlight forthcoming information. As a *prereading* activity, use them to direct students' attention to important concepts, ideas, and details presented in the chapter. Students can use outlines and questions *during* the reading to organize information and then *after* the reading to check their comprehension and to engage in critical thinking.

Summaries and ***reviews*** at the ends of sections and chapters highlight key concepts presented in the body of the text. The language used in reviews and summaries is often more readable because the sentences are shorter and more concise. Teach your ELLs to read summaries and reviews *before* reading a textbook section or chapter. Prereading these sections helps all students organize their thinking about the content they are about to read. It allows them to form a base upon which to build the concepts and supporting details presented in the body of the text.

Glossaries are a bonus feature for all students. For ELLs, they can be a lifeline. Make your students aware that the words or phrases highlighted by color or bolding in the body of the text are important to understanding the concepts. Show how these key words are explained in a glossary at the end of the textbook, as margin notations, or at the beginning or end of each chapter. Some textbooks include a bilingual glossary; if yours does not, encourage your ELLs to make liberal use of *bilingual dictionaries* for additional clarification.

Text organizers are particularly valuable to ELLs because they offer a great deal of information in the fewest number of words. They call attention to key information by showcasing it in boxes, bulleted or numbered lists, and sentences written in bold or different colored ink. Students should recognize that these elements signal significant material presented in a linguistically simplified form.

Graphics present information in chart, table, or diagram formats. They facilitate comprehension by visually contextualizing printed words. ELLs can gather content data by learning to analyze the information displayed in these graphics.

Visuals in textbooks are designed to appeal to students, capture their attention, offer them contextual support, and enrich their understanding of concepts. As with graphics, students should understand that visuals are more than mere decoration or page fillers—that is, real information is offered in the maps, pictures, and illustrations included in the text. ELLs and struggling readers should be encouraged first to scan visuals and graphics to activate or build background knowledge and then to use these features to help clarify the meaning of the written text.

STRATEGY 71   TEACH READING IN REVERSE

IN CONCEPT

Reading in reverse is a scaffolding strategy that previews concepts in order to prepare students to mentally organize a forthcoming reading. It literally reverses the order of the traditional reading approach, which generally proceeds like this:

- Teacher activates background knowledge.
- Students read the text.
- Students answer the questions in the text.
- Teacher and students discuss information in the text.
- Teacher and students apply information to real-life and/or past learning.

Figure 9.3 The Traditional Model for Reading a Textbook

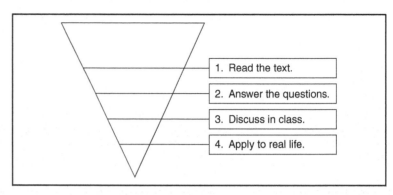

Figure 9.4 A New Model for Reading a Textbook : Reading in Reverse

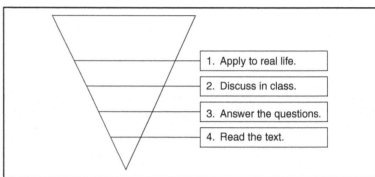

This widely practiced model, shown graphically in Figure 9.3, asks students to do the most difficult, dense part of the lesson first, before enough scaffolding is in place to support their attempts to read the text. Assigning students the text reading before the activities that would embed the information in context means that students lack the strong foundational base to support their comprehension. There is a better way to do this.

In the reading in reverse strategy, students complete a series of prereading steps that create a strong scaffold for comprehension. This approach places the hardest part, reading the text, at the end of the activity, rather than at the beginning.

IN PRACTICE

Figure 9.4 shows the reversed order of reading. Step 1 is *application*: Talk about real-life experiences related to the reading topic, or do something concrete to make it meaningful. The application and extension sections at the end of the chapter or in your teaching guide can help you find ideas.

Step 2 uses *discussion* to introduce the topic, key concepts, and content-specific vocabulary. You create a strong foundation for textbook comprehension when ELLs first hear new content words and phrases spoken in authentic contexts and see them written on the board.

Step 3 involves *reading the summary and questions* at the end of the chapter to focus student attention on "the big picture"—the main ideas and purpose of the reading. This is also the time to focus on the textbook aids. Preview the headings and subheadings as a guide to the chapter's organization and the pictures and graphics as a source of information.

In Step 4, students do the actual *reading*. At this point you return to the traditional model, following the reading sequentially with questions, class discussion, and real-life application. The strategy of reverse reading supports students' efforts and facilitates their comprehension of concepts as they read the textbook.

To demonstrate how this works with an actual reading, look now at the short reading "Nomads" in Figure 9.5. As you read, think about the four-step process by focusing on these questions:

1. How would you introduce the topic of nomads? How would you relate this material to concrete, real-life experiences?
2. How would you apply these ideas to a class discussion of nomads?

FOCUS ON CONTENT

Social Studies

Nonfiction gives true information. "Nomads" tells about people who travel from place to place. Preview the pages. What do the pictures and headings tell you about nomads?

NOMADS

What Are Nomads?

Nomads are people who do not live in one place. They move from place to place to find food and water. They carry their homes with them on their **journeys**. In **prehistoric** times most people were nomads. They hunted animals and looked for seeds and plants to eat.

Are All Nomads Hunters?

Some nomads today are hunters, but most are herders. They travel with herds of sheep, goats, or camels. They look for places that have grass and water for their animals. These nomads often live in tents. They travel in large family groups called tribes.

journeys, long trips
prehistoric, before people started writing down history

◄ This cave painting shows prehistoric nomads hunting elk.

Woman herder with long-haired lamb ►

MAKE CONNECTIONS

1 How large is your family group? Count your family members.
2 Are there nomads in your home country? Explain.

38

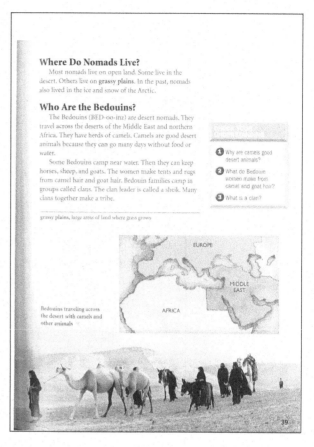

Where Do Nomads Live?

Most nomads live on open land. Some live in the desert. Others live on **grassy plains**. In the past, nomads also lived in the ice and snow of the Arctic.

Who Are the Bedouins?

The Bedouins (BED-oo-inz) are desert nomads. They travel across the deserts of the Middle East and northern Africa. They have herds of camels. Camels are good desert animals because they can go many days without food or water.

Some Bedouins camp near water. Then they can keep horses, sheep, and goats. The women make tents and rugs from camel hair and goat hair. Bedouin families camp in groups called clans. The clan leader is called a sheik. Many clans together make a tribe.

1 Why are camels good desert animals?
2 What do Bedouin women make from camel and goat hair?
3 What is a clan?

grassy plains, large areas of land where grass grows

Bedouins traveling across the desert with camels and other animals

39

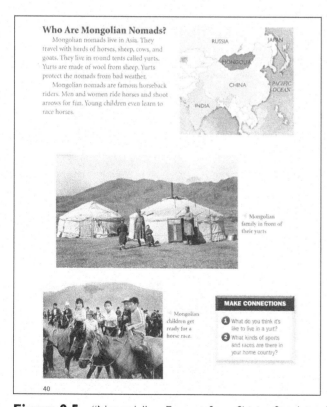

Who Are Mongolian Nomads?

Mongolian nomads live in Asia. They travel with herds of horses, sheep, cows, and goats. They live in round tents called yurts. Yurts are made of wool from sheep. Yurts protect the nomads from bad weather.

Mongolian nomads are famous horseback riders. Men and women ride horses and shoot arrows for fun. Young children even learn to race horses.

◄ Mongolian family in front of their yurts

◄ Mongolian children get ready for a horse race.

MAKE CONNECTIONS

1 What do you think it's like to live in a yurt?
2 What kinds of sports and races are there in your home country?

40

▲ Sioux hunters chasing buffalo

Are There Nomads in North America?

There are very few nomads left in North America. Before 1850, there were many nomads. The Sioux, for example, hunted buffalo on the plains. They used buffalo meat for food. They made tents and blankets from buffalo skins. The tents were called tepees.

The Inuit, who live in the most northern part of North America, were also nomads. In summer they lived in tents by the sea and fished. In winter they hunted seals and polar bears. They used small boats called kayaks. Today most Inuit live in towns or villages. They are no longer nomads.

▲ This tepee is made of buffalo skins.

1 What animals did the Sioux hunt?
2 What animals did the Inuit hunt in the winter?

◄ Inuit hunting in a kayak

41

Figure 9.5   "Nomads," an Excerpt from *Shining Star*, Introductory Level

3. How would you preview the reading?

4. How would you go about the reading itself?

Figure 9.6 offers ideas for each of the prereading steps. How do they compare with yours?

Step 1. Apply to real life.

   Talk about the following:

   • personal experience with moving
   • immigration experiences
   • experiences with frequent moves to seek employment, other reasons
   • migrant worker experiences

Step 2. Discuss in class.

   Talk about the following:

   • Is moving from place to place "fun"? Why/why not?
   • Does it feel different if the move is voluntary or forced?
   • Compare leaving school, friends, and family behind to taking it all with you. (This is the time to introduce the word and the concept of *nomads*.)
   • Look at pictures in the text to compare differences among nomad homes and students' homes.

Step 3. Read the questions—and the section and subsection headers.

   Ask the following:

   • What is this section about?
   • What information will this section focus on?
   • What is the main Idea of this section?

Step 4. Read the text.

   • Read one section at a time.
   • Follow each section reading by discussing the questions in Step 3.

Figure 9.6 Suggestions for Reading "Nomads" in Reverse

STRATEGY 72   READ TEXT IN SMALL SEGMENTS AND HIGHLIGHT MAIN IDEAS

IN CONCEPT

Today's textbooks are impressive in their size and weight and the amount of information they present. Students will find them less intimidating when they are taught strategies to break long text passages into smaller, learnable segments. You can use these techniques singly or in combination as you implement the reverse reading strategy.

IN PRACTICE

Technique I

T-notes, shown in Figure 9.7, are really a simplified form of an outline that ELLs can use as a reference while they are reading. The left column represents a main idea, and the

Figure 9.7 T-Note Format

Main Ideas	Details/Examples
1. _____	1. _____ 2. _____ 3. _____
2. _____	1. _____ 2. _____ 3. _____
3. _____	1. _____ 2. _____ 3. _____

right column lists supporting details and/or examples. You can ask for volunteers among your more advanced students to make and share sets of T-notes. Everyone benefits from this technique: ELLs have a clear outline to guide their reading, and volunteers get extra credit while reinforcing their own understandings.

Figure 9.8 shows T-notes for the first sections of the "Nomads" reading. Referring to the organized presentation and concise language of the outline facilitates ELLs' comprehension as they read.

The T-note format is user-friendly, easy to learn, and readily adaptable to multiple tasks. Figure 9.9 uses this format to outline a segment on water quality from an earth science textbook.

Figure 9.8 T-Notes for the Reading "Nomads"

Main Ideas	Details/Examples
1. Nomads are groups of people who . . .	1. move from place to place 2. take homes with them 3. move to find food and water
2. Nomads are hunters or herders . . .	1. now most are herders 2. travel with sheep, goats, camels 3. look for grass and water for the animals 4. travel in large family groups (tribes)
3. Nomads are people who live . . .	1. in the desert 2. on grassy plains 3. in ice and snow (long ago)
4. Bedouins are . . .	1. desert nomads 2. travel across the Middle East and northern Africa deserts 3. herd camels 4. family groups called clans 5. sheik is leader of clan 6. many clans make a tribe

Figure 9.9   T-Notes for Science:
Factors Affecting Water Quality

Main Ideas	Details/Examples
1. Appearance and taste	1. cloudiness 2. odor 3. color 4. minerals and chemicals
2. Acidity	1. measured in pH—0 to 14 2. pure water is neutral—pH of 7 3. lower pH = more acid 4. higher pH = more base
3. Hardness	1. based on 2 minerals—calcium and magnesium 2. hard water doesn't make suds 3. deposits from hard water clog water pipes and machines
4. Disease-causing agents	1. contamination from E. coli bacteria 2. comes from human and animal waste
5. Standards of quality	1. set by the EPA 2. standards set concentration limits 3 concentration = amount of 1 substance in a certain amount of another substance 4. example: alphabet soup—number of letters per liter of soup

T-notes serve as a reference and an aid to learning not only during the reading process but also later as a review. Students can use them individually or in small groups to study for exams. T-notes are a simple but effective strategy that helps to streamline the reading and learning process for ELLs and perhaps for other struggling readers in your classes.

Technique II

Learning logs are structured content journals based on reading assignments from the textbook. Students use them while they are attempting to complete assigned pages. Figure 9.10 shows two variations of a format for learning logs. Note that the more traditional and self-stigmatizing "What I Didn't Understand" has been replaced with positive phrases such as "Questions I Have," "Things I Want to Know," and "Clueless."

Because of the way that learning logs are structured, it is important to designate some class time to address the issues, questions, or difficulties that the students have noted in their logs. Students, meeting in small groups, can help each other by exchanging understandings, answering each other's questions, and clarifying vocabulary. Encourage their independence, but offer your support as needed. Students should note in their logs the new understandings they derive from these discussions.

Learning logs are valuable because they engage language learners in the process of negotiating knowledge and increasing their understanding of the text. The logs also provide an excellent source of information for ongoing or summary review of material. And they can serve teachers as additional input for student assessment.

Learning logs, like T-notes, are highly adaptable and can be used by students for a range of activities that go beyond text readings. In science, for example, the first column could be adapted for use with in-class experiments or demonstrations. In math, learning logs can be useful during lessons in which new concepts, applications, and/or vocabulary are presented. In literature, learning logs can record characters as they are

Text Pages	What I Understood	New or Difficult Vocabulary	Questions I Want to Know

Text Pages	I Get It	I Think I Get It	I Don't Have a Clue

Figure 9.10 Two Formats for Learning Logs

introduced or reactions to plot developments. In all subject areas, learning logs can be used when videos or other media are being utilized to contextualize or enrich understandings. The uses of learning logs are limited only by the imagination and creativity of the teacher.

Technique III

Grouping students heterogeneously to discuss a text is another effective means to help ELLs understand main ideas and important concepts. (Rules for successful group work are addressed in Strategy 87 in Chapter 10.) Group work facilitates reading comprehension because the give and take of peer discussion embeds the written words in context. ELLs—indeed, all students—have the opportunity to clarify difficult or confusing concepts as they negotiate meaning. Group work also supports ELLs' language development by providing an authentic context in which to hear and use new vocabulary. And it lowers all students' affective filters as it prepares them to participate in class discussion. Group work is a powerful strategy for learning.

STRATEGY 73   REINFORCE LEARNED READING STRATEGIES

IN CONCEPT

Reading instruction at the secondary school level is often not a part of mainstream content class curriculum. However, teachers can help ELLs and struggling readers become better textbook readers by reinforcing previously learned reading strategies.

IN PRACTICE

Technique I

Review learned reading strategies on an ongoing basis. Begin a lesson by previewing the material again. Draw students' attention to a specific graphic or photo in the text, and ask them what they can tell you about it. Ask students to reread the headings and subheadings and then make general statements about the content. Ask them to focus on bolded phrases or bulleted lists to give some supporting details about the content. Students who remember to do these previews on their own will facilitate their own comprehension.

Technique II

You can help all your students become better readers by demonstrating and reviewing the concept of making connections as you read. Good readers continually interact with the text as they read. They anticipate and predict what is about to come. They also relate an event, character, or concept to themselves, to something they have previously read, or to something they know in the real world. In addition, they ask themselves questions to monitor their understanding and seek to clarify points of uncertainty. And they synthesize and summarize what they have just completed reading.

Your students will benefit from frequent review of these reading techniques as they begin each textbook chapter. By actively promoting the *predict–read–question–summarize* approach, you will help your students internalize it to become better readers.

STRATEGY 74   USE ORAL READING EFFECTIVELY

IN CONCEPT

Oral reading as a comprehension strategy can be used effectively but more often is not. Round robin reading, for example, in which students take turns reading aloud to their peers, frequently results in situations that are more embarrassing than educational. Other oral reading practices have proven far more instructive (Ediger, 2000; Rasinski & Hoffman, 2003).

IN PRACTICE

Technique I

When *teachers* read aloud, they model fluency, pacing, intonation, and pronunciation. They can also add drama to make a passage more engaging. As students follow along in their books, teachers can model aloud what good readers do silently when they read—pausing at appropriate points to make predictions, ask questions, clarify, make connections, and summarize.

Technique II

A twist on oral reading is the *hot potato reading* technique. As you read a passage, stop at a particular point, and designate a student to finish the sentence. Walking around the room as you read and handing off a "baton" requires students to focus on the material being read. To reduce anxiety, allow students to return the baton to you after a single word or to hold on to it and continue reading the full sentence or more.

Technique III

It has been well established that reading comprehension and retention rise when readers simultaneously see and hear information as in *closed-captioned video*, which has been proven an effective technique for developing reading skills both for nonnative speakers and for preliterate native-speaking adults (Bean & Wilson, 1989; Goldman & Goldman, 1988; Neuman & Koskinen, 1992). Interestingly, one way that a competent reader brings comprehension to a difficult text is by reading it aloud. Hearing the printed words, even when reading them to yourself, assists in producing meaning.

ELLs also benefit from seeing and hearing text in other ways. They learn pronunciation of unfamiliar words, and they may make new associations of words in their oral and written forms, words known in spoken form but not recognized in writing because they are spelled so differently from the way they are pronounced, like those in Figure 6.7 in Chapter 6. Another advantage relates to *homophones*, words that are pronounced the same but are spelled differently and have different meanings (e.g., *peace/piece* and *straight/strait*), and *homographs*, words that are spelled the same but are pronounced differently and have different meanings (e.g., *wind, lead,* and *bow*). Simultaneously seeing and hearing words like these in context may help students to understand, retain, and apply their meanings.

Students who read well can be offered extra credit to read segments or entire chapters of the textbook into a tape recorder. The bonus again is that the readers are reinforcing their own learning while helping others—and helping themselves, too, with extra credit. Language learners can then listen to the tape while reading the text, at home if possible or, if not, in school. This multimedia approach facilitates comprehension and offers ELLs greater access to important content concepts.

WORKING WITH YOUR TEXTBOOK

The Objective: Help Students Become Competent Note Takers

The Rationale: Few students are offered direct instruction in how to take notes. It is a skill that successful students simply acquire and refine during their academic years. In today's educational environment, note-taking skills, like learning strategies, must become a part of classroom instruction. And like learning strategies, they are an essential key to academic success.

STRATEGY 75   TEACH HOW TO TAKE NOTES

IN CONCEPT

As students advance through the grades, the importance of taking good notes in an increasingly efficient and automatic manner intensifies. ELLs, in particular, need formats and techniques that put the most information into the fewest number of words. Explicit instruction in note-taking skills will help all students become better note takers.

IN PRACTICE
Technique I
T-notes are a useful format for teaching students the basics of note taking. Prepare a set of T-notes in which main ideas have already been listed in the left column, as shown in

Figure 9.11   Using T-Notes to Teach
Note-Taking Skills

Main Ideas	Details/Examples
1. Nomads are groups of people who	1. move from place to place 2. _____ 3. _____
2. Herder nomads...	1. travel with _____ 2. look for places with ___ 3. live in _____
3. Nomads are people who live (where?)	1. in the desert 2. _____ 3. _____
4. Bedouins	1. are _____ 2. travel _____ 3. herd _____ 4. _____ 5. _____ 6. _____

Figure 9.11. Give your students an in-class or home assignment of completing the Details/Examples column. Students will benefit from seeing one or two examples in that column to model what to look for. Once learned, T-notes are an ideal format in which to record information from class instruction and text readings.

T-notes can also be used to teach the concept of getting the main idea. In this instance, students' T-notes show items in the Details column, and the students must find the main idea that the details represent.

Technique II

Graphic organizers (discussed at length in Chapter 10) are an excellent format for note taking because they visually convey large amounts of information in the fewest number of words. ELLs can use a web (see Figure 10.13 in Chapter 10) or a matrix (Figure 10.20) to note the main ideas and supporting details of a reading. Other graphics that work well for note taking are graphs, charts, maps, diagrams, timelines, and sequenced pictures, all illustrated in Chapter 10.

Technique III

Early in the school year, try teaching a lesson with the combined objectives of finding important information and taking notes. Give students a photocopied section of several pages from their textbook, and read it with them in a section-by-section process. Reread the first subsection aloud to them after they have finished reading it silently. Discuss what is important, explaining your reasoning about how you distinguish the details from the main ideas. Be sure to explain the *why* and *why not* behind your thinking. Finally, use a highlighter pen to show students how to highlight key words, phrases, and sentences in the passage. Repeat this *read–discuss–highlight* procedure with each successive subsection, encouraging greater student input as the lesson continues. Follow up with an at-home assignment of transferring the highlighted areas into a set of notes.

STRATEGY 76   TEACH HOW TO CONDENSE TEXT FOR NOTES

IN CONCEPT

Effective note takers do not copy whole sentences from the text. To make note taking an efficient academic tool, students must learn to condense text so that their notes contain only key words and phrases that convey important information.

IN PRACTICE

Working with T-notes or an appropriate graphic, model the wording of the notes you would take for a subsection of the text. Demonstrate which words and phrases to omit or shorten. Be sure students understand the concept of *condensing*. After hearing "Write in complete sentences" for their entire school careers, students may need assurance that condensing is appropriate and desirable in note taking.

Using abbreviations is another important element of condensing for notes. Explain to students the art of abbreviating commonly used words—*because, therefore, leading to, compared to*, for example. You can create a class set of abbreviations and also encourage students to create their own—a practice they may not know is acceptable.

WORKING WITH YOUR TEXTBOOK

The Objective: Use Alternative Resources for True ELL Beginners

The Rationale: Teachers often ask what to do in class with the true ELL beginner. How can a grade level textbook be used by a newcomer who has just begun to learn English? The answer is as obvious as it is unsatisfying: ELLs at early stages of language development cannot successfully use a grade level textbook. Certain approaches, however, may help students gain *some* knowledge of content while they are developing their English language skills.

STRATEGY 77   FOCUS ON SIMPLE LANGUAGE AND GRAPHICS

IN CONCEPT

The fact that beginner ELLs will not comprehend a grade level textbook doesn't mean that they cannot learn anything at all from it. You can help them derive some information by directing their attention to the parts of the textbook that are high in context and low in linguistic demand.

IN PRACTICE

Beginners should focus on only selected parts of textbook chapters—headings, subheadings, and all the visuals, including charts, tables, maps, photos, graphics, diagrams, and bulleted and/or boldfaced lists. They can write, even in their native language, words and phrases that they believe relate to the information they see. In the process, beginners should be encouraged to make ample use of a bilingual or picture dictionary.

STRATEGY 78   PAIR ELL BEGINNERS WITH VOLUNTEER BUDDIES

IN CONCEPT

In almost every class, certain students are *nurturers* and may enjoy working one-on-one as volunteer buddies with ELL beginners, another win–win situation for both sides. Beginners appreciate the help and support of a peer, and nurturers feel gratified and satisfied.

IN PRACTICE

Volunteer buddies can work with ELLs on some of the strategies presented in previous sections of this chapter. The buddies can help ELL beginners focus on getting information from charts, tables, diagrams, maps, pictures, and other illustrations in their textbook. Buddies can also assist with vocabulary by demonstrating the meanings of words, synonyms, and idioms and by prompting frequent use of personal, bilingual, and picture dictionaries. Bilingual buddies can help locate cognates in the language detective activity (Strategy 60 in Chapter 8). Most important of all, they can offer support, encouragement, and perhaps even friendship.

You may think the buddy system would be most valuable if the volunteer is bilingual in English and the beginner's native language or is at least at a more advanced level of English language development. Although this type of pairing can be beneficial, it is also fraught with risk. Reliance on translation of vocabulary and concepts may place an undue burden on the buddy and lead to the beginner's dependence on the translation and the translator. It can sometimes even slow the language learner's development of English reading skills. In reality, any willing student can offer enough help and support to make a difference.

STRATEGY 79   USE ALTERNATIVE BOOKS AND OTHER MEDIA

IN CONCEPT

For true ELL beginners, you or your reading resource specialist can seek out alternative media to supplement the regular classroom textbook. If your school or district has no objection, you might consider using content texts written specifically for ELLs, trade books on key topics, Internet websites, or alternative texts.

IN PRACTICE

Textbooks written specifically for ELLs offer even more context than grade level texts and contain many language-supporting features. They make frequent use of review and reinforcement and often include DVDs, PowerPoint presentations, and other ancillary material. Resources of this type are available for many secondary school topics in science and social studies. Also available are many books of fiction and nonfiction written at high interest/low readability levels. ELL and reading resource teachers, as well as the media specialists at your school, should be able to help you locate texts of these types and also trade books on key topics, Internet websites, native-language trade books and magazines, and alternative textbooks.

Be aware, however, that using an alternative textbook, especially one written for a lower grade, may be stigmatizing. It sends a subtle, unintended message that those who use it are less capable than their peers. In addition, using a native-language textbook may violate state laws concerning classroom use of a language other than English. But even if no legal issues are involved, students using native-language textbooks may become dependent on them to the point of not wanting to attempt using the regular classroom text. Much like using a translator, using native-language textbooks may ultimately impede the development of English language skills.

The use of native-language textbooks presents an additional difficulty when your ELL beginners are from several language backgrounds. If you can't find suitable textbooks for all of their languages, is it fair to find native-language textbooks only for some? Despite these disadvantages, it is important to note that for ELL beginners entering U.S. secondary schools in the middle of a school year, native-language resources can mean the difference between learning some content and learning none.

There is no magic formula to help true ELL beginners in your content class. These strategies are probably the best you can use at this stage of language development because, at the very least, they allow the students to learn *some* content while they are learning English and they show that you care.

IN SUMMARY: WORKING WITH YOUR TEXTBOOK

Reading a textbook is a daunting task for ELLs and struggling readers. Students arrive in your classes with differing levels of language ability and differing sets of reading and literacy skills. They need a variety of strategies that show them how to interact with the text to derive meaning—techniques that embed written words in context and focus thinking on main ideas and supporting details. You can ease the challenge for your students by using the strategies in this chapter to scaffold their content reading as they learn English.

QUESTIONS FOR DISCUSSION

1. Which of the *12 Guidelines for Practice* presented at the end of Chapter 1 inform the strategies in this chapter?
2. Cite and summarize additional research that gives theoretical and/or experiential support to the strategies discussed in this chapter.
3. Examine the textbooks you use in your classes to see which textbook aids they contain. Plan a lesson to teach students how these aids can facilitate comprehension. How can you determine if students are already using these aids?
4. Using a textbook with which you are not familiar, examine a chapter following the steps in Figure 9.1. How successful were you in getting the gist of the chapter?
5. Read the "Nomads" passage again, this time focusing on the types of problematic vocabulary discussed in Chapter 8. Look for words and phrases that might cause confusion: synonyms, idioms, and familiar words used in new ways.
6. Plan a reading in reverse lesson to introduce a reading or a new topic from a textbook. Select a reading or topic, and then follow the three preliminary steps to reading. Explain the reasoning behind your choices. Work individually if you are now teaching a class or in pairs if you are not.

REFERENCES AND RESOURCES

Bean, R. M., & Wilson, R. M. (1989). Using closed-captioned television to teach reading to adults. *Reading Research Instruction, 28*(4), 27–37.

Calderón, M. (2007). *Teaching reading to English language learners, grades 6–12: A framework for improving achievement in the content areas.* Thousand Oaks, CA: Corwin Press.

Daniels, H., & Zemelman, S. (2004). *Subjects matter: Every teacher's guide to content-area reading.* Portsmouth, NH: Heinemann.

Dornan, R., Rosen, L. M., & Wilson, M. (2005). Lesson designs for reading comprehension and vocabulary development. In P. A. Richard-Amato & M. A. Snow (Eds.), *Academic success for English language learners: Strategies for K–12 mainstream teachers* (pp. 248–274). White Plains, NY: Pearson Education.

Echevarria, J., Vogt, M., & Short, D. J. (2007). *Making content comprehensible for English language learners: The SIOP model* (3rd ed.). Needham Heights, MA: Allyn & Bacon.

Ediger, M. (2000, August). *Evaluation of round robin approaches in teaching reading.* ERIC Education Resources: ED444124. Available at *http://www.eric.ed.gov/PDFS/ED444124.pdf*

Fitzgerald, J., & Graves, M. (2004). *Scaffolding reading experiences for English language learners.* Norwood, MA: Christopher-Gordon.

Goldman, M., & Goldman, S. (1988). Reading with closed captioned TV. *Journal of Reading, 31*(5), 458.

National Captioning Institute. (2003). *Using captioned television in reading and literacy instruction.* Retrieved February 19, 2010, from *http://www.ncicap.org/classroom.asp*

Neuman, S., & Koskinen, P. (1992). Captioned television as comprehensible input: Effects of incidental word learning from context for language minority students. *Reading Research Quarterly, 27*(1), 95–106.

Peregoy, S. F., & Boyle, O. F. (2001). *Reading, writing, and learning in ESL: A resource book for K–12 teachers* (pp. 257–411). New York: Addison Wesley Longman.

Rasinski, T., Blachowicz, C., & Lems, K., (Eds.). (2005). *Fluency instruction: Research-based best practices.* New York: Guilford Press.

Rasinski, T., & Hoffman, J. V. (2003). Oral reading in the school literacy curriculum. *Reading Research Quarterly, 38* (4), 510–522.

The TechConnection

http://dww.ed.gov/index.cfm
The Doing What Works website translates research-based practices into practical tools to improve classroom instruction.

REINFORCING LEARNING: ACTIVITIES AND ASSIGNMENTS

The lesson has been taught, the textbook read. Now come the in-class and at-home assignments to reinforce and extend the learning, assignments that ELLs often find challenging. For teachers, planning activities for ELLs that are cognitively complex but linguistically simplified may present an almost-equal challenge. This chapter presents assignment strategies that offer language learners alternative means to improve their performance outcomes.

ASSIGNMENTS TO PROMOTE STUDENT SUCCESS

The Objective: Good Assignments Begin with Good Directions

The Rationale: Have you ever been a student in a class in which you were given directions that you didn't understand? You probably sat there with a growing sense of anxiety because you had absolutely no idea what to do. You may have looked around—were you the only one who didn't get it? Perhaps you quietly checked with several of your peers, only to discover that they didn't understand either. These memories of anxious moments may have you feeling a little uneasy even now. Anxiety is never a good way to begin an assignment.

STRATEGY 80 GIVE CLEAR DIRECTIONS

IN CONCEPT

Successful activities begin with clear directions. Students need to approach each assignment with a complete understanding of process and product. When you follow the simple, five-step plan summarized in Figure 10.1, you can be sure that your instructions will always be clearly understood by all your students.

Figure 10.1   Clear Directions in Five
Steps

1. *Say* the directions clearly.
2. *Write* them and leave them in view.
3. *Model* the process and the product.
4. *Check* comprehension.
5. *Ask* for questions.

IN PRACTICE

1. *Say* the directions. Explain them as explicitly as you possibly can. State what you want students to do in a simple, step-by-step manner. If the directions are complex, use the one-step approach: Tell students that after they complete the first step, you'll tell them what they'll be doing next.

2. *Write* the directions on the board, on chart paper, or on an overhead transparency. Written words reinforce spoken language and help language learners process what they are being asked to do. Keep the written directions in view so students can refer to them as needed during the assignment.

3. *Model* the process and the product. Demonstrate how to begin, and explain the choices you make to reach the final product. Show students what a finished product should look like; show several good variations as well as examples of poor products. Adding these visual elements to your directions is essential for your ELLs because it bypasses the need for wordy explanations. It also gives all students a clear understanding of your expectations.

4. *Check* comprehension by asking the students to repeat, step by step, what they are expected to do. Start by asking, "So what's the first thing we're going to do?" Go through each step of the activity, adding detail or correcting as needed. Point to each step of the written directions as students review them orally. It is important that the students *themselves* explain the steps they are going to take to complete the project. After all, they are the ones who will be doing the activity.

5. *Ask* for questions: "Question time. Who's got a question for me?" The clarity of your directions may leave your students *without* any questions.

Clear directions start students out right. This five-step approach lets students focus immediately and confidently on the work to be done—no lost time, no unnecessary anxiety. You maximize your students' opportunity for success when you give clear, detailed directions before every assignment, including homework.

ASSIGNMENTS TO PROMOTE STUDENT SUCCESS

The Objective: Modify Whole Class Assignments to Make Language Comprehensible

The Rationale: ELLs will be able to demonstrate their content knowledge when the output required for the assignment matches their level of English language development. Modifying assignments by lowering language demands does *not* mean that you are lowering the cognitive challenge or your expectations. Instead, it recognizes the difficulties that ELLs face in developing English language competency at the same time that they are attempting to learn content in English.

The types of modifications you choose should consistently challenge your ELLs with incrementally complex language. The strategies that follow are widely adaptable and can be applied to many homework tasks and in-class activities.

STRATEGY 81   OFFER A WORD BANK

IN CONCEPT

For assignments that require simple, short answers to a series of questions, consider using a word bank, especially with students who are in the early stages of English language development. Word banks are lists of content-related word or phrase choices that students can use to correctly answer the assigned questions. You will promote critical thinking and encourage thoughtful consideration of answer choices when you include at least three extra words or phrases that closely relate to the topic.

IN PRACTICE

Word banks work well with many straightforward questions used to check comprehension after textbook readings. They are also well suited to assignments that ask students to label—for example, items on maps in social studies or parts of a diagram in science, such as that of the eye in Figure 10.2.

Word banks can be used in conjunction with many of the strategies that follow. They allow ELLs to focus their attention on content by lowering the language demand.

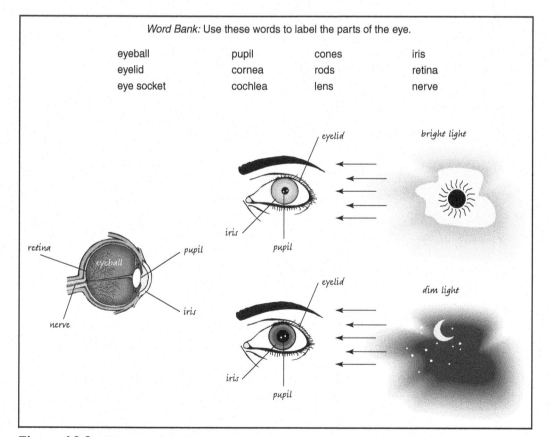

Figure 10.2 Diagram of the Eye

STRATEGY 82   PARE DOWN QUESTIONS AND ASSIGNMENTS

IN CONCEPT

Textbook sections usually end with a set of questions to check comprehension and to encourage critical thinking about the material. An assignment that seems reasonable for other students may feel overwhelming to your ELLs. They will respond better if you assign fewer questions or give fewer assignments, focusing on those that are either more conceptually important or less linguistically complex.

IN PRACTICE

Technique I

Textbook questions aim to check students' understanding of broad concepts and specific details. Some questions are conceptually more central to the topic than others. By assigning only the more important questions, especially in combination with one or more of the other strategies presented in this chapter, you enable your ELLs to focus their efforts on the concepts that are most critical to their understanding.

Technique II

A second approach is to select questions that are linguistically easier to complete. Questions vary in the amount and type of language required to answer them—some needing only a single word or short phrase, others requiring longer, more linguistically complex responses. Particularly for students in the early stages of English language development, consider assigning only questions that are linguistically simple to answer, perhaps in combination with a word bank. For questions involving a longer, more complicated written answer, use one of the alternative assignments described later in this chapter.

STRATEGY 83   PARAPHRASE THE QUESTIONS

IN CONCEPT

Textbook questions are often written at a level of academic English that is difficult for ELLs. Simplifying the wording of questions helps them focus on the content required to respond.

IN PRACTICE

Consider this set of questions:

What are the advantages and disadvantages of using solar energy?

What are the advantages and drawbacks of geothermal energy, hydroelectric power, tidal power, and wind power?

Language learners may be overwhelmed by the density of these questions. Instead, rewrite them in a linguistically more accessible format:

What is good and bad about these things:

1. Solar energy
2. Geothermal energy
3. Hydroelectric power

ENERGY/POWER	GOOD	BAD
Solar		
Hydroelectric		
Geothermal		
Tidal		
Wind		

Figure 10.3 A Response Format That Focuses on Content

4. Tidal power
5. Wind power

When you combine the streamlined question with the simplified response format shown in Figure 10.3, ELLs can really show what they know.

STRATEGY 84   ALLOT EXTRA TIME

IN CONCEPT

Every assignment is twofold for ELLs: They must first decode the language and then deliver the content. They clearly need more time to get their work done.

IN PRACTICE

With this double burden in mind, allow additional time for ELLs to complete readings and assignments. Divide their assignments into smaller chunks, too. Remember that they are learning English at the same time that they are learning *in* English. Extra time lowers stress and makes content feel more learnable for them.

STRATEGY 85   SEPARATE CONTENT FROM LANGUAGE

IN CONCEPT

Although you probably require good grammar and complete sentences as a normal part of your regular assignments, remember that if ELLs could write that way, they wouldn't be classified as ELLs. Separating content from language allows teachers to better assess ELLs' understanding of content.

IN PRACTICE

Evaluate ELL assignments for accuracy of content information only. Focus on key content words or phrases that signify some grasp of the assigned topic, and ignore grammar and spelling errors. Look for the positive—even by trying to pronounce an unrecognizable word phonetically to see if you can bring meaning to it. Using a simple rubric—such as the one discussed in Chapter 11, Strategy 105—helps keep the focus on content. It's important to think about the *message* being delivered, not about the *means*.

STRATEGY 86   OFFER MODELS AND OUTLINES

IN CONCEPT

Many written assignments follow a stylized paragraph format. For these, consider giving ELLs a model, outline, or formatted page to follow. This strategy also appeals to struggling native English-speaking students who, like ELLs, often feel more able to tackle an assignment when they don't have to face a completely blank page.

IN PRACTICE

Think about the kinds of written assignments you give. Most assignments ask students to classify, identify, list, explain, describe, predict, compare, and/or contrast in language much like that in Figure 10.4. Student responses to these tasks follow a basic pattern that can be modeled to lighten the linguistic load. Figures 10.5 and 10.6 illustrate response models for questions in science and social studies, respectively.

Many types of written assignments lend themselves to modeled formatting. Figure 10.7 shows two formats, one for beginners and the other for more advanced levels, that can be

---

- Describe the process by which _____ causes _____.
- Describe the factors that affect _____.
- Describe the characteristics of _____.
- Describe how _____ [changes, uses] _____.
- Describe conditions that cause _____.
- Describe how _____ form _____.
- Name and describe [two] kinds of _____.
- List factors that affect _____.
- List and explain the main types of _____.
- Identify and explain the effects of _____.
- Explain why _____ is Important to _____.
- Give examples of how _____ uses _____.

Figure 10.4   Typical Writing Assignments That Can Be Modeled

---

Figure 10.5   Modeled Response to a Comprehension Question: An Example from Earth Science

Question

Name and define the three major types of interactions among organisms.

Modeled Response

The first type of interaction is called _____.
This means _____.

The second type of interaction is called _____.
This means _____.

The third type of interaction is called _____.
This means _____.

<table>
<tr><td>

Question

What was the goal of the Open Door Policy in China? Did it succeed?

Modeled Response

The goal of the Open Door Policy in China was to_____

_____. It [was, was not]

successful because_____

_____.

</td></tr>
</table>

Figure 10.6 Modeled Response to a Comprehension Question: An Example from Social Studies

For Beginners:	**For Intermediates**
Name of Experiment: _____	**Title:**
We wanted to show that _____ _____.	**Hypothesis:**
We used these materials: _____, _____, _____, _____,	**Equipment:** (Include list of possibilities: Bunsen burner, graduated beaker, test tube, chemical names, etc.)
The first thing we did was _____ _____	
The second thing we did was _____ _____.	**Procedure:** (Include list of verb possibilities: mix, pour, add, stir, shake, heat, etc.)
The third thing we did was _____ _____.	**Observations:** At the beginning of the experiment, the _____ was _____. After _____, the _____ became _____.
What happened was _____ _____.	
This happened because _____ _____.	**Conclusion:** Combining _____ with _____ causes _____.
This shows that _____ _____.	[Heating _____ causes it to _____.] [Adding _____ to _____ produces _____.]

Figure 10.7 Modeled Response for Science Lab Reports

used for reporting on science experiments, demonstrations, or activities. With an already-structured language pattern, ELLs can concentrate on cognitively processing the *content* required for the response instead of first having to focus on creating the language to convey that content. Of equal importance, repeated exposure to formatted patterns teaches ELLs how to formulate appropriate responses when this scaffolding strategy is removed.

STRATEGY 87   DO MORE SMALL GROUP WORK

IN CONCEPT

ELLs can often do assignments in pairs or small groups that they would be unable to do individually. Think of it as an equation: $1 + 1 > 2$. Group work is beneficial for many additional reasons as well.

Figure 10.8 Rules for Successful Group Work

1. Select an appropriate task.
2. Establish ground rules for group work.
3. Group students heterogeneously.
4. Give clear directions.
5. Announce a time frame for completion.
6. Monitor the groups as they work.
7. End with a whole class sharing.

Working in pairs or small groups promotes concept acquisition through social interaction. Small groups offer an authentic, nonthreatening environment that encourages the negotiation of meaning. ELLs gain the opportunity to use academic language and new content vocabulary in a meaningful way; they can clarify their understandings through exchanges of questions and information in a low-risk environment with native English-speaking peers. Group work also personalizes and adds a social element to students' learning and instruction, often bringing about more positive attitudes toward content and class work. It ultimately raises students' feelings of self-confidence, too. In pair and small group work, one plus one really does add up to more than two.

IN PRACTICE

Technique I

Many teachers are reluctant to engage in frequent group work because they worry about loss of control. You can minimize your anxiety and maximize success by following the guidelines outlined in Figure 10.8.

1. Good group work starts with selecting *an appropriate task*. And what exactly is an appropriate task? It is one in which students must work together because each student in the group has only part of the information needed to reach the final product. Students must interact in a cooperative manner to figure out how to make all the pieces work together as a whole.

A good way to understand the concept of an appropriate task is to examine a task that is definitely *not* appropriate. In this unsuccessful group experience, the teacher tells the students that they are going to work in groups to review material from a content reading. Each student in the group gets a worksheet with the same five questions on it and directions to work together to answer the questions.

After several minutes of silence, one student asks the others in the group, "So what did you put for Question 1?" As one student offers an answer, the others quickly write it down. When handled in this way, the task itself necessitates no negotiation of meaning, no communication or cooperation, no need to exchange any information. This is not group work; it is simply an individual task with students sitting in a group.

In good group work, students must rely on other group members' input and information to complete the task. Such tasks are challenging, creative, interesting, and widely adaptable for use in content classrooms. Figure 10.9 illustrates an appropriate task to review content information, in this instance about forest biomes. Students in each group receive envelopes containing information printed on slips of paper. The students work together to categorize items based on characteristics and examples. Review tasks may also ask students to arrange items sequentially or classify items by types and subtypes. Group review is an ideal way to consolidate learning.

Group tasks can promote critical thinking, as shown in Figure 10.10. Here students use the items in their envelopes to make groupings based on as many different sets of shared characteristics as they can think of. One student records the groupings on paper so that

Students sit in groups of three. Each student receives an envelope containing slips of paper with details about forest biomes. Together the students work to sort the details into their appropriate categories.

Group A
Student 1

| Coniferous Forests |
| Location: temperate zone |
| Poor acidic soil |
| Examples: spruce, cedar |
| Trees shed leaves seasonally. |
| Examples: hickory, ash |
| Trees have buttressed trunks. |
| Located in climates with four different seasons |
| Examples: teak, mahogany |

Group A
Student 2

| Deciduous Forests |
| Trees produce cones. |
| Examples: maple, oak |
| Thin, nutrient-poor soil |
| Trees have shallow root systems. |
| Location: tropical zone |
| Biome with the greatest diversity |
| Examples: cypress, balsa |

Group A
Student 3

| Rain Forests |
| Examples: fir, hemlock |
| Location: subarctic regions |
| Trees have needles. |
| Examples: beech, birch |
| Triangular-shaped trees |
| Rich, fertile soil |
| Trees produce seeds. |

Figure 10.9   Group Task: Review the Characteristics of Forest Biomes

Directions: Classify these animals into different groups based on common features or behaviors. How many different classifications can your group think of? Write a list of the animals in each grouping, and specify what they have in common. Then reuse the animals to make another grouping.

Each group receives this envelope:

ape, dog, rabbit, mouse, cat, whale, mole, zebra, horse, giraffe, anteater, goat, monkey, kangaroo, koala, elephant, human being

Figure 10.10   Group Task: Stretch Your Thinking to Classify These Mammals

items can be reused. During class discussion, students then share their lists and explain the basis for each grouping. Tasks like these can generate extra enthusiasm by naming winners for the most groupings, the largest grouping, and the most unusual grouping.

2. Good group work follows a *set of class rules* that have been generated through class discussion before the first group work session takes place. The rules should include these, among others: (a) Stay in your seat; (b) use conversational voices; (c) disagree politely; (d) stay on task.

The rules should be displayed prominently and permanently for teachers to refer to as needed during group sessions. A quirk of human nature makes students more willing to comply with "Remember rule number 2 about using conversational voices" than with the perceived accusation "Your voices are way too loud."

3. Divide the class into *heterogeneous groupings*. Each group should reflect the general mix in the classroom, including diversity of gender, ability, language, and ethnicity. ELLs extend their zone of proximal development (see Chapter 1) by working with more advanced peers, who themselves have the opportunity to reinforce and extend their own understandings.

4. Introduce the topic and task, and give *explicit directions*. Follow up with a clarification check to make sure students know exactly what to do. Use the five-step approach outlined in Strategy 80 in this chapter.

5. Give students a *time frame* for completing the task. People of all ages seem to focus better under the pressure of a deadline. Allocate the minimum amount of time you think the task will take, and announce frequently how many minutes remain to complete the work. If students groan about not being able to finish, you can always extend the time as needed.

6. *Monitor the task* by walking around the room as students work. Many students are more willing to seek clarification from their teacher in the security of small group settings. Consider this a golden opportunity to answer student questions and offer individual help.

7. Bring closure to group work through *whole class sharing*. Even if the group work is ongoing, students should report what they have achieved in this session. Students are naturally curious about the progress and products of the other groups.

If you'd like to do more group work in your classroom, follow these rules and start small. Start with short, paired assignments, and build up to major group projects over time. You'll see that small group activities bring big results.

Technique II

Arrange your classroom to be conducive to group work. A group-ready physical arrangement of desks or tables and chairs precludes the need for students to move into assigned groups, saving time and averting commotion.

STRATEGY 88 TRY PEER TUTORING

IN CONCEPT

ELLs often need a little help to complete an assignment. At the same time and in every class, certain students enjoy the role of helping others. Peer tutoring pairs willing students with ELLs who can use a little coaching on an as-needed basis.

IN PRACTICE

Peer tutoring not only gives ELLs (and other students, too) the opportunity for personalized attention from a more advanced student who is not the teacher, but also offers a rewarding solution for students who consistently complete individual assignments early. These students may be pleased to help others with the task they've finished; they benefit from doing so because explaining to others clarifies and expands their own conceptual knowledge and acts as a strong aid to retention. A final advantage of peer tutoring is that you, the teacher, benefit from your small cadre of assistants who can give you more flexibility to monitor your students' understanding and progress.

ASSIGNMENTS TO PROMOTE STUDENT SUCCESS

The Objective: Differentiate Instructional Activities and Assignments

The Rationale: Academic activities and assignments must promote cognitive challenge. To meet the needs of ELLs' linguistic and conceptual development, teachers must offer differentiated assignments that maintain a high level of cognitive challenge and, at the same time, lower language demand. These assignments should be viewed as stepping-stones on the path toward academic success in an English language environment. The goal is to move ELLs toward full participation in the mainstream activities and assignments required of all students.

STRATEGY 89   ASSIGN DIFFERENT MEANS OF COMPLETING AN ASSIGNMENT

IN CONCEPT

Good teaching recognizes that students within any class function at different levels of ability. It also recognizes two basic psychological principles: Failure breeds failure, and nothing succeeds like success.

IN PRACTICE

After a whole class introduction, such as brainstorming or a reading review, differentiate the way different levels of students will complete the assignment: Advanced level students work individually; intermediate level students work in pairs or triads; and ELLs and other struggling students work in a group directly with you or a qualified other, such as an aide, the ELL or reading resource teacher, or a parent volunteer. For students at this level, supported assignments offer the best chance for success.

STRATEGY 90   USE DIAGRAMS, MAPS, AND CHARTS AS ASSIGNMENTS

IN CONCEPT

Students are often required to engage in factual, descriptive content writing. ELLs can convey much of the same information alternatively through graphic or visual means.

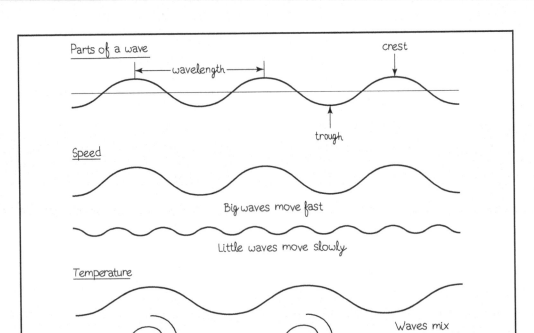

Figure 10.11   All About Waves

IN PRACTICE

ELLs can label a diagram, map, chart, or drawing in place of expository writing. In sub-sequent assignments, they can supplement the information with more detailed descriptive words and explanatory phrases. For example, students could expand the drawings of the eye shown in Figure 10.2 to include additional functional or descriptive data. For other types of diagrams, students can classify items by color coding or can indicate relation-ships among elements by adding arrows. Figure 10.11 uses separate drawings to label and explain a type of ocean movement.

STRATEGY 91   USE SEQUENCED PICTURES AS ASSIGNMENTS

IN CONCEPT

ELLs can show conceptual understanding by drawing or arranging a set of pictures. While other students are completing an assignment in standard paragraph form, language learn-ers can be doing the same assignment through graphics.

IN PRACTICE

Sequenced pictures can depict steps or stages, or they can be as simple as before and after. As in the previous strategy, students can supplement pictures with additional written in-formation. ELL beginners can label parts of each picture, with or without a word bank. ELLs at higher levels can add descriptive and explanatory words, phrases, and sentences.

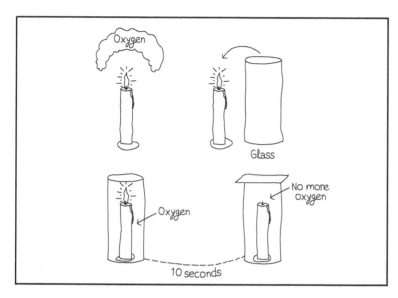

Figure 10.12   Sequenced Pictures of a Science Experiment

Figure 10.12 shows a series of sequenced pictures detailing the process and results of an in-class science experiment. The drawings reflect a clear understanding of the experiment in a way that would have been unattainable for this student in a written report.

 ## STRATEGY 92   USE GRAPHIC ORGANIZERS AS ASSIGNMENTS

IN CONCEPT

It is likely that you make frequent use of graphic organizers as a routine part of your teaching. Now consider using them as alternative assignments for your ELLs.

Certain graphic organizers are widely adaptable, whereas others are more tightly structured. It is important to predetermine the most appropriate graphic format to convey the information that the other students will be expressing in written form. As a differentiated assignment, graphic organizers are challenging and interesting and allow ELLs to convey a large amount of content information in a linguistically simplified form.

IN PRACTICE

Technique I

The *cluster* or *web*, illustrated in Figure 10.13, is valuable for explaining topics with multiple elements and for showing relationships among elements. Figure 10.14 uses a web to show details about the groups in the "Nomads" passage in Chapter 9, Figure 9.5.

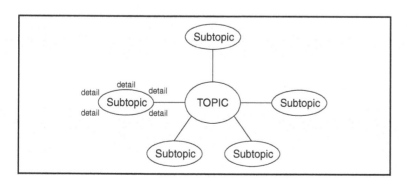

Figure 10.13   The Cluster or Web

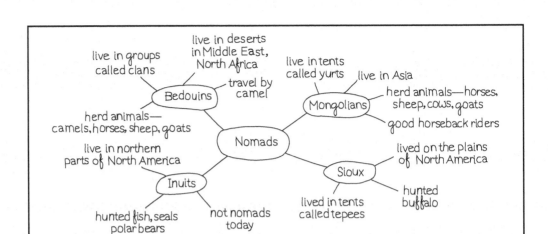

Figure 10.14   The Web in Action: Nomads

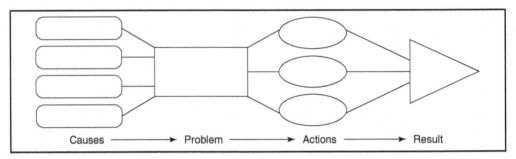

Figure 10.15   The Problem-Solving Organizer

Webs are widely adaptable to all content areas. In social studies, webs can show the complex causes of an event or factors influencing immigration to the United States in the early 1900s. In science, students can use a web to categorize, classify, and describe types and subtypes of substances. In math, students can depict properties of geometric shapes. And in language arts, webs can display details about settings and characters in a novel.

Technique II

A more tightly controlled form of clustering is the *problem-solving organizer*, shown in Figure 10.15. It is a concept map structured around a central issue or problem, showing multiple and sequential instances of cause and effect that result from direct relationships and linear patterns. Figure 10.16 uses this format to graphically depict sources of water pollution in the United States, actions taken to deal with the problem, and the effects of these actions.

In science and social studies, ELLs can complete this type of graphic to demonstrate their understanding of conceptual relationships based on details from their T-notes (see Strategy 72, Chapter 9) or as an alternative to written reports on environmental and societal issues, such as those listed in Figure 10.17. The problem-solving organizer is an ideal way for students to express complex ideas and relationships in a linguistically simplified manner.

Technique III

Venn diagrams are used to show similarities and differences among concepts, events, people, or things. The Venn diagram in its most common form, comparing and contrasting two elements, is well known and often used. Students like it and may enjoy the challenge of completing the triple Venn diagram, shown in Figure 10.18. Like other graphic organizers, Venn diagrams reduce language demand to single words and short phrases and allow ELLs to focus on content.

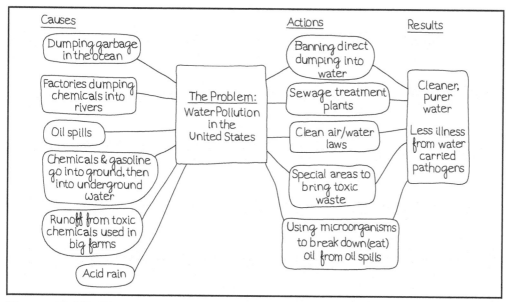

Figure 10.16   The Problem-Solving Organizer in Action: Water Pollution in the United States

Environmental Issues	Societal Issues
Global warming	Slavery
Air or water pollution	Reconstruction of post–Civil War South
Recycling	Rise of labor unions
Endangered species	The Cold War
Depletion of tropical rain forests	Terrorism

Figure 10.17   Some Topics Appropriate for Problem-Solving Organizers in Science and Social Studies

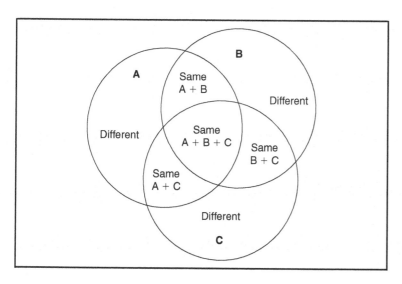

Figure 10.18   Venn Diagram Comparing Three Things

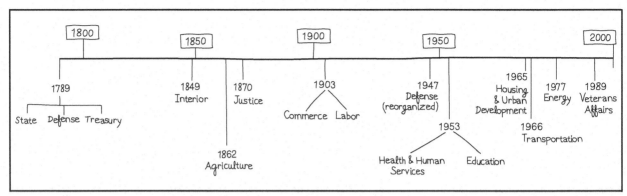

Figure 10.19 The Executive Branch: Executive Departments Timeline

Technique IV

Timelines graphically depict chronological sequences and temporal relationships. They can record developments over periods of time as short as seconds or as long as millennia—for example, the chemical change of matter within seconds, historical development over a single century, or the evolution of human beings over hundreds of thousands of years. The timeline in Figure 10.19 shows the year that each department in the executive branch of U.S. government was created. In subsequent assignments, students can add information to explain the function and focus of each department.

Students can also draw parallel timelines to compare two or more chains of related activity over simultaneous time periods, as in timelines representing developments in land, sea, and air transportation from 1800 to 2000. Or students can expand a segment of a timeline to add greater detail to a short period within the longer timeline. Timelines are readily adaptable, simple to create, and convey a great deal of information in very few words.

Specimen ↓ / Qualities →	Luster	Cleavage	Hardness	Color	Other
A					
B					
C					
D					
E					

Figure 10.20 The Matrix in Science: Comparing Minerals

Nomads	Hunter/Herder	Country/Area	Type of Land	Animals	Tents	Other
Bedouins						
Mongolians						
Sioux						
Inuits						

Figure 10.21   The Matrix in Social Studies: Nomads

Technique V

The *matrix*, also known as semantic feature analysis (Anders & Bos, 1986), is a form of attribute charting. This grid format visually compares key variables of a set of related items. Items to compare are listed in the first column, and qualities to evaluate are listed across the top row. Figure 10.20 shows a matrix for a science lab, comparing characteristics and qualities of five different mineral substances. In social studies, the matrix can compare the character and achievements of selected presidents or the demographic, geographic, and economic data of several countries or regions. Figure 10.21 illustrates the matrix used to show key information again from the "Nomads" passage in Chapter 9. In language arts, the matrix is suitable for noting roles, backgrounds, personality traits, and relationships of characters in a novel. In math, it can be used to compare qualities of geometric shapes.

Information in matrix grids can take a variety of forms. Students can use a plus or minus sign to denote the presence or absence of an element or a number to specify an exact amount or percentage. They can write in descriptive words or short phrases or can give specific representative names. The matrix is versatile and widely adaptable.

STRATEGY 93   BUILD LANGUAGE FROM GRAPHICS

IN CONCEPT

Graphic organizers and other differentiated assignments are productive means for ELLs in the early stages of English language development to show what they know. However, if ELLs were to do only this type of written assignment, they would make slow progress in developing the language and literacy skills required for academic success. Language learners can move from graphics to higher linguistic levels through formatted models, outlines, and sentences that help ELLs transition to independent writing and also offer examples of good sentence and paragraph structure.

IN PRACTICE

Technique I

All graphic organizers can be formatted to build language. Figure 10.22 and 10.23 present samples of formatted models that students can use to convert information from their time-lines and Venn diagrams to complete sentences. Figure 10.24 offers a generic model for the more inherently complex problem-solving organizer, which may require modifications to fit specific topics. You may also want to use the T-notes format discussed in Strategy 72 (Figure 9.7, Chapter 9) or the models or outlines shown in Figures 10.5 to 10.7 earlier in this chapter.

Technique II

At this early stage, ELLs may also need assistance with certain academic words and phrases in their writing. They, and others as well, will benefit from posted lists of common words

Figure 10.22 Using Timelines to Build Language

> **Stage I**
>
> In _____, _____ occurred.
>   [year]   [event]
>
> _____ was invented by _____.
>   [product]
>
> _____ was born.
>   [person]
>
> _____ gained independence.
>   [country]
>
> **Stage II**
>
> _____ began in _____ and ended in _____.
>   [event]   [year]   [year]
>
> **Stage III**
>
> _____ began in the _____
> [Trend or movement]   [ordinal number (first/third/middle)]
>
> _____ of the _____.
> [period (decade/quarter/half)]   [century]

Figure 10.23 Using Venn Diagrams to Build Language

> **Stage I**
>   To compare:
>   [X] were _____, and [Y] were, too.
>   To contrast
>   [X] were _____, but [Y] were _____.
>
> **Stage II**
>   When we compare _____ to _____, we can
> see that some things are the same and some things are different.
>   The things that are the same are _____
> _____
> _____.
>
>   The things that are different are _____
> _____
> _____.

CHAPTER 10 Reinforcing Learning: Activities and Assignments 153

Stage I
The problem was _____.
The causes were _____, _____,
and _____.
The actions taken were _____, _____,
and _____.
The result is _____.

Stage II
    The [issue, problem] of _____
has [several, four, many, etc.] causes. The causes are _____
_____
_____.
    [People, agencies, the government, etc.] have tried to deal
with this [issue, problem] by _____
_____
_____.
    These actions have [helped, not helped] because _____
_____
_____.
    The [issue, problem] of _____ [has
been resolved, needs more action, is unchanged, is growing, etc].

Figure 10.24   Using the Problem-Solving Graphic to Build Language

and phrases associated with writing in your discipline. Additionally, phrases to make writing more cohesive—for example, the lists of transition words shown in Figure 10.25—provide support to help students become better writers. With enough practice and repetition, students can move from the model to effective independent writing.

Showing Addition
  First, second, third
  Additionally, in addition to
  Also
  Another reason
  Furthermore
  The most important reason
  Finally

Showing Chronological Order
  First (second, etc.)
  Next
  Then
  After that
  Finally

Showing Contrast
  On the other hand
  In contrast
  However
  But, yet
  Rather, rather than

Showing Similarity
  Likewise
  Similarly
  In a similar way

Giving Examples
  For example
  For instance
  Such as
  One example of this is _____.
  Another example is _____.

Showing Cause and Effect

Cause	→→→	Effect
X _____.	So,	Y _____.
X _____.	Consequently,	Y _____.
X _____.	As a result,	Y _____.
X _____.	Therefore,	Y _____.

Figure 10.25   Transition Words for Writing Assignments

Figure 10.26 Matching Graphic
Organizers and Writing Genres

Type Of Graphic Organizer	Writing Genre
Venn Diagram	Expository: Compare/Contrast
Timeline	Narrative: Logical/Sequential
Matrix	Expository: Compare/Contrast
Web, Cluster, T-Notes	Expository: Various
Problem-solving Organizer	Expository: Cause and Effect

STRATEGY 94 USE GRAPHIC ORGANIZERS BEFORE WRITTEN WORK

IN CONCEPT

For ELLs at an intermediate level, graphic organizers can serve as a forerunner to written work. Completing an appropriate graphic allows ELLs to first focus exclusively on content before becoming involved with more complex linguistic demands.

IN PRACTICE

ELLs should learn that the graphic organizers discussed earlier relate closely to expository and narrative writing genres generally used in content classes. You can display a chart showing these relationships, as depicted in Figure 10.26. An appropriate graphic, when completed, becomes the basis for planning, organizing, and refining the written piece. This approach is another way to support students as they navigate the path to good academic writing.

IN SUMMARY: ASSIGNMENTS THAT PROMOTE STUDENT SUCCESS

Assignment strategies for ELLs depend upon choosing what is appropriate both to the content and to each student's level of language development. Students need to start with simple tasks that are highly context-embedded before moving on to more complex ones. Remember that academic language develops slowly over a long period of time.

Differentiated assignment strategies allow students to demonstrate their content knowledge while they are building language skills. These assignments balance high levels of cognitive challenge with low levels of language demand so that language learners can begin to experience academic success. Even minimal changes, such as the inclusion of a word bank, can mean the difference between feelings of failure and the beginnings of success.

Try to view assignments as your ELLs might see them. Anticipating areas of language difficulty and making appropriate modifications will go a long way in helping your language learners demonstrate their comprehension of the content you have taught. The small investment of time and effort in putting these ideas to work in your classroom will yield big returns for you and your students.

QUESTIONS FOR DISCUSSION

1. Which of the *12 Guidelines for Practice* presented at the end of Chapter 1 inform the strategies in this chapter?

2. Cite and summarize additional research that gives theoretical and/or experiential support to the strategies discussed in this chapter.

3. All of the assignment strategies presented in this chapter help to extend students' understanding by maintaining high cognitive challenge while lowering linguistic demand. Many of the strategies also support ELLs in other areas. Which of the assignment strategies do you think specifically raise learner self-confidence? Which raise student motivation? Which lower anxiety?

4. Choose an appropriate graphic organizer, and use it to depict concepts presented in this chapter.

5. Working individually if you are now teaching or in pairs if you are not, choose an assignment, and modify it for ELLs. Create different levels of modification for beginners, intermediates, and advanced ELL students.

REFERENCES AND RESOURCES

Anders, P. L., & Bos, C. S. (1986). Semantic feature analysis: An interactive strategy for vocabulary development text comprehension. *Journal of Reading, 29,* 610–617.

Brinton, D. M., & Master, P. (Eds.). (1997). *New ways in content-based instruction.* Alexandria, VA: TESOL.

Bromley, K., Irwin-De Vitis, L., & Modlo, M. (1995). *Graphic organizers: Visual strategies for active learning.* New York: Scholastic Professional Books.

Cohen, E. (1994). *Designing groupwork: Strategies for the heterogeneous classroom.* New York: Teachers College Press.

Forte, I., Pangle, M. A., & Drayton, A. (2001). *ESL content-based language games, puzzles, and inventive exercises.* Nashville, TN: Incentive Publications.

Kagan, S. (1989). *Cooperative resources for teachers.* San Juan Capistrano, CA: Resources for Teachers.

Lyman, F. (1997). Think-pair-share: An expanding teaching technique. *MAA-CIE Cooperative News, 1*(1), 1–2.

Zemelman, S., Daniels, H., & Steineke, N. (2007). *Content area writing: Every teacher's guide.* Portsmouth, NH: Heinemann.

The TechConnection

Use the term *graphic organizers* in your search engine to access many websites from which you can download blank formats of every possible type for all content areas.

STRATEGIES FOR CLASSROOM PRACTICE: ASSESSMENT

CHAPTER 11

CLASSROOM ASSESSMENTS: DID THEY LEARN WHAT YOU TAUGHT?

Increased emphasis on school accountability has turned the spotlight on student assessment. The attention of all shareholders—students, teachers, administrators, and parents—is now focused on annual standardized tests that determine whether students have met state and local standards. The importance of *classroom* assessment practices, however, should not be overlooked.

The purpose of assessment is to inform teachers about the progress and achievement of their students: where they are now and what they need next. Results from statewide assessments are neither timely nor specific enough to serve this purpose. Well-written teacher-made tests, however, *can* provide this information. They can serve as an instructional tool to maximize learning and ultimately raise performance levels on high-stakes tests.

Good classroom tests assess students' understanding of concepts the teacher has taught; they contain questions that do not come as a surprise to students. Good tests are made up of items that vary in type and content demand, balancing simple, factual questions with questions that elicit higher level reasoning skills and critical thinking. Good tests also differentiate among students' varying levels of understanding and depth of knowledge. Classroom tests that meet these criteria are not easy to create under the best of circumstances. In classes with ELLs, the challenge is even greater.

Creating classroom tests that allow ELLs to show what they know puts teachers on the horns of a dilemma because essay questions require high-level *writing* skills and multiple-choice questions require high-level *reading* skills. The question for teachers, then, is twofold: How can teachers create good tests that, first, meet the criteria set out here and, second, evaluate ELLs' mastery of subject matter in a way that separates content knowledge from English language knowledge? This important question is best answered after a brief exploration of the difficulties that essay questions and multiple-choice questions present for ELLs and the pitfalls of writing good multiple-choice questions.

ESSAY QUESTIONS, MULTIPLE-CHOICE QUESTIONS, AND LANGUAGE DEMAND

Essay questions require English language *writing* skills that are generally beyond the level of most ELL students. In the multistep process of essay writing, students must first decode what the question is asking; then mentally retrieve, select, and organize content knowledge to address the question; and finally structure that information in a cohesively written answer. The fact that some native English-speaking students struggle with essay responses offers an insight into the degree of challenge this format presents to ELLs.

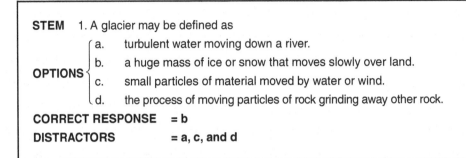

STEM 1. A glacier may be defined as

OPTIONS
- a. turbulent water moving down a river.
- b. a huge mass of ice or snow that moves slowly over land.
- c. small particles of material moved by water or wind.
- d. the process of moving particles of rock grinding away other rock.

CORRECT RESPONSE = b

DISTRACTORS = a, c, and d

Figure 11.1 Parts of a Multiple-Choice Question

Multiple-choice questions require English language *reading* skills that are generally beyond the level of ELL students. Multiple-choice questions often use more complex sentence structure and different synonyms from those appearing in the original text.

Well-written multiple-choice questions demand critical analysis of four or more options in order to select the best answer. (Multiple-choice question terminology is shown in Figure 11.1.) Wordy options or those with subtle distinctions, such as the examples in Figure 11.2, effectively prevent ELLs from demonstrating their content knowledge. For ELLs, a multiple-choice test of several pages presents a formidable reading load. And questions that combine option choices, such as those shown in Figure 11.3, increase the reading load even further. Questions like those require students to first read and comprehend the information in the answer choices, then match the correct facts to the question, and finally weed out the varying number of incorrect choices. Combining option choices in multiple-choice questions simply adds an additional level of confusion for many students, not only the ELLs.

1. The Battle of Antietam was important because
   a. the South regained all of Virginia but Stonewall Jackson was killed.
   b. Confederate troops abandoned Kentucky and increased Grant's determination to win.
   c. Richmond was saved from capture and Northern forces retreated.
   d. the Confederate retreat gave Lincoln the occasion to issue the Emancipation Proclamation.
2. The people known as "Copperheads" were
   a. policemen exempt from fighting to maintain order in Northern cities.
   b. miners from the North who formed a fighting unit in the Union Army.
   c. men who deserted shortly after being paid for enlisting in the Confederate Army.
   d. Democrats demanding an immediate armistice and peaceful settlement of the war.
3. The North and South had different opinions about tariffs. Choose the statement that is true:
   a. The North wanted high tariffs because it helped sell tobacco and cotton in foreign countries.
   b. The North wanted high tariffs because it made the price of foreign goods higher.
   c. The South wanted high tariffs because it helped factories make better goods.
   d. The South wanted high tariffs because it was good for foreign trade.

Figure 11.2 Typical Multiple-Choice Questions About the American Civil War

Figure 11.3 Confusing Option Choices

Changes in energy consumption in the United States during the
past 100 years are due to
    (a) population growth.
    (b) industrialization.
    (c) modernization.
    (d) medical advances.
A. Both (a) and (b)
B. Both (b) and (c)
C. All but (d)
D. None of the above
E. All of the above

Figure 11.3 Confusing Option Choices

Multiple-choice tests are challenging for ELLs for still another reason: The format is unique to the American school system. The majority of students from other countries have had no experience with this common type of test before their arrival in U.S. classrooms. That lack of familiarity with the format makes multiple-choice tests even more difficult for ELLs.

The Pitfalls of Multiple-Choice Tests

The single reason that multiple-choice tests have become the preferred test format is that they are easy to score. It is their primary advantage, and with so many demands on teachers' time, it is an important one. This type of test, however, has many inherent disadvantages and pitfalls. Although there are only a few rules for writing good multiple-choice questions, there are many ways to write bad ones.

High-stakes standardized tests generally avoid the pitfalls because they are generated, field-tested, and analyzed by professional test makers. But classroom teachers have neither the time nor the expertise to create tests with this level of sophistication. Consequently, multiple-choice tests created by teachers for classroom use are often flawed.

The foremost problem with teacher-made multiple-choice tests lies in the challenge of writing questions that assess students' deep conceptual understandings. Higher order questions that assess critical thinking and problem solving may produce options that are overly long, confusing, silly, or illogical. The question in Figure 11.4, for example, seeks an inferential judgment. The stem is wordy and complicated, and the options are indistinct, confusing, and open to interpretation.

Distractors present another area of concern: They must seem like reasonable choices with appeal to those who don't know the correct answer. To be a true test of students' knowledge, questions must have distractors that are chosen by at least some of the test takers, unlike those in Figure 11.5.

Based on the past relationship between Shoshanah and her
mother, we could predict that the years to come would find them
    a.   distant but with episodes of closeness.
    b.   close but with episodes of distance.
    c.   in a generally unsatisfying relationship.
    d.   in a generally satisfying relationship.

Figure 11.4 A Poor Attempt to Assess Critical Thinking

Figure 11.5 Unreasonable Distractors

Wild animals are considered domesticated when they
a. enjoy being with people.
b. are toilet trained.
c. eat burgers and fries.
d. are taught to work for human beings.

Figure 11.6 Assessing Factual Knowledge: Best Use of Multiple-Choice Questions

A nation with a population that is not increasing is
a. Peru.
b. Guatemala.
c. Sweden.
d. Kenya.

On the positive side, teachers have an abundance of good option choices for testing simple facts—the who, what, when, where, and how questions. There will never be a shortage of dates, names, places, and definitions to use as distractors to the correct answer. Testing the type of knowledge shown in Figure 11.6 is using the multiple-choice format to its best advantage.

However, even in the best multiple-choice application, the issue of backwash—the effect that tests have on actual learning—remains. A perennial question from students is "Is this going to be on the test?" The answer to that question determines whether or not they will make the effort to learn that particular set of data. But even without this question, students quickly perceive what they actually need to study for classroom tests. If teachers discuss concepts, relationships, and implications in class but test just the facts, students know that it's just the facts that really count, and those are what they study and learn. That is backwash.

Multiple-choice tests also create negative backwash on the way students process information. The format requires students simply to recognize and select the correct option when they read it. In the world outside the classroom, those who are asked a question (other than "May I take your order?") are not often given choices from which to select a correct response. They are expected to *produce* an answer. In real life, people need to engage in high-level cognitive processing to become effective problem solvers. Multiple-choice testing does not give them much practice toward this end.

Teacher-made multiple-choice questions present still more potential pitfalls. The wording of the stem may point to the correct option, as shown in Figure 11.7, or the

A network of all the feeding relationships in an ecosystem is called a
a. ecological pyramid.
b. energy chain.
c. food web.
d. energy web.
[Options a, b, and d can be eliminated because they would require the stem to end with *an* instead of *a*, leaving c as the only grammatically correct choice.]

Figure 11.7 Stem Wording That Points to the Correct Answer

Of the following, the factor most likely to result in a decrease in the size of a specific population is

    a.   improved medical care.

    b.   increased food availability.

    c.   famine.

    d.   industrialization.

[The three distractors are all positive factors. Only the correct choice—c. famine—is negative.]

Figure 11.8 Options That Highlight the Correct Answer

options themselves may point to the correct choice, as in Figure 11.8. Also, information in one test question may inadvertently offer a clue that helps answer another question on the test. In addition, questions that include the words *never* or *always* may penalize the more knowledgeable students who think of exceptions that lead them away from the intended choice. And guessing and cheating are factors as well. In sum, multiple-choice tests may not be the best indicator of students' true knowledge.

SEPARATING LANGUAGE FROM CONTENT IN ASSESSMENTS

The Objective: Modify Testing Techniques

The Rationale: To assess ELLs' real understanding of content, teachers must create tests that assess content knowledge separately from English language knowledge. This means finding formats for assessment that go beyond essay and multiple-choice questions. One approach involves modifying testing techniques; simple changes can make big differences in student performance on tests.

 ## STRATEGY 95   OFFER TRUE–FALSE QUESTIONS

IN CONCEPT

The ELLs in your class will be more able to demonstrate their content knowledge when you create a parallel test for them by replacing the stem and options of multiple-choice questions with a linguistically simplified format. True–false questions are one way to do this.

IN PRACTICE

You can change the multiple-choice question shown in Figure 11.7 to a complete sentence that uses the multiple-choice stem plus any one of the options, as shown in Figure 11.9. To ensure that these questions are not just random guesses, however, for every question marked *false*, students must cross out the part that makes it incorrect and write in its place the word or phrase that corrects it. No credit should be given to a false question that is not properly corrected.

Original Multiple-Choice Question

A network of all the feeding relationships in an ecosystem is called a

    e. ecological pyramid.

    f. energy chain.

    g. food web.

    h. energy web.

Substitute True–False Question:

T (F) A network of all the feeding relationships in an ecosystem is called ~~an energy web~~ *a food web.*

Figure 11.9   Changing a Multiple–Choice Question into a True–False Question

STRATEGY 96   USE IDENTIFICATION QUESTIONS

IN CONCEPT

Identification questions can assess knowledge of a large amount of information while significantly lowering the amount of reading involved. This format offers teachers the additional advantages of being easy to write and simple to score.

Forest Biomes

Write the letter of the forest biome to which each statement below applies.

    C = Coniferous forests

    D = Deciduous forests

    R = Rain forests

_____1. Location: temperate zone

_____2. Location: subarctic regions of North America, Europe, Asia

_____3. Location: tropical zone

_____4. Location: climate with four different seasons

_____5. Trees have buttressed trunks

_____6. Trees are triangular shaped

_____7. Trees produce seeds

_____8. Trees shed leaves seasonally

_____9. Trees have needles

_____10. Trees have shallow root systems

_____11. Soil: poor, acidic

_____12. Soil: thin, nutrient poor, nutrients recycled back into trees

_____13. Soil: rich, fertile

_____14. Examples: cypress, balsa, teak, mahogany

_____15. Examples: maple, oak, beech, ash, hickory, birch

_____16. Examples: hemlock, fir, spruce, cedar

_____17. Biome with the greatest biodiversity

Figure 11.10   Using Identification Questions to Lower the Amount of Reading

IN PRACTICE

For tests that assess understanding of two or more contrasting concepts, as in Figure 11.10, replace multiple-choice questions with a format in which a series of simple statements must be labeled with the concept they describe. This format minimizes reading and allows students to demonstrate knowledge of a large body of simple, factual information.

STRATEGY 97   GIVE COMPLETION QUESTIONS

IN CONCEPT

Completion questions, using the multiple-choice stem but replacing the options with a space or blank lines, are another means of linguistically simplifying multiple-choice tests. Completion questions offer several advantages: They lower the reading and language demand so ELLs can focus on content. They avoid the negative backwash of multiple-choice questions by having students actually produce an answer rather than just recognize it. And completion questions can be used in conjunction with a content word/phrase bank as a supplement for students in the early stages of English language development.

IN PRACTICE

Technique I
ELLs will respond more easily to the three questions in Figure 11.2 if they are changed to the completion format shown in Figure 11.11. In these questions, all the blanks intentionally appear at the end of the stem, making them cognitively easier to process than blanks appearing at the beginning or in the middle of the sentence.

Technique II
The cloze technique involves a series of completion-type questions. In the content cloze format, the teacher composes several paragraphs on a topic and then systematically deletes key content words or phrases, replacing them with blanks for the student to complete. Figure 11.12 shows the use of a cloze passage to assess knowledge of the circulatory system in the human body. Again, beginner and low-intermediate-level ELLs could use a word bank for assistance.

Giving ELLs true–false, identification, and completion questions in place of multiple-choice puts the focus where it belongs: on content, not on reading ability. These other types of questions offer the additional benefit of avoiding many of the pitfalls of multiple-choice testing. And from the teacher's perspective, they are easier to write than multiple-choice questions and almost as fast to score.

Figure 11.11 Using Completion Questions to Put the Focus on Content

1. The Battle of Antietam was important because _____
   _____ .

2. "Copperheads" were people who _____
   _____ .

3. The North wanted _____(high or low?) tariffs because
   _____ .

Circulation

Circulation is the pumping of blood around the body. The _____ is the main organ of the circulatory system. It never rests. It _____ and _____ in a regular, even motion, about _____ times a minute. It makes the blood travel around your body bringing _____ to muscles and other parts of the body.

Tubes that carry blood around the body are called _____. There are three types of tubes that carry blood—arteries, veins, and capillaries. Each type has a different job to do. Arteries _____ (what do they do?).

Veins _____ (what do they do?).

And capillaries _____ (what do they do?).

Blood is made of four main parts. The largest part of blood is called _____. Its job is to _____.

The three other parts of the blood are (1)_____ whose job is to_____;

(2) _____ whose job is to _____

_____; and (3) _____ whose job is to _____

_____.

Figure 11.12   The Cloze Technique

STRATEGY 98   USE GRAPHICS TO EXPRESS KNOWLEDGE

IN CONCEPT

Information from essay questions can also be linguistically simplified. In place of sentences and paragraphs, ELLs can use visuals and graphics for their responses.

IN PRACTICE

In response to an essay question, ELLs can demonstrate their understanding of complex concepts and relationships with graphic organizers, T-lists, sequenced pictures, or labeled diagrams and maps. Many of the strategies in Chapter 10 can be used effectively for assessment.

STRATEGY 99   BEND THE RULES

IN CONCEPT

Teachers give little thought to the standard rules of testing that have existed for many decades. There are, however, some rules concerning communication while testing that you may want to revisit and consider modifying.

IN PRACTICE

Technique I

Start with allowing ELLs to use a *bilingual dictionary* for words they are unsure of in English. *Offer clarification* of test items that puzzle ELLs. *Answer questions* that don't influence or give away content. *Substitute a synonym* for an unknown word. *Paraphrase directions* that confuse ELLs. For a complicated test, consider having a bilingual student, parent, or volunteer *translate the directions* into the students' native language. It might even be feasible to *translate the questions* themselves. In addition to any of these modifications, you might also *allow rewrites and test corrections* to improve grades and demonstrate more complete understanding.

Technique II

Shorter tests feel more doable for ELLs. Try using *flexible timing.* Think about dividing the test into several shorter sections given separately. You can also *select only concepts of primary importance.* Question 2 in Figure 11.2 is an example of a question that could reasonably be eliminated.

Another means to shorten a test and decrease the reading load is to *reduce the number of options* on each multiple-choice question. This has the additional advantage of giving ELLs practice with this question type without overwhelming them. In combination with any of these strategies, you could also allow ELLs to *use their textbooks* during the test. For beginners, you might even consider noting a page number next to each question.

Technique III

A seemingly radical idea is to *pair* two ELL students for the test. Working together may allow them to complete more of an exam than either one of them could do individually. In this case, the test is actually helping them learn. It may also be possible for you to give sections of a test as an *individual oral exam* if time allows. Oral language is often an easier modality for ELLs to use to convey content knowledge.

Technique IV

Finally, consider adding a section at the end of all classroom multiple-choice tests called *Explain Yourself.* Here students can offer explanations to justify their choice of an answer—perhaps a question for which two options seemed equally true, or one in which none seemed right. For ELLs whose language development is not yet at a stage to explain themselves, you can substitute "I need to talk to you about question number _____." An explanation, written or oral, may be good enough for you to give partial or even full credit.

SEPARATING LANGUAGE FROM CONTENT IN ASSESSMENTS

The Objective: Don't Test at All!

The Rationale: Not testing at all doesn't *really* mean not giving any tests. It means using alternative assessment techniques and measures in place of, or as a complement to, more traditional forms of tests. It is a productive way of evaluating ELLs' content knowledge.

A caveat to alternative testing is that the alternative formats themselves may present their own sets of language demands for ELLs. And because they don't necessarily look or feel like tests, students and their parents may need an explanation in order to understand how these techniques are being used for assessment.

STRATEGY 100   USE PERFORMANCE-BASED ASSESSMENT

IN CONCEPT

Performance-based assessments allow students to demonstrate their content knowledge through concrete examples: writing samples, projects, visuals and graphics, oral reports, PowerPoint and other presentations, and portfolios. To increase students' ability to produce high-quality results, teachers must clearly explain their criteria of evaluation, as discussed in Strategies 106 and 107 in this chapter.

IN PRACTICE

Before the assessment, give students copies of the scoring rubric, checklist, point distribution chart, or anything else that will be used for grading. Students' product outcomes, especially those of ELLs, will benefit from the students' seeing models and examples of work that meet high standards.

STRATEGY 101   USE PORTFOLIOS FOR ASSESSMENT

IN CONCEPT

Portfolio assessment has gained popularity among teachers and school administrators in recent years. Used in conjunction with other forms of evaluation, portfolio assessment offers students an additional means of demonstrating their developing understanding. Portfolio evaluation involves a process of shared responsibility and participation for students and teachers. It is an approach to classroom assessment that feels almost democratic.

IN PRACTICE

In class discussion, students and teachers make decisions about standards for selection of portfolio items and about criteria for evaluation. Throughout the grading period, teachers and students confer, discuss, and assess the pieces of work that will go into the students' portfolio collections as evidence of their achievements.

Portfolios invite students to become active participants in their own evaluations. They empower students as well by enabling them to demonstrate content competence through a wider range of measures than paper-and-pencil tests provide. Portfolio collections document growth of both content knowledge and language skills over a period of time.

STRATEGY 102   USE INFORMATION JOURNALS FOR ASSESSMENT

IN CONCEPT

Like portfolios, information journals (also called content journals or learning logs) can be used as a valid means of evaluation. For ELL students who write in them on a regular basis, information journals will show progress over time.

IN PRACTICE

Students use information journals to record content information. Entries are wide-ranging across all content areas. Sentence starters such as "I discovered that . . . ," "I learned that . . . ," and "I saw that . . . " can help students get started.

Information journals that use a structured, concise, and objective format such as learning logs (see Chapter 9, Figure 9.10), T-notes (see Chapter 9, Figure 9.7), and K–W–L charts (see Chapter 5, Figures 5.2–5.3) will simplify the evaluation process. Students may be extra motivated to work on their information journals knowing that they are being used for assessment purposes.

STRATEGY 103   TRY SELF-ASSESSMENT AND PEER ASSESSMENT

IN CONCEPT

Self-assessment and peer assessment constitute a powerful and positive tool when used as an adjunct to other forms of evaluation. Students develop an understanding that it is normal to find some concepts easier to learn than others, and it is also normal for even quick learners to still have questions. Students feel empowered by contributing to their own evaluations. In fact, they often assess themselves more rigorously than their teachers might.

Teachers who routinely use self- and peer assessment—at the end of chapters or units or at the end of the week, month, or grading period—find that it opens and maintains a line of communication with their students. Through their insights and observations, students often help teachers develop ideas for more effective teaching. Few assessment techniques are as positive as this one.

IN PRACTICE

Teachers can create individual checklists that students complete to reflect their personal feelings about comprehension of text or topic, contributions to class or group work, and areas of strength, weakness, and/or improvement. Figures 11.13 and 11.14 show examples of checklists in which items can be changed or added as needed. Teachers can get additional feedback from student self-assessments by including an area for extra explanation and input, either at the bottom, as in Figure 11.14, or by adding a fourth column to the checklist in Figure 11.13. An even more individually expressive format for self- and peer assessment involves completing a set of open-ended questions, as shown in Figure 11.15.

Textbook: Chapter 12	☹	😐	☺
WEEK OF _____ I understood the reading. I highlighted the text. I used a dictionary. I worked with a friend.			

Figure 11.13   Self-Assessment Checklist I

Textbook: Chapter 12	Usually Not	Sometimes	Almost Always
WEEK OF_____ I understood the assigned reading. I highlighted the text. I made note cards. I made vocabulary cards. I participated in class discussions. I asked for help when I was unsure.			
I also want to tell you that _____ _____ _____			

Figure 11.14 Self-Assessment Checklist II

1. The concepts I understood were _____.
2. The concepts I didn't understand were _____.
3. I think I improved in _____.
4. I think I need more improvement in _____.
5. I need special help with _____.
6. The kind of help I need is _____.

Figure 11.15 Open-Ended Self-Assessment

SEPARATING LANGUAGE FROM CONTENT IN ASSESSMENTS

The Objective: Grade English Language Learners to Promote Success

The Rationale: The issue of grading ELLs is a complex one. It seems like a double penalty to give ELLs a low grade in social studies, math, science, or language arts because their English language skill level prevents them from expressing their knowledge. It is well-known that students who regularly get low grades see themselves as failures and, as such, make even less effort to achieve. On the other hand, is it fair to your native English-speaking students who have worked hard to earn good grades if you use a different system to grade your ELLs?

Grading ELLs requires a delicate balance. It makes little sense to grade down ELLs who, based on their language proficiency level, have no chance of completing an assignment to grade level standards. Neither does it make sense to accept lower level work from ELLs who are capable of producing a better product. Teachers need to be clear about their goals for instruction and about the academic and linguistic levels of their students; then, based on the instruction provided and the students' backgrounds, teachers need to give grades that reflect standards that students have a reasonable chance of achieving.

You can reduce grading issues to some degree by modifying your regular tests and using alternative assessments. With more opportunity and varied means for ELLs to show what they know, you will gain more accurate feedback to use in grading them. Beyond this are several other ways to make grading fairer for your ELLs.

STRATEGY 104 FOCUS ON CONTENT ONLY

IN CONCEPT

Just as the focus was on content in ELLs' oral participation and written assignments discussed in Strategies 54 and 85, it is equally important to focus on content in all forms of assessment. Separating content knowledge from the language used to express it allows teachers to more fairly evaluate ELLs' conceptual understandings.

IN PRACTICE

When you evaluate students' test responses and other forms of written work, look closely for key content words in short answers. You may find enough there to give at least partial credit, even if the whole answer is not completely comprehensible to you. An additional option is to invite the student to elaborate on an answer orally.

STRATEGY 105 GRADE WRITTEN WORK WITH A RUBRIC

IN CONCEPT

A teacher-made rubric can make grading easier for you and fairer for your students. Unlike state- or districtwide rubrics that are designed to assess all levels of writing skills from virtual perfection to near-total lack of skills, rubrics created for daily classroom use more narrowly reflect the highest to lowest expectations for *your* student population. Your own personal rubric prevents perfection from being the enemy of the good.

IN PRACTICE

The simple rubric shown in Figure 11.16 takes a holistic view of student writing. It challenges students to do their best and, at the same time, rewards them for their efforts at their current level of ability. The benefits of rubric scoring are many.

Rubrics allow students to experience success by having their written products evaluated against reasonable standards, not against perfection. Teachers who use rubrics to evaluate writing find that they focus on what is *there*, rather than what is *not* there. Students can recognize the expectation of excellence, but within the boundaries of *realistic achievement* for the group. As students progress in their English language development, expectations rise. Rubrics can reflect these higher standards by including additional elements for evaluation, as shown in Figure 11.17.

Figure 11.16 A Usable Rubric

3	Meaningful content on assigned topic Errors do not interfere with reader comprehension
2	Some meaningful content on assigned topic Errors require some rereading for reader comprehension
1	Little meaningful content on assigned topic Errors require frequent or constant rereading for reader comprehension

A single rubric can be used with all types of writing—homework questions, short answers on tests, research reports, virtually any written product. Teachers find that familiarity with their own rubric and the rubric scoring process makes grading writing assignments much quicker and easier, even those sets of essays that teachers often dread.

The process is simple. Start with a rapid scan of student papers to separate them into two piles—the betters and the *"worsers."* Read the worsers first. This group will receive scores of 1 or 2, or perhaps 1+ if you feel a paper is better than a 1 but not quite a 2. When you finish reading the papers in the first group, move on to the second set, scoring those 2, 2+, or 3. You *just read*—you do not correct anything on any paper. Resist that temptation; simply focus on the two qualities of the rubric—the amount of meaningful content and the readability of what is written there.

3	Meaningful content on assigned topic **+ with many supporting details** Errors do not interfere with reader comprehension
2	Some meaningful content on assigned topic **+ with some supporting details** Errors require some rereading for reader comprehension
1	Little meaningful content on assigned topic **+ with few or no supporting details** Errors require frequent or constant rereading for reader comprehension

3	Meaningful content on assigned topic **+ with many supporting details** **+ presented in an organized manner** Errors do not interfere with reader comprehension
2	Some meaningful content on assigned topic **+ with some supporting details** **+ presented in a loosely organized manner** Errors require some rereading for reader comprehension
1	Little meaningful content on assigned topic **+ with few or no supporting details** **+ presented in an unorganized manner** Errors require frequent or constant rereading for reader comprehension

Figure 11.17 Rubrics Reflecting Rising Expectations

STRATEGY 106   USE FOCUS SCORING FOR WRITTEN WORK

IN CONCEPT

An adjunct to rubric scoring is *focus scoring,* also called single or primary trait scoring. Here, a single, preannounced element is evaluated in addition to the rubric score.

IN PRACTICE

Focus scoring offers the flexibility of focusing student attention on one specific element that you have emphasized in your teaching or that you want to encourage in student writing. Single traits can range from basic to complex—for example, correct capitalization of proper nouns, proper scientific notation, or an opening sentence stating the overall topic and position.

In advance of the assigned writing, announce the focus trait you will be evaluating in addition to your rubric scoring. Students will find that concentrating on one trait at a time is much more doable and less anxiety-producing than trying to write a faultless paper.

STRATEGY 107   WRITE INTERACTIVE COMMENTS

IN CONCEPT

Interactive comments, highlighted in Figure 11.18, are those in which the reader *as a person* directly addresses the writer *as a person* as if in conversation. These comments respond to the *content* of the writing, not the quality. They make writers feel that their ideas have been read and affirmed, creating an affectively positive writing environment.

Look at the two comments in Figure 11.19. Both comments are positive. However, the first is an evaluation coming from a higher authority whereas the second, an interactive comment, makes the writer feel validated because it is a personal reaction from the reader that speaks directly to the writer. It makes the writer want to write more, just to be rewarded with more comments like it.

> Interactive comments are those in which
> the reader *as a person*
> responds to
> the writer *as a person*
> as if in conversation.

Figure 11.18 Interactive Comments

> "Excellent writing!"
>
> "I loved reading this!"

Figure 11.19 Widely Differing Comments

IN PRACTICE

Interactive comments at the end of each student's paper present the reader's overall reaction to the writing. Comments should attempt to mention something specific that you particularly liked, as in "I loved your description of _____. I could almost see it!" Your reactions should be honest but phrased in a positive manner. Try softening a negative comment with something like one of these:

"I like what you wrote about _____. I wish you had written more."

"I think you may have some good things to say about _____, but I had a hard time reading your handwriting."

Perhaps even more importantly, interactive comments, in the form of questions and comments in the margins of students' work, can develop student writing skills better than all the corrections you might make on those papers. If, as you read, you think to yourself that very little detail is included in the paper, try writing specific questions, such as those shown in Figure 11.20 , to guide students toward the kinds of detail they might have included. Most students who read the traditional teacher comment "Needs more detail" have no idea what they omitted or what they might have included. Similarly, instead of "This doesn't address the topic," try something like "This is interesting. Can you explain how it applies to _____?" Write interactive comments in the margins and at the end as you read each paper for rubric scoring. One strategy for writing interactive comments is called TAG, outlined in Figure 11.21 . It systematically focuses on the positive at the same time that it helps improve student writing skills.

Tune in to the thoughts and reactions that go through your head while you are reading. After a bit of practice, your comments will flow quite readily. Combining rubric and focus scoring with interactive comments creates a powerful evaluation program that takes the dread out of assessing a set of papers. And wouldn't you be surprised, as one teacher was, if your students asked whether they could revise their papers to respond to your queries?

Figure 11.20 Interactive Comments Promoting Writing Skills Development

Try these questions instead of "Needs more detail."

What issues did they disagree on?

Why did they disagree?

How many men were lost in the battle?

How many months did this take?

What types of work were they involved in?

What color did it change to? Why did this happen?

Which other materials did we use in the experiment?

What else made him look frightening?

Can you give some more examples?

Figure 11.21 TAG: An Interactive Comment Strategy

T	Tell something you liked
A	Ask a question
G	Give a suggestion

STRATEGY 108   GIVE GRADES FOR PROGRESS AND EFFORT

IN CONCEPT

Progress and effort grades are another strategy to be considered. They are a means of showing students that you recognize the difficulties they are going through.

IN PRACTICE

Progress grades focus on ELLs' individual growth and development instead of evaluating them against expectations set for native English-speaking students. You can develop a system—perhaps an asterisk following the grade—to denote that you are using an alternative grading system. Including some positive comments will also make ELLs feel more successful, even if their actual grades are low.

Effort grades, used in tandem with content grades, show ELLs that you recognize their persistence, even in the face of less-than-acceptable outcomes. If your school has a large number of ELLs, this might be something that the administration could consider adopting as a schoolwide grading system.

STRATEGY 109   OFFER EXTRA CHANCES AND SELF-GRADING OPTIONS

IN CONCEPT

People learn from their mistakes, or at least they try to. Students should be allowed to learn from their mistakes, too.

IN PRACTICE

Technique I
Consider allowing ELLs to retake a test, to correct an assignment, or to hand in a second or even third draft of a piece of writing. Your interactive comments, as well as partner or small group editing meetings after papers and tests have been returned, will give students ideas for improvement.

Technique II
ELLs can be offered opportunities to collaborate with peers *before* they submit their work for grading. Both writer and editor(s) can earn an improved grade for their work. Partner or small group peer discussion and correction can have a positive effect on grades.

Technique III
Have your students self-evaluate their work. What grade do they think they realistically deserve? Your first thought may be that students will overvalue their products, but in reality many students will grade themselves more harshly than you will.

IN SUMMARY: SEPARATING LANGUAGE FROM CONTENT IN ASSESSMENT

Combining strategies that modify grading procedures with those that use scaffolded or alternative assessment approaches will produce a more accurate picture of your ELLs' actual content knowledge, allowing them to show what they know and earn grades that better reflect their understanding. They will find themselves more motivated to learn when you evaluate them in ways that place success within their reach. You will be opening their door to academic achievement.

QUESTIONS FOR DISCUSSION

1. Which of the *12 Guidelines for Practice* presented at the end of Chapter 1 inform the strategies in this chapter?

2. In pairs, examine a teacher-made multiple-choice test. Can you find any pitfalls? How would you eliminate the pitfalls that you found?

3. In pairs, choose a test that one or both of you have used in your classrooms, and analyze it through the eyes of an ELL. What would have been especially difficult or confusing? Identify specific questions that are high in language demand, and determine ways to decrease the linguistic load so that ELLs could more easily demonstrate their understanding of the content.

4. Using a student textbook in a content area of your choice, create a test for a class, and then modify it for your ELLs. Pair up with a colleague, and critique each other's tests.

5. Obtain a set of student papers containing expository writing. Grade them holistically, using the process explained in Strategy 105, and then add interactive comments. (Note: Your instructor may want to photocopy a set of three or four student papers to do this as a whole class assignment.)

6. What are the relative benefits and disadvantages of using modified paper-and-pencil tests on the one hand and alternative assessment techniques on the other? Consider the issues of reliability and validity, structure, and creativity.

REFERENCES AND RESOURCES

Alvermann, D. E., & Phelps, S. F. (2005). Assessment of students. In P. A. Richard-Amato & M. A. Snow (Eds.), *Academic success for English language learners: Strategies for K–12 mainstream teachers* (pp. 311–341). White Plains, NY: Pearson Education.

De Fina, A. A. (1992). *Portfolio assessment: Getting started.* New York: Scholastic Professional Books.

Gibbons, P. (2005). Writing in a second language across the curriculum. In P. A. Richard-Amato & M. A. Snow (Eds.), *Academic success for English language learners: Strategies for K–12 mainstream teachers* (pp. 275–310). White Plains, NY: Pearson Education.

Haley, M., and Austin, T. (2004). *Content-based second language teaching and learning: An interactive approach.* Boston, MA: Allyn & Bacon.

O'Malley, J. M., and Valdez Pierce, L. (1996). *Authentic assessment for English language learners: Practical approaches for teachers.* Reading, MA: Addison-Wesley.

Stiggins, R., Arter, J. A., Chappius, J., & Chappius, S. (2004). *Classroom assessment for student learning: Doing it right—using it well.* Portland, OR: Assessment Training Institute.

Valdez Pierce, L. (2003). *Assessing English language learners.* Washington, DC: National Education Association.

CHAPTER 12

THE BIG ONE: PREPARING FOR HIGH-STAKES TESTS

Teachers in every state of the United States face the twin issues of accountability and high-stakes testing. Performance results on standardized or state-designed assessment instruments affect decisions about promotion, curricular tracking, and graduation for students. In many states, test results determine teacher, school, and district ratings, which are often tied to differential school or district funding bonuses. Poor showings may result in corrective actions ranging from schoolwide restructuring to providing students with alternative school choices. Never before have the stakes of testing been so high.

With increased reliance on accountability and testing, teachers and administrators have become deeply involved in creating new programs and innovative approaches to improve the performance levels of their students—their native English-speaking students, that is. For better or worse, however (and there really are two sides to this issue), ELLs also must face these tests.

In the past, potentially low-scoring ELLs were simply excused from high-stakes testing. Now, the No Child Left Behind Act (NCLB) of 2001 mandates that virtually all ELLs participate in the same statewide assessment instruments as their native English-speaking peers. However, the testing results of ELLs at early stages of English language development are exempted.

Although it seems unrealistically optimistic to expect ELLs to achieve the same level of performance on an exam as native English speakers, it is equally pessimistic to believe that they are destined to fail. Teachers can maximize the performance potential of their ELLs on yearly state-mandated tests by using a combination of strategic approaches throughout the school year:

- Incorporating into daily procedures a variety of the instructional strategies presented in Part II of this text to facilitate content comprehension
- Using the classroom assessment strategies discussed in Chapter 11 to build students' ongoing experience in test taking
- Explicitly teaching test-taking skills
- Ensuring that the most appropriate and beneficial test accommodations are being made available to ELLs

These last two strategic approaches are the subject of this chapter.

MAXIMIZING STUDENT POTENTIAL ON STANDARDIZED TESTS

The Objective: Familiarize Students with the Format and Process of Multiple-Choice Testing

The Rationale: Experience counts in tests, as it does in life. Students become better test takers through repeated exposure. ELLs in particular need practice to become familiar with the format and process of multiple-choice tests, as this test type is uncommon outside the United States.

STRATEGY 110   TEACH HOW TO APPROACH A MULTIPLE-CHOICE QUESTION

IN CONCEPT

The process of reading the stem and option choices (see Chapter 11, Figure 11.1 for multiple-choice terminology), eliminating incorrect options, and then bubbling-in the chosen response on a separate answer sheet may completely bewilder ELLs. Frequent practice with this type of test will sharpen students' skills and make them more comfortable with the multiple-choice test design.

IN PRACTICE

Technique I

Acquaint ELLs with the multiple-choice question format by starting small. Offer questions with only two option choices per question. Increase to three options shortly thereafter. Starting small will start ELLs on a positive testing path.

Technique II

Giving two parallel sets of questions is another way to familiarize ELLs with multiple-choice questions. Use any of the linguistically simplified question formats discussed in Chapter 11 so that ELLs can demonstrate their actual content knowledge. *At the same time*, give them multiple-choice questions with exactly parallel content. For example, students could see a true–false question in tandem with a two-option multiple-choice question, as in Figure 12.1, or a completion question along with a three-option multiple-choice question, as shown in Figure 12.2. By explicitly demonstrating the correspondence between a question in simplified format and a multiple-choice question's stem

Figure 12.1   Parallel Test Questions: True-False with Multiple-Choice

> T   F   A glacier may be defined as a huge mass of ice or snow moving slowly over land.
>
> A glacier may be defined as
>   a. turbulent water moving down a river.
>   b. a huge mass of ice or snow that moves slowly over land.

_____ is a nation with a population that is not increasing.

A nation with a population that is not increasing is
  a. Peru
  b. Sweden
  c. Kenya

Figure 12.2 Parallel Test Questions: Completion with Multiple-Choice

and options, you will help your students begin to make sense of the multiple-choice process.

Technique III

To clarify students' understanding even further, allocate time for practice in scrutinizing distractors. Show students how to analyze each set of distractors; have them circle the word or phrase that makes each item incorrect.

Decreased options, parallel formats, and distractor analysis will all help ELLs develop processing skills to successfully respond to standard four-option questions. Continued practice will lower students' anxiety and improve their performance on high-stakes tests.

STRATEGY 111   TEACH HOW TO USE THE ANSWER SHEET

IN CONCEPT

ELLs also need to become familiar with the process of using a Scantron sheet for answering multiple-choice questions. You may or may not remember the anxiety these separate answer sheets provoked when they were first introduced. Scantron sheets are a new experience for most ELLs, and bubbling-in answers on a separate sheet raises their anxiety levels, too, just as it did for early users. Here again, ELLs will benefit from repeated practice.

IN PRACTICE

Photocopy Scantron sheets, or create your own bubble answer sheets for classroom tests (see *The TechConnection* at the end of this chapter) so that ELLs can practice transferring answers from the question page to the answer sheet. Instruct students to check frequently that the number on the answer sheet corresponds to the question number they are responding to, especially if they have skipped a question.

An obvious test-taking strategy is to answer as many questions as possible in the allotted amount of time. Teach ELLs to tackle first the questions they find linguistically and conceptually easy and to skip over difficult questions, reserving them for whatever time remains at the end of the test. However, for any question they skip, they need to know how critical it is to skip that number line on the bubble sheet. Suggest that students make a light mark next to the number of the skipped question to remind themselves not to use it for the following question and to return to it at the end.

STRATEGY 112 FAMILIARIZE STUDENTS WITH PREDICTABLE PATTERNS AND PHRASES

IN CONCEPT

When ELLs understand the design of the multiple-choice format and answer sheet, practice sessions can focus on familiarizing them with the common word patterns of test directions.

IN PRACTICE

Written directions on standardized or statewide tests often differ from those that students are accustomed to reading on classroom tests. The wording of directions for a given task can also vary from one test to another. As a result, it may not be apparent to ELLs that the two sets of directions in Figure 12.3, for example, are asking them to do the same thing. Practice that familiarizes ELLs with the variations in word patterns will allow them to focus their linguistic efforts on finding answers to the questions instead of trying to figure out what the instructions are asking them to do.

Figure 12.3 Same Task, Different Directions

> **Directions on a standardized test:**
>
> Choose the word or group of words that means the same, or nearly the same, as the underlined word. Then mark the space for the answer you have chosen on your answer sheet.
>
> **Directions on a classroom test:**
>
> Bubble-in the letter of the word or phrase that is closest to the meaning of the underlined word.

STRATEGY 113 TEACH THE FACTS-WITHOUT-FLUFF STRATEGY

IN CONCEPT

Math word problems on standardized tests often present a challenge to ELLs, not because of the math skills involved but because of the vocabulary. The *Facts-Without-Fluff* strategy teaches students to look beyond cumbersome vocabulary to reveal the data needed to solve the problem.

IN PRACTICE

Look at the linguistic complexity of the problem presented in Figure 12.4. The challenge here clearly lies in the English, not the math. ELLs can learn to show what they know in math through explicit instruction in how to strip away the fluff to get to the facts they need. Demonstrate making word substitutions and deletions, "translating" *stable manager* to *someone*, for example. Figure 12.5 shows the process and results of focusing on the data in Figure 12.4 to solve the problem, a strategy students can practice in pairs or small groups throughout the school year.

A stable manager had a 78.3-foot length of braided leather line to use to replace the fraying reins on his horse bridles. Which equation could be used to find L, the number of lengths of rein measuring 3.7 feet, that could be cut from the 78.3 feet?

A. $78.3L = 3.7$

B. $78.3 = 3.7L$

C. $L = (3.7)(78.3)$

D. $\dfrac{L}{78.3} = 3.7$

Figure 12.4   Is it the math or the English that's hard?

Facts with All the Fluff

A stable manager had a 78.3-foot length of braided leather line to use to replace the fraying reins on his horse bridles. Which equation could be used to find L, the number of lengths of rein measuring 3.7 feet, that could be cut from the 78.3 feet?

The Facts Without the Fluff

Someone ... had 78.3 feet ... of *something* ... to do *something*.

Which equation to use to find L?

L = the number of 3.7-foot lengths (*parts, pieces, things, units*) in the 78.3 feet

Figure 12.5   The Facts-Without-Fluff Strategy

STRATEGY 114   TEACH TEST-TAKING SKILLS

IN CONCEPT

At this point, ELLs can join the rest of the class when you teach test-taking skills. All students will benefit from learning testing strategies to improve their "odds."

It should be recognized here that teachers' real goal is to help students become competent in the content of the test and not to become better test takers. However, it is a legitimate endeavor to teach students to be *test wise*.

IN PRACTICE

The first thing students need to know about any test is whether or not wrong answers are penalized. In tests that assess penalties for wrong answers, students should consider guessing only if they can eliminate two of the options. If there are no penalties for guessing, the best strategy is to answer all questions.

Give students practice in looking for clues before guessing an answer. Demonstrate how you would begin, by eliminating any option known to be wrong. Then search for other possible clues. Look at the length of the remaining options; often the longest is the best choice. Look also for similarities: If two options are close in meaning, it is likely that neither will be the correct choice. Look next for two options that are opposites: Choose one as the answer. Finally, if none of these approaches result in clues to the answer, students should select the same letter as their guess for all unknown questions throughout the test. Consistency offers the best statistical odds for a correct guess.

STRATEGY 115   GIVE SHORTER TESTS MORE FREQUENTLY

IN CONCEPT

ELLs become better test takers through repeated practice. There are many good reasons to establish a pattern of twice monthly mini-assessments, rather than saving everything for "the big one."

IN PRACTICE

Shorter tests, given more often, allow ELLs to focus on understanding smaller amounts of material. They also serve as grade indicators: Students know how they are doing throughout the grading period, averting the surprise of failure at the end of the period. In addition, more frequent tests offer students multiple opportunities to improve their grades. And they let teachers know whether students have a good grasp of concepts or whether review, reteaching, and/or additional individual services are needed.

Perhaps most important of all, frequent tests help students prepare for major exams. Each test and quiz raises students' comfort level with understanding and following directions, choosing correct responses, and using appropriate test-taking strategies. At the same time, increased exposure to shorter tests may serve to decrease students' overall anxiety toward test taking.

MAXIMIZING STUDENT POTENTIAL ON STANDARDIZED TESTS

The Objective: Use All Reasonable, Allowable Accommodations for English Language Learners

The Rationale: ELLs' performance outcomes on high-stakes standardized tests generally more accurately reflect their English language proficiency than the actual knowledge or skills the test purports to measure. To address this very real difficulty, NCLB specifies modifications in test materials and procedures, organized into four areas of accommodations for ELLs: accommodations in presentation, response, setting, and timing. States vary in which accommodations they permit. Teachers who implement legal accommodations to their fullest extent can maximize their ELLs' performance outcomes.

STRATEGY 116   USE ACCOMMODATIONS IN PRESENTATION

IN CONCEPT

Modifications in the realm of test presentation involve *communications* between teachers or test administrators and students before and during a test. Accommodations of this type are designed to offer clarification for ELLs in several different ways.

IN PRACTICE

Technique I

Prior to test administration, test directions may be translated into students' native languages. They may also be recorded in advance by qualified teachers, parents, or other community volunteers.

In addition, teachers may conduct a linguistic preview of test questions to reduce the need for clarification during actual testing sessions. The unusual vocabulary in the math problem shown in Figure 12.4, for example, could be simplified to that shown in Figure 12.6. Nothing mathematical has changed—only the linguistic ability needed to understand what the question is asking.

Linguistic items such as confusing synonyms, unfamiliar terminology or phrasing (e.g., *given that* in math), and questions that are overly long or structurally complex (e.g., "One can say that it is generally not true that ...") can be rewritten in simplified form and included as part of the test, either in the test booklet itself or as a separate handout.

Technique II

During test administration, test directions may be read aloud, repeated, paraphrased, and/or simplified. Students may also request clarification while they are taking the test. Teachers or test administrators may answer questions that extend ELLs' comprehension of the question, provided that their responses will not offer help with the answer. They could, for example, clarify vocabulary in the math problem in Figure 12.4. Test results will more accurately reflect ELLs' content knowledge and skills when teachers explain, rephrase, or simplify vocabulary, synonyms, idiomatic phrases, or cultural references that are extraneous to the content knowledge being assessed.

Figure 12.6 Now the Focus Is Math

Which equation could be used to find L, the number of lengths of string measuring 3.7 feet, that could be cut from a length of string measuring 78.3 feet?

a. $78.3L = 3.7$

b. $78.3 = 3.7L$

c. $L = (3.7)(78.3)$

d. $\dfrac{L}{78.3} = 3.7$

STRATEGY 117   USE ACCOMMODATIONS IN RESPONSE

IN CONCEPT

Accommodations in response are those that involve *how* a student may respond to a test. Accommodations of this type attempt to address potential difficulties that ELLs may encounter in reading and answering test questions.

IN PRACTICE

The most valuable modification in the response category is to allow ELLs to use reference aids, such as bilingual dictionaries and glossaries. Students can use commercially published editions, or they can bring to the test preapproved word lists, vocabulary journals, or dictionaries that they have created throughout the school year.

Other modifications in response may be logistically difficult to implement. For example, although ELLs may be allowed to mark answers directly in their test booklets, this option makes scoring more difficult, time-consuming, and costly. Other problematic modifications are to bring in a qualified interpreter if one is locally available, to allow ELLs to respond in their native language, or—for large language groups—to offer the test in the students' native language. Unless your school or school district has unusual resources, these accommodations are difficult to institute and may present almost as many problems as they attempt to solve.

STRATEGY 118   USE ACCOMMODATIONS IN SETTING

IN CONCEPT

Accommodations in setting are those that involve *where* a test may be given. Accommodations of this type reduce distractions for ELLs and lower their levels of test-related anxiety.

IN PRACTICE

ELLs may be offered the option of taking standardized tests in a separate location, in small groups, or even individually. They may also be given preferential seating, such as facing a teacher or sitting in the front of the room. Additionally, tests may be administered in a classroom that is familiar to the students—their own homeroom or their English language development classroom. And a teacher whom the students know and feel comfortable with may be chosen as test administrator.

STRATEGY 119   USE ACCOMMODATIONS IN TIMING AND SCHEDULING

IN CONCEPT

Accommodations in timing and scheduling are those that involve *when* a test is given. Giving ELLs extra time or modifying their schedule to complete tests is a sensible adjustment. Because ELLs must expend additional time and effort decoding the language of a test before they can demonstrate their content knowledge, it seems fair to schedule their tests in a way that extends their time to complete them. Accommodations in time and schedule compensate ELLs for the increased language burden and produce a more accurate assessment of their content achievement levels.

IN PRACTICE

Options for scheduling that allow ELLs extra time include extended test time on the same day, shorter test sessions over several days, or some combination of the two. Tests can also be scheduled at a time of day that is beneficial to the students. And extra breaks or longer breaks can be included in the test schedule.

Even though all of these options offer ELLs more time to separate language from content on tests, the extra time to focus may also prolong students' feelings of test-related anxiety. It is important to achieve a good balance.

STRATEGY 120   SELECT A COMBINATION OF THE MOST EFFECTIVE ACCOMMODATIONS

IN CONCEPT

Effective accommodations balance the needs of ELLs and the resources of districts, schools, and test administrators. Combining modifications that are practical and relatively easy to implement with ones that offer ELLs the maximum benefits produces a short list of recommendations.

IN PRACTICE

- Test ELLs separately, in small groups and in a familiar location.
- Schedule a reasonable amount of additional time for ELLs to take the test.
- Allow ELLs use of bilingual reference aids.
- Simplify directions, word usage, and long, complicated questions.
- Encourage ELLs to seek clarification during the test.

These accommodations seem reasonable, workable, and cost-effective. School resources will not be unduly burdened, and test outcomes for ELLs will be more accurate. It is a win–win situation: Students, teachers, and schools will all benefit from the results.

Finally, it should be said that no accommodation, no matter how advantageous to ELLs, should be used if it has not been previously practiced in a classroom test situation. The day of a high-stakes test is not the time to surprise students with new approaches to test taking.

IN SUMMARY: MAXIMIZING STUDENT POTENTIAL ON STANDARDIZED TESTS

Teaching students to perform well on tests starts with sound content instruction. But often, good test takers are made, not born.

ELLs' performance on standardized tests can improve through practicing how to approach multiple-choice questions, understanding the patterns and phrases used in test directions, and learning test-taking strategies. Before test administration day, teachers and school administrators should work with the district to agree on the best possible set of accommodations. ELLs should also know what accommodations will be available to them on test day.

Bringing together the strategies for assessment with the strategies for instruction will help your ELLs reach their fullest potential on their path to academic success.

CONCLUSION

Yes, the challenge is here. Teachers must find ways first to facilitate ELLs' understanding of subject-specific content and then to create instruments and opportunities that will accurately evaluate the learning that has taken place. The strategies of instruction and assessment detailed in this volume have given you the means to help you meet that challenge.

Start by choosing strategies that appeal to you and are appropriate for your students and the content you teach. Then integrate them into your instructional routines. Add more strategies on a regular basis. And experiment with them; try them out with the whole class, not just the ELLs. Integrate different types of strategies: learning strategies, instructional strategies, textbook strategies, assignment strategies, and assessment strategies. Evaluate their effectiveness, and eliminate those that don't appear to work well with your student population. Discuss them with your colleagues, and share ideas and applications. Above all, keep trying. You, like your students, will be encouraged by the rewards of success.

And you *will* be rewarded. By choosing to use these strategies, you will start your ELLs on the path of achievement. With each small accomplishment, they will build their academic self-confidence and begin to identify themselves as capable learners. To you, their teacher, will go the credit for making the extra effort to help these students become successful participants in the academic environment that is such an important part of their daily lives.

Indeed, it is a challenge. But it is an exciting and rewarding challenge—one that is well worth embracing.

QUESTIONS FOR DISCUSSION

1. Which of the *12 Guidelines for Practice* presented at the end of Chapter 1 inform the strategies in this chapter?
2. How has high-stakes testing affected the education of ELLs? What has changed since implementation of NCLB in 2001? If you have been teaching since before NCLB was enacted, draw upon your own observations. If you have entered the profession since that time, interview several classroom teachers to gain insights in this area.
3. Research and report your state and/or district rules for standardized assessment, test content, and accommodations as they relate to ELLs.
4. Working in small, geographically diversified groups of peers, compare the accommodations used in your schools. Do all schools in your district or county use similar sets of accommodations? Are they all used in the same ways? If your comparisons show nonuniform accommodation usage, how do you think the variations might affect test results?
5. Formulate a personal philosophy for testing ELLs. What do you believe would constitute best practices for ELLs taking high-stakes tests? Justify your beliefs.

REFERENCES AND RESOURCES

Cizek, G. J., & Burg, S. S. (2005). *Addressing test anxiety in a high-stakes environment: Strategies for classrooms and schools.* Thousand Oaks, CA: Corwin Press.

Gottlieb, M. (2006). *Assessing English language learners: Bridges from language proficiency to academic achievement.* Thousand Oaks, CA: Corwin Press.

Pearlman, M. (2002). *Measuring and supporting English language learning in schools: Challenges for test makers.* Presentation at the National Center for Research on Evaluation, Standards, and Student Testing (CRESST) Conference, Los Angeles, CA.

TESOL. (2005). *Position paper on assessment and accountability of English language learners under the No Child Left Behind Act of 2001 (Public law 107-110).* Retrieved March 9, 2010, from http://tesol.org/s_tesol/bin.asp?CID=32&DID=4720&DOC=FILE.PDF

The TechConnection

www.cresst.org
The website of the National Center for Research on Evaluation, Standards, and Student Testing has a dedicated section just for teachers, as well as conference abstracts and presentations.

www.ncela.gwu.edu/
The website of the National Clearinghouse for English Language Acquisition (NCELA) provides resources related to the assessment of and accountability for English language learners.

www.catpin.com/bubbletest
This website allows you to design and print practice bubble-test answer sheets for your students and suggests that you create an answer key on a clear transparency using a permanent pen to mark the correct answers.

GLOSSARY OF ACRONYMS

English language learner, or *ELL*, is the term used consistently in this text. However, many other terms are in general usage. The related acronyms listed here are used in various school districts in the United States and by state and federal education agencies. The terms refer to individuals, classes, programs, concepts, and agencies.

Individuals

LEP	Limited English proficient
NEP	Non-English proficient
PEP	Partially English proficient
FEP	Fluent English proficient
ELL	English language learner
EL	English learner
NES	Non-English speaker
LES	Limited English speaker (or speaking)
FES	Fluent English speaker (or speaking)
NNS	Nonnative speaker
NS	Native speaker
LMS	Language minority student

Classes and/or Programs

ESL	English as a second language
ESOL	English for speakers of other languages
EFL	English as a foreign language
EAL	English as an additional language
ELD	English language development
ELA	English language arts
SDAIE	Specially designed academic instruction in English
SEI	Structured English immersion
SEIP	Structured English immersion program
SI	Sheltered instruction
ESP	English for specific (or special) purposes
EOP	English for occupational purposes

EAP	English for academic purposes
IEP	Intensive English program
CELT	Content-based English language teaching
CLAD	Cross-cultural, language, and academic development
LCD	Linguistically and culturally diverse

Concepts

BICS	Basic interpersonal communication skills
CALP	Cognitive academic language proficiency
ELP	English language proficiency
L1	First [native] language
L2	Second [target] language
SLA	Second language acquisition

Agencies

CABE	California Association for Bilingual Education
CAL	Center for Applied Linguistics
CREDE	Center for Research on Education, Diversity, and Excellence
NABE	National Association for Bilingual Education
NAME	National Association for Multicultural Education
NCELA	National Clearinghouse for English Language Acquisition
NCBE	National Clearinghouse of Bilingual Education (now NCELA)
OELA	Office of English Language Acquisition
TESOL	Teaching (or Teachers of) English to Speakers of Other Languages

BOOK CLUB

WELCOME!

And thank you for making *120 Content Strategies for English Language Learners* your book club selection. I congratulate you on choosing to support your own professional development through meetings, discussion, and study. I hope you enjoy the process and the results.

You have probably spent a good deal of time talking about the challenges you face with your students, particularly your English language learners (ELLs). Even before you begin reading, you might consider developing a group list of specific issues and difficulties in reaching and teaching the ELLs in your classes. Then as you read, you can check back with this list on a regular basis to see which challenges you now feel more able to address.

THE GOAL

The overall goal of an educational book club is for its members to engage in reflective teaching. As you read each chapter, think about the instruction you offer your students in the classroom. Then with your peers, discuss and develop deeper understandings and more effective practices. Through these directed teacher conversations about teaching and learning, you will become a more accomplished teacher.

QUESTIONS, QUESTIONS, QUESTIONS

Before You Begin

Before reading the first chapter, think about these questions:

- Do I believe that I am effectively teaching *all* my students?
- Do I believe that I am effectively involving *all* my students?
- Do I believe that I am creating a risk-free environment in my classroom?
- Do I believe that I am sensitive to linguistic and cultural diversity among my students?
- Do I believe that I make the content I teach meaningful and relevant to my students' lives?
- Do I believe that I set realistic but cognitively challenging instructional goals for my ELLs?
- Do I believe that I engage in reflective teaching practices?

For Part I: Theory and Culture

Chapter 1

1. Research the numbers of ELLs in your district and in your school. What languages are represented and in what percentages? How have these numbers changed in recent years? What are the projections for the coming years?

2. Clarify through discussion each of the second-language acquisition theories. Which of them have you been practicing in your classroom?

3. If you have ever studied a foreign language, how successful were you in learning it? Can you explain your success or lack of it based on these theories, principles, and guidelines?

4. Discuss in detail Bloom's taxonomy. Think about the questions you ask in your classroom. What percentage of them would you classify as knowledge and comprehension?

5. Examine the *12 Guidelines for Practice* at the end of Chapter 1. How do they fit with your pedagogical philosophy? Are there any that you particularly espouse?

Chapter 2

1. When you think about the classroom behaviors of your ELLs, are there any that you now understand better through the lens of their culture?

2. Discuss ways you can help your ELLs adjust more readily to your school culture.

3. Have you experienced any additional cultural influences on learning in your content area beyond those discussed in this chapter? (I'd really love it if you'd let me know!)

For ALL Strategy Chapters in Parts II and III

As you read each chapter, do an honest self-assessment of your current instructional practices by asking yourself this question: Have I been using some of the strategies in this chapter, and if so, how effectively have I been using them? (Share with peers your responses to these self-evaluations only if you feel comfortable doing so.)

For Part II: Instruction

Chapter 3

1. What accommodations in curricular objectives and standards have you been making for your ELLs and your struggling readers? How will these accommodations change in light of the information in this chapter?

2. Create a two-tiered planner for a unit you will soon be teaching. Compare the items you selected for your essential tier with the others in your group. After discussion, are there modifications you believe you should make?

Chapter 4

1. Think back to your days as a student. What types of learning strategies did you use to achieve your goals? How did you learn to use them? How effective do you believe those strategies were?

2. Analyze the learning strategies that you now use most frequently. Do you use different strategies for different types of tasks?

3. Which strategies would you like to try out in your classroom? How will you use each one (be specific)? How will you evaluate its effectiveness?

Chapter 5

1. Select a lesson you have taught that began with a particularly effective introduction to build and activate background knowledge. Describe the strategies you used and the reasons you believe they were effective.
2. Look at Strategy 21, "Preview the Material." How does this relate to the content you teach? With what specific content or unit might you use the preview strategy to benefit your ELLs?
3. Which strategies would you like to try out in your classroom? How will you use each one (be specific)? How will you evaluate its effectiveness?

Chapter 6

1. Prepare a text passage, and read it aloud to your group as if your group were your class; follow the practices set forth in Strategies 24 and 25. After the reading, have your colleagues give you verbal feedback or a written critique.
2. Audiotape a lesson in which you are actively teaching, and analyze it using the checklist in Figure 6.6. What advice would you give yourself to facilitate your ELLs' comprehension of your oral language? Within your group, compare and critique each other's analyses of the recorded lessons.
3. Discuss the ideas presented about classroom routines. Are there new routines you could institute to lower language input for your ELLs and, at the same time, make your class time more efficient?
4. Discuss the techniques you currently use to review instructional content. Are you satisfied with the frequency and effectiveness of your review practices? Are there review strategies that you really liked in this chapter? How will you use them?

Chapter 7

1. With a partner, practice announcing, "It's question time. Who's got a question for me?" with your voice going down at the end. Be sure these words sound like a statement rather than a question.
2. Working in pairs or small groups, develop sets of cognitively challenging questions that require lowered language output for use in your classrooms (refer to Strategy 43).
3. With your group, discuss classes you have taken in which you did enjoy participating and ones in which you did not. Evaluate what the instructor did or did not do to encourage/discourage participation. Can you come up with a list of at least five practices that encourage classroom participation and five practices that are sure to discourage participation?
4. Which strategies would you like to try out in your classroom? How will you use each one (be specific)? How will you evaluate its effectiveness?

Chapter 8

1. What do you currently do when you find an unfamiliar word in a book you are reading? How often do you look it up in a dictionary? Do you remember the word and its meaning after you have looked it up? What strategies could you use if you wanted to be sure you would remember the word?
2. Discuss the different phrases you use to give the same directions or to refer to a single concept or process.
3. Prepare a list of additional domain-specific and domain-crossing usages of familiar words, similar to the examples illustrated in Figures 8.2 and 8.3.
4. Talk about the ways you now teach vocabulary. How effective do you believe they are? Which strategies in this chapter will you try? Why?

Chapter 9

1. Choose content topics that will soon be introduced to your students. As a group, discuss ways to apply the reading in reverse strategy. Refer to Strategy 71 to review the four-step process.
2. Do you believe your students are aware of the aids in their own textbooks? Try involving the students in a discussion about the purpose of textbook aids and the ways they might benefit from using them.
3. Introduce a new textbook chapter to your students by following the steps in Figure 9.1. Were your students successful in getting the gist of the chapter?
4. Which strategies, other than reading in reverse, would you like to try out in your classroom? How will you use each one (be specific)? How will you evaluate its effectiveness?

Chapter 10

1. Think about and list the in-class and at-home assignments you give. Rate each on a scale of 1 to 5 in terms of difficulty for ELLs. Consider both cognitive challenge and linguistic complexity. You may decide with your group to give each type of assignment one combined rating or to rate the two elements separately.
2. For each assignment you rated as linguistically complex, create a linguistically simplified form for your ELLs.
3. Choose several assignments you will be giving to your class. Modify them for ELLs. Create several levels of modification for beginners, intermediates, and advanced ELL students.

Overall Question for Instructional Strategies

Think back to a lesson you have taught that was less successful than you anticipated. Can you identify any specific factors that may have caused difficulty? Recast the lesson now in terms of the strategies presented in this book.

For Part III: Assessment

Chapter 11

1. Examine several of your own teacher-made multiple-choice tests. Can you find any pitfalls? How would you eliminate the pitfalls you found?
2. Analyze through the eyes of an ELL one or more tests that you have used in your classroom. Which questions would have been especially difficult or confusing, and which now seem too high in language demand? Which strategies could you use to modify these questions in order to allow ELLs to better demonstrate their understanding of the content?
3. Consider your classroom tests in general. What kind of backwash do you think they are creating?
4. Discuss the concepts of holistic scoring and interactive comments. Have you tried these approaches, and if so, with what results? If you like the ideas, give them a try. Then discuss your own and your students' reactions to the techniques.
5. Think about an expression of praise you received that was particularly meaningful to you. Why was it so? What elements of praise make it rewarding and motivating to students? Plan some specific expressions of effective praise to use with your students.

Chapter 12

1. How do you believe NCLB has changed the way you teach and test? How in particular has it affected ELLs? Discuss what is good and bad about these changes.

2. What test accommodations for ELLs are used in your school or district? Do you believe these accommodations are reasonable and effective? Do all schools in your district use the same sets of accommodations? If they do not, how do you think the variations might affect test results?

3. Formulate a personal philosophy for testing ELLs. What do you believe would constitute best practices for high-stakes testing of ELLs? Justify your beliefs.

And the Final Question

Reflect upon the effectiveness of the strategies you have implemented since you started to read this book. What have been your triumphs and your difficulties?

Reflect for a moment now upon the difficulties. What next steps are you considering to make improvements in these areas?

A PARTING THOUGHT FROM ME TO YOU

Collaborating with other professionals, airing and discussing issues, sharing attempts (successful and otherwise), and reinforcing learning is a major benefit of participating in a book club. I encourage you to continue meeting to share the new strategies that you will implement and the outcomes you will encounter.

I am honored that you chose this book to study, and I hope you consider yourselves to be more accomplished professionals as a result. I wish you continued success and satisfaction in your teaching careers. Good luck!

APPENDIX I

ADDITIONAL RESOURCES FOR TEACHERS

The books on this list provide good reading for all aspects of teaching ELLs. The books are broad based and simply too good to be listed in the reference section of any single chapter.

Cary, S. (2007). *Working with second language learners: Answers to teachers' top ten questions* (2nd ed.). Portsmouth, NH: Heinemann.

Dong, Y. R. (2004). *Teaching language and content to linguistically and culturally diverse students: Principles, ideas, and materials.* Greenwich, CT: Information Age.

Freeman, Y. S., Freeman, D. E., & Mercuri, S. (2002). *Closing the achievement gap: How to reach limited–formal schooling and long-term English learners.* Portsmouth, NH: Heinemann.

Herrell, A. L., & Jordan, M. (2007). *Fifty teaching strategies for English language learners* (3rd ed.). Upper Saddle River, NJ: Pearson Education.

Kottler, E., & Kottler, J. (2001). *Children with limited English: Teaching strategies for the regular classroom.* Thousand Oaks, CA: Corwin Press.

Vaughn, S. S., Bos, C. S., & Schumm, J. S. (2010). *Teaching students who are exceptional, diverse, and at-risk in the general education classroom* (5th ed.). Boston: Allyn & Bacon.

Walter, T. (2004). *Teaching English language learners: The how-to handbook.* White Plains, NY: Pearson Education.

The TechConnection

www.ncela.gwu.edu

The National Clearinghouse for English Language Acquisition & Language Instruction Educational Programs (NCELA) collects, analyzes, synthesizes, and disseminates information about language instruction educational programs for ELLs and related programs. It is funded by the U.S. Department of Education's Office of English Language Acquisition, Language Enhancement & Academic Achievement for Limited English Proficient Students (OELA) under Title III of the No Child Left Behind (NCLB) Act of 2001.

http://iteslj.org

Published since 1995, this monthly Internet journal offers articles, research papers, lesson plans, teaching ideas, and classroom activities of interest to content teachers and teachers of English as a second language.

www.cal.org

The website of the Center for Applied Linguistics gives access to topics of interest to secondary school teachers and to many related resources for ELL development.

www.ncela.gwu.edu/files/rcd/BE021775/Glossary_of_Terms.pdf

This resource explains and defines terms related to all aspects of teaching linguistically and culturally diverse students.

SELECT STRATEGIES THAT SUPPORT LANGUAGE SKILLS

Strategy	Title	Reading	Writing	Speaking	Listening
13	Begin with brainstorming	X	X		
16	Personalize the lesson			X	
17	Make analogies	X		X	
18	Spark interest			X	
21	Preview the lesson	X			
42	Don't fall into the "Does everyone understand?" trap			X	
43	Select question types			X	
44	Plan questions in advance			X	
45	Promote active listeners				X
47	"Pre-Pair" to respond			X	
48	Try Numbered Heads			X	
49	Use Think–Pair–Share			X	
50	Allow extra wait time			X	
51	Give credit for trying			X	
52	Offer face savers			X	
53	Watch for student readiness			X	
54	Focus on content			X	
55	Combine questioning strategies for best results			X	
58	Look beyond content-specific words to teach	X			
60	Turn your students into "language detectives"	X			
61	Have students develop a personal dictionary	X	X	X	
62	Use concept-definition maps	X			
63	Demonstrate the value of a student- friendly dictionary	X	X		
65	Get into a Pair–Define–Explain routine				X
66	Use online resources for vocabulary growth	X			
67	Set up a Word of the Week program	X	X	X	
68	Make your students into word wizards	X	X	X	
70	Teach textbook aids	X			
71	Teach reading in reverse	X			